TESI GREGORIANA

Serie Teologia

—— 7 ——

JACOB NANGELIMALIL

The Relationship
between the Eucharistic Liturgy,
the Interior Life and
the Social Witness of the Church
according to
Joseph Cardinal Parecattil

EDITRICE PONTIFICIA UNIVERSITÀ GREGORIANA
Roma 1996

Vidimus et approbamus ad normam Statutorum Universitatis

Romae, ex Pontificia Universitate Gregoriana
die 15 mensis iunii anni 1995

R.P. Prof. PHILIP J. ROSATO, S.J.
R.P. Prof. AUGUSTINE THOTTAKARA, C.M.I.

ISBN 88-7652-695-1

GREGORIAN UNIVERSITY PRESS
Piazza della Pilotta, 35 – 00187 Rome, Italy

ACKNOWLEDGEMENTS

With a heart filled with great joy and legitimate satisfaction, the author presents this thesis to the Faculty of Theology of the Pontifical Gregorian University. It is a matter of rare privilege to undertake research on the works of Joseph Cardinal Parecattil who initiated the author to the priestly life, and with whom, on various occasions, he came in close contact and by whom he was inspired.

First and foremost profound gratitude is expressed to the Eucharistic Lord for the constant grace to complete this laborious task. Next, the author thanks his parents and his brother and sisters for their prayer and support. Sentiments of deep thanks are owed as well to Rev. Philip J. Rosato, S.J., the director of this dissertation. Without his skilled guidance and loving encouragement as «Doktor Vater», this work would not have been completed. In every meeting with him the author experienced his theological understanding and fatherly care. The author is also grateful to Rev. Augustine Thottakkara, who introduced him to the richness of Indian philosophy, and carefully read his thesis, providing him solid criticism and creative suggestions.

The author acknowledges his indebtedness to all the professors of the Gregorian University for the theological formation he received from them. Expressions of loving gratitude are offered to His Eminence Antony Cardinal Padiyara, the Major Archbishop of Ernakulam-Angamaly of the Syro-Malabar Church for his unrelenting paternal concern and blessing. Thanks are due to His Excellency Jacob Manathodath, the Auxiliary bishop of the Metropolitan Archdiocese of Ernakulam. Many thanks also to all fellow priests of his archdiocese, especially to those who are now in Rome. The author gratefully acknowledges the scholarship granted by the Congregation for the Oriental Churches for his studies in Rome.

Sincere thanks to my friends at the Collegio Maria Immacolata, Collegio Urbano, Divino Amore Sanctuary, and to Sister Helen who painstakingly controlled the manuscript. Gratitude is expressed to Mr. Albert De Biesme and his collaborators of «Institut de presse missionnaire» for their financial support. And finally, thanks to the superiors of Collegio Maria Immacolata, to my loving friends in India and abroad as well as to all whose prayers and advice have contributed to the successful completion of this thesis.

Cardinal's House,   Jacob Nangelimalil
Ernakulam, Cochin-682031
Kerala, India
January 26, 1996

PRESENTATION

One of the most appealing aspects of my serving as professor of dogmatic theology at the Pontifical Gregorian University in Rome is the direction of doctoral students from many local churches dispersed over the globe. For, if in preparing courses and seminars for the baccalaureate and licentiate students, I invariably elucidate revealed truths with the aid of arguments based on my own intellectual, cultural and ecclesial experiences, I am drawn out of myself and am faced with unknown yet astoundingly enriching perspectives through the research undertaken by the doctoral candidates. Thus, when Fr. Jacob Nangelimalil, a presbyter of the Syro-Malabar archdiocese of Ernakulam-Angamaly in Kerala, presented me the first results of his study of the writings of Joseph Cardinal Parecattil (1912-1987) concerning the connection between the participation of Christians in the Eucharist and their ensuing spirituality and social engagement, I came to fathom, by means of reasoning derived from experiences quite different from my own, the vivid intellectual stimuli provided for India by the documents of Vatican II on the sacred liturgy, on the relationship of the Catholic Church to non-Christian religions, and on the task of the Church in the modern world.

These initial impressions were confirmed by each ensuing chapter on these aspects of the thought of Cardinal Parecattil which Fr. Nangelimalil bought to my desk. I especially remember the moment when I first read the following passage from an undated sermon, entitled «The Holy Eucharist», offered by Parecattil at the conclusion of the Forty-hours devotion held in a parish of the archdiocese: «We should abide by the virtues of truth, justice and mercy [...] love of neighbour in all actions. Some may question the relevance of these things in a sermon on the occasion of the forty hour adoration. But, in a Eucharistic life one learns these kinds of practical lessons». I was astounded by these words, since the lectures I had hitherto held and the articles I had already written on the link between sacramental orthodoxy and sacramental orthopraxy were all inspired by my attendance at the International Eucharistic

Congress held in 1976 in Philadelphia, my native city, and based on the theme «The Eucharist and the Hungers of the Human Family». Thus, I found the manner in which Cardinal Parecattil conjoins this sacrament to a life-style marked by truth, justice, mercy and charity to reflect perfectly the insights articulated in the unforgettable addresses given there by Dom Helder Camara, Fr. Pedro Arrupe and Mother Teresa of Calcutta.

In the entire doctoral thesis which is now to appear in the series «Tesi Gregoriana», Fr. Jacob Nangelimalil explains in a clear, systematic and thorough manner what Cardinal Parecattil, influenced by his theological training, his cultural and socio-political concerns and his episcopal responsib-ility, meant by «a Eucharistic life» and by «the practical lessons» which are learned through it. What emerges in these vigorous pages is a distinctive Eucharistic thought-pattern which is both Scholastic and pragmatic, ontologically grounded and apostolically oriented, informed as much by a Christian friendship with Giambattista Montini, who as Paul VI was the spiritual father of the Catholic community, as by an indelible affinity to the moral ideals of Mahatma Karamchand Gandhi, who was the inspired leader of the Indian nation. Confronted both with the innate complexity and with the prophetic force of the Eucharistic theology of Parecattil, Fr. Nangelimalil opts to depict his writings neither as traditionally Catholic in a strict sense nor as innovatively syncretic in an exaggerated sense. Instead, he presents the thought of Parecattil as deeply rooted in the post-Tridentine theology in which he was formed and in the efforts at adaptation which he was called to undertake as a post-Vatican II bishop in a newly independent and rapidly developing Asian Country.

In effect, the historical, expository and valuative sections of this thesis manifest that F. Jacob Nangelimalil is an adept young scholar who has brought an original research project to most professional and felicitous conclusion. Furthermore, the consistent point of view which he maintains with regard to the Eucharistic thought of Parecattil, who himself feared that his distinctive interweaving of Catholic doctrines and Indian social ideals could indeed be deemed by many as totally irrelevant to a genuine ecclesial spirituality and by many more as too audacious on the part of a responsible churchman, is to be admired. May this first publication of Fr. Nangelimalil on the thought of a faithful, courageous and committed Syro-Malabar theologian not be his last, for the insights of Joseph Cardinal Parecattil on the Eucharist, and on other doctrinal themes, need to be further illumined and promulgated and competently developed and enhanced.

Pontifical Gregorian University   Philip J. Rosato, S.J.
Rome, January 19, 1996

GENERAL INTRODUCTION

In the twentieth century, consistent interest has been shown in Eucharistic theology on the part of the official and the theological magisterium. A number of notable Papal statements and theological books led to the formulation of the documents of Vatican II, and many others have appeared in the post-Conciliar period. The major themes in contemporary Eucharistic theology have also had their influence on, and been developed by, bishops and theologians of the Syro-Malabar Church, an Oriental Church in India, founded by the apostle St. Thomas. This Church, which follows the East-Syrian Eucharistic liturgy, has always accepted many theological positions of the West, even if since Vatican II it has attempted to inculturate its faith and worship by adapting appropriate elements from the Indian culture and the Hindu religion. Nevertheless, its Eucharistic theology has not been confined solely to an explanation of the enactment of the sacrament, but has also treated its effects in the spiritual life and the social witness of Christians. Of the recent theologians of the Syro-Malabar Church who have contributed to the formulation of its Eucharistic theology, Joseph Cardinal Parecattil has emerged as the most prominent.

This thesis investigates the Eucharistic theology of Joseph Parecattil, insofar as it effects the spiritual life and the social witness of the members of the Syro-Malabar Church. Joseph Parecattil, the late Metropolitan of Ernakulam in Kerala, India, was born on April 1, 1912, and died on February 20, 1987. He became a bishop in 1953, and a cardinal in 1969. Since he had earned a doctorate in systematic theology on the basis of his thesis *Augustine vs. Pelagius on Grace*, he was a constant teacher and writer throughout his pastoral ministry. In the last years of his life, he was the president of the Pontifical Commission for the Revision of Oriental Canon Law. The project reached its fruition on October 18, 1990, a few years after his death.

In his Eucharistic theology Parecattil systematically developed the idea that, through the celebration of this sacrament, divine grace nourishes the spiritual life of the faithful and stimulates their social action. Although a few general descriptions of the manner in which he presented the Christian faith do exist, the present study represents the first systematic and detailed analysis of an aspect of his theology. It attempts to expose his Eucharistic theology as grounded on two main interests: 1) the renewal of the Syro-Malabar Eucharistic liturgy; and 2) its actual and eventual impact on the spiritual life and the social witness of the members of the Church. It is beyond the scope of this study to treat extensively the reflections of Parecattil on various other branches of Catholic theology, although they may be mentioned in passing, insofar as they are related to his Eucharistic thought.

The primary sources of this study are: 1) *A Call to Support the Rights of Minorities*; 2) *As I See Myself (Ñān Ente Dṛṣṭiyil)*; 3) *Augustine vs. Pelagius on Grace*; 4) *Letters to Children (Kuṭṭikalkulla Kattukal)*; 5) *Letters to Priests (Vaidikarkulla Kattukal)*; 6) *Letters to the People (Janannlkulla Kattukal)*; 7) *Letters to Sisters (Sahodarimārkulla Kattukal)*; 8) *Liturgy as I See It (Liturgy Ente Dṛṣṭiyil)*; 9) Pastoral and official letters, sermons and discourses.

A triple method, that is historical, expository and critical, is employed in this study. First, the historical and intellectual influences on the Eucharistic theology of Parecattil are examined. This is followed by a systematic presentation of his thought by means of a detailed analysis of major texts from the corpus of his writings. Finally, a critical evaluation is made of the strengths and limits of his reflections.

The three major parts of the thesis comprise six chapters. The first part contains two chapters, the second part, three, and the third part, one.

Chapter One, «Liturgical, Spiritual and Social Background of the Eucharistic Theology of Joseph Parecattil», deals with his gradual acquisition of theological insights during his formation and first years of priestly service. This topic is developed in three subdivisions: 1) The Eucharistic Theology and Spirituality of the Syro-Malabar Church: Their Roots in the Liturgical Celebration of the Sacrament; 2) The Post-Tridentine and Neo-Thomistic Eucharistic Theology and Spirituality; 3) Religious and Social Context of India: The Need of Eucharistic-centred Social Action.

The Syro-Malabar Church, in which Joseph Parecattil was educated, was so greatly influenced by East-Syrian theology that its Eucharistic liturgy was almost identical with that of the Chaldean Church. Yet, the theological training which Parecattil received in the Latin Seminary at Kandy and the

Eucharistic devotion he practised there exposed him to the intellectual and spiritual trends prevalent in the Western Church in the early twentieth century. Furthermore, from his earliest years Parecattil was familiar with the reality of religious pluralism in India where followers of different faiths live together. The socio-political life of India in the first half of the twentieth century was dominated by the stormy struggle for independence which was led by Mohandas Karamchand Gandhi (1869-1948) who advocated the moral principles of *Satyam* (truth) and *Ahimsā* (non-violence). All these factors exerted a quite evident influence on Parecattil as he articulated his understanding of the Eucharist.

Chapter Two is entitled «Various Prospects on the Eucharist Proposed by Vatican II: Their Impact on Joseph Parecattil». It explains how he came to be convinced that 1) the active participation of the laity in the Eucharist would be facilitated by the painstaking yet courageous restoration, revision and adaptation of the previous Missals; 2) Christian spirituality is centred on the free response to the grace of this sacrament; and 3) the Eucharist leads Christians to a form of social involvement which shares in the suffering and grief of all the children of God.

Having been a participant at all four sessions of Vatican II, Parecattil was impressed by the readiness of his fellow bishops to promote the renewal of Catholic theology by encouraging scholars to formulate new expressions of the Church's teaching. The innovative stance of Vatican II in recognizing the inherent value of non-Christian religions also exerted considerable influence on Parecattil. Then, in the years after the council, while the Indian Church was introducing some experiments, so that the Christian liturgy could be enhanced by the introduction of suitable rituals of Hinduism, Parecattil called for similar measures of renewing the Syro-Malabar Eucharistic liturgy, with the hope of fostering greater Hindu-Christian dialogue. Vatican II also encouraged the faithful to be engaged in human welfare activities especially in schools and hospitals, since they are «to give generous service of the most varied kinds to all manner of people» (LG 46). As the archbishop of Ernakulam, Parecattil tried consistently to link this Conciliar teaching to the illuminative and strengthening aspects of Eucharistic grace.

Chapter Three, entitled «The Eucharistic Writings of Joseph Parecattil in the Pre-Vatican II Period», deals with his pertinent writings before 1962. In this period Parecattil reflected on: 1) how a sincere participation of the baptized in the Eucharistic liturgy joins their lives to the self-sacrifice of Christ; 2) how the Eucharist becomes the centre of Christian spirituality which entails an existential worship of God in all the activities of the faithful; and 3) how the Church should attribute a Eucharistic interpretation especially to the social involvement of its members on behalf of justice and charity.

Joseph Parecattil firmly maintained that, by means of an active participation in the Eucharistic liturgy, the faithful offer themselves, along with the self-sacrificing Jesus, to the Father. He pointed out that the first and foremost effect of participation in the Mass is the reception of Eucharistic grace which manifests itself in the spiritual life and the social witness of the Christians.

Chapter Four, «The Application of the Teachings of Vatican II to the Eucharistic Liturgy, Spirituality and Social Action of the Syro-Malabar Church», studies: 1) Parecattil's desire to comply with the proposals of Vatican II concerning the restoration, revision and adaptation of the liturgy by enacting them in the Syro-Malabar Church; 2) his views on the renewal of Christian spiritual life through Eucharistic grace; and 3) his understanding of the social mission of the Church as the means of extending the selflessness of Jesus Christ who is present in the Eucharist. The chapter analyzes the writings of Parecattil in the period from 1963 to 1969.

Parecattil contributed to the formulation of the documents of Vatican II through his specific interventions and general participation in the discussions. Thereafter, he laboured particularly to bring about the renewal of the Eucharistic liturgy of the Syro-Malabar Church. Because of the ecumenical teaching of the Council, he described Eucharistic grace as the stimulus to strive for the reunion of all Christians. Moreover, he noted that in the modern context ecumenism also entails working for better understanding among followers of different religions. As members of the mystical body of Christ, Christians have the responsibility to promote the welfare of the weaker members of society.

Chapter Five, «An Indian Eucharistic Theology: Meeting of Hindu and Christian Religious Experiences», analyzes 1) how the Syro-Malabar Eucharistic liturgy is adapted to the Indian genius; 2) how an Indian Eucharistic spirituality can be described as a synthesis of Hindu and Christian religious experiences; and 3) how bread and wine symbolise various kinds of labour, and indicate the unity which exists between worship and work. This chapter focuses on the thought of Parecattil in the period from 1970 to 1987.

Parecattil was actively involved in the attempts to reform the Syro-Malabar Eucharistic liturgy. His substantial contribution was the *Bhāratiya Pūjā* (Indian Mass). At this stage, he emphasized the universal effect of the Eucharist which contains Christ who has redeemed and justified all humanity by the blood he shed on the Cross. He applied this truth to Hindus who seek «release from the trials of the present life by ascetical practices, profound meditation and recourse to God in confidence and love» (NA 2), and thus presented the Eucharistic Christ as the fulfilment of the Hindu search for God. He maintained that an Indian spirituality entails a proper synthesis of Hindu and Christian elements. He also claimed that the unity between worship and work could be noted in the Eucharistic bread and wine which are the products of human labour. Strengthened by the sacrament, Christians work for their own sustenance as well as for that of their needy neighbours.

Chapter Six, entitled «The Eucharistic Theology of Joseph Parecattil as an Inspiration and a Challenge to the Syro-Malabar Church», intends critically to evaluate his approach to the theme of this study. It offers: 1) an assessment of the positive aspects of his Eucharistic theology; 2) an attempt to propose some means by which the limitations of his understanding of the relationship between Eucharistic liturgy, spiritual life and social action may be overcome, and his valid insights enhanced.

The most important positive aspect of the Eucharistic theology of Parecattil is that it is based on a study of the liturgy itself. He stressed the indispensable role of the faithful in the celebration of the Eucharist. He forcefully showed that Christian spirituality is continually strengthened and activated at the Eucharist. Furthermore, Parecattil held that the reception of the Eucharist leads Christians to be engaged in the social life of India, especially in helping the poor.

However, Parecattil did not treat certain prominent aspects of Eucharistic theology in depth. The eschatological dimension of the Eucharistic liturgy is hardly mentioned, and his concept of Eucharistic spirituality seems to be more concerned with the sanctification of individuals than with that of the Church. Furthermore, his presentation of the social dimension of the Eucharist appears not to be adequately related to the various other forms of the presence of Christ. In regard to these matters, the author proposes a few thoughts which, if developed in a systematic way, could render the views of Parecattil an even more solid foundation for the future Eucharistic theology of the Syro-Malabar Church.

Although this introduction, in order to be synthetic, has in one sense already indicated both the content of the Eucharistic teaching of Parecattil and some of its considerable merits and limits, there is another sense in which these opening words reveal little. For, they intend only to interest the reader in coming to know and respect a thinker who, although trained rigorously in Western thought-patterns and raised to the cardinalate in the

Church because of his loyalty to it, underwent an almost unimaginable transition in the course of this century. He changed from being a classical theologian fascinated with the history of dogma to being a revisionist, oriented to its future fully inculturated form in his own country and in all the churches of the world which are inserted in age-old and precious religious traditions. Thus, the pages of this study relate the story of a theological conversion which even if it could have been more radical in some ways was, and indeed remains, a symbol of the Catholic Church as a more conscientious and fraternal pilgrim on the way to salvation with the rest of humankind.

Because in the person of Joseph Cardinal Parecattil, the decision of the whole Church to continue its pilgrimage in a new way is exemplified, this study attempts to ask and to respond to the following question: what led a piously educated and officially approved son of a long-standing Oriental Church in Asia to end his years dressed in such a way that his pectoral Cross rested against saffron robes, and that his pastoral heart and administrative capabilities inspired him to prepare a revised Eucharistic ritual in which he pronounced the words of institution of Jesus at the Last Supper along with the Hindu blessing that God show the way from darkness into light, and from lies and hostility to truth and non-violence?

PART ONE

ORIGIN OF THE EUCHARISTIC THEOLOGY OF JOSEPH PARECATTIL

CHAPTER I

Liturgical, Spiritual and Social Background
of the Eucharistic Theology of Joseph Parecattil

The ideas of reknown ecclesiastics are often rooted in the sound found-ational experiences of their formative years. This is particularly true of Joseph Parecattil, the former leader and spokesman of the Syro-Malabar Church. He attributed his theological insights regarding the Eucharist to the religious training he received in his family and in Catholic schools and seminaries. This formation led him to a detailed understanding of the theo-logy of the sacrament, as it was expressed in the traditions of both the East and the West. Whereas the Eucharistic liturgy of the Syro-Malabar Church was almost identical with that of the East-Syrian Church of Chaldea, the *Mass of the Roman Rite* reflected the post-Tridentine mentality prevalent in the Western Church since the Reformation. Besides these Christian influ-ences, the religio-social context of Indian society was a factor which conditioned him in his formulation of a Eucharistic theology appropriate for Christians living in a different, but vital spiritual atmosphere.

The chapter is divided into three parts, the first of which deals with the theology and spirituality of the Eucharist based on the three anaphorae of the early East-Syrian tradition: a) The *Anaphora of Addai and Mari*; b) The *Anaphora of Theodore of Mopsuestia*; and c) The *Anaphora of Nestorius*. The *Anaphora of Addai and Mari* is the most ancient and unique of all the Eucharistic prayers, and is in use even today in the liturgy of the Syro-Malabar Church. Hence, the theology and spirituality connected with it have permeated the mentality of this Church and therefore of Parecattil who was raised in it. In the past, the anaphorae of Theodore and Nestorius were in use in the Syro-Malabar Church, whereas today attempts are being made to restore them.

The second part addresses the influence which post-Tridentine and neo-Thomistic theologies exerted on Joseph Parecattil. In the post-Tridentine theology, the sacrificial nature of the Eucharist and the ontological nature of the real presence of Christ in the sacrament were stressed. Since the fifteenth century when Western missionaries first came to India, the Syro-Malabar Church has had contact with this theology. From his youth, therefore, Parecattil, was familiar with the theology proposed by the Western Church and engaged in a thorough study of it while at the Major Seminary in Kandy.

The third part depicts the religio-social context of India in the first half of the twentieth century. Since India is a land of noted religious pluralism, with Hinduism as the major factor, Christians have necessarily to preach and to live by the Gospel in this particular context. During the time of the religious training of Joseph Parecattil the social and economic conditions of India were not as encouraging as they would later be. The vast majority of the population existed under the poverty line. The political sphere was stormy because of the drive toward independence from Great Britain. Mahatma Gandhi pressed for political change by means of a non-violent and spiritually oriented form of protest. Parecattil inevitably had to consider these religio-social factors while formulating his Eucharistic theology, a fact which explains his sensitivity to the moral dimension of sacramental grace.

1. The Eucharistic Theology and Spirituality of the Syro-Malabar Church: Their Roots in the Liturgical Celebration of the Sacrament

The spirituality of the Syro-Malabar Church is mainly sacramental in nature, since it is based primarily on an accurate study of liturgical and devotional texts. The celebration of the Mass is the most intensive expression of Christian faith, and it is the most efficacious help for the Christian life[1]. At the celebration of the Eucharist, God the Father sanctifies the world in Christ and in the Spirit, and the members of the Church offer themselves to the Father through Christ and in the Spirit. All the activities of the Christian life are in fact related to the Mass, and are directed to it. The faithful share in the unique self-sacrifice of Christ as they participate in the Eucharist, for they consume his sacramental body, and drink his sacramental blood under the signs of bread and wine. By participating in the Eucharist,

---

[1] J.A. JUNGMANN, *The Mass*, 236.

the Church of Christ grows as a community united by the Holy Spirit[2]. Frequenting daily Mass and Holy Communion are the sources of spiritual nourishment which provide the sanctification both of individual Christians and of the whole Church[3].

Born at Kidangoor in India on April 1, 1912 to parents of the Syro-Malabar Church, Joseph Parecattil was introduced to the Christian religion through the personal love and sacred solidarity of his family: «What I am today is the result of God's grace and of the virtues of my parents»[4]. Through praying with him and initiating him into the Christian way of life, they taught him the fundamentals of Syro-Malabar spirituality which is based on the East-Syrian Eucharistic liturgy[5]. In order to understand the liturgical and spiritual nature of the Eucharistic theology to which Parecattil was exposed from the youth, it is necessary, at first, briefly to investigate the East-Syrian form of worship and the three anaphorae on which it is based.

The East-Syrian Eucharistic liturgy had its origin and was initially developed in Edessa[6] which, although somewhat influenced by the tradition of Antioch, can be considered an independent source. The liturgy of the East-Syrian Church differed in many respects from the West Syrian Rite of Antioch[7]. Since Edessa was under the Persian dominion and thus outside the Roman Empire, the East-Syrian liturgy did not reflect traces of the Greek and Roman cultures[8]. On the other hand, this liturgy comprised a

---

[2] J.H. EMMINGHAUS, *The Eucharist*, xvi.

[3] P. YOUSIF, «An Introduction to the East Syrian Spirituality», 3.

[4] J. PARECATTIL, *As I See Myself (Ñān Ente Dṛṣṭiyil)*, I, 79.

[5] At the dawn of the twentieth century Syro-Malabar spirituality had already assumed a peculiar nature incorporating components from different spiritual heritages. It shaped itself into a hybrid fruit; with a mixture of the East Syrian (Chaldean), Western and Indian elements. St. Thomas, the apostle, came to India in 52. A.D. and founded seven Christian communities. It was the beginning of the Indian period which lasted for three centuries, until the coming of the Chaldeans.

In the fourth century the Indian Church came in contact with that of Chaldea through the Christians who came from Persia under the leadership of Thomas of Cana, Mar Sapor and Mar Prot (Cf. A. M. MUNDADAN, *Indian Christians' Search*, 7). Soon, the latter took control of the Syro-Malabar Church liturgically and juridically. The governance of the Church was under the dominion of the bishops and priests from Chaldea. The Chaldean bishops being unfamiliar with the local language and religious practices, naturally propagated the Chaldean liturgy in the Syro-Malabar Church.

[6] D. ATTWATER, *The Christian Churches*, I, 195.

[7] A. FORTESCUE, *The Mass*, 84-85; W.F. MACOMBER, «A Theory», 235.

[8] R.J. GALVIN, «Addai and Mari Revisited», 384.

mixture of elements from the Judeo-Christian, Assyro-Babylonian and Iranian cultures[9].

East-Syrian Eucharistic theology and liturgy are closely related to the names of Addai and Mari, Theodore of Mopsuestia, and Nestorius[10]. The East-Syrian Eucharistic liturgy is celebrated with the *Anaphora of Theodore of Mopsuestia* from the Annunciation to Palm Sunday, and with that of *Addai and Mari* from Easter to the Annunciation. The *Anaphora of Nestorius* is used only on five feast days of the liturgical year: Epiphany, St. John the Baptist, Greek Doctors, Wednesday of the Rogation and Passover Thursday[11].

Addai is considered to have been either the Apostle Thaddeus or one of the seventy disciples of Jesus[12]. Tradition also relates that St. Thomas the Apostle sent Addai to Edessa to preach the Gospel of Christ there[13], whereas he himself went to India[14]. In turn, Mari was later sent by Addai so as to introduce Christianity in Mesopotamia[15].

The *Anaphora of Addai and Mari* is believed to have originated in Edessa[16]. Since it represents a quite primitive form of Eucharistic anaphorae, many theologians consider it as the most ancient of such prayers which exists today[17]. Theological opinion varies regarding its date of origin. Many consider it to have originated in the third century while some others hold on to its later origin[18]. As its title indicates, it could have been formulated by Addai and Mari[19], or by later authors who attributed it to them[20]. Furthermore, the term «Apostles» could stand either for the Apostles of Christ or for Addai and Mari themselves[21].

---

[9] W.F. MACOMBER, «A History of the Chaldean Mass», 107-108.

[10] W.F. MACOMBER, «The Sources for a Study», 524.

[11] P. YOUSIF, «Divine Liturgy», 218-219.

[12] W. WIGRAM, *Introduction to the History*, 26.

[13] J.M. NEALE, *A History of the Holy Eastern Church*, I, 141.

[14] P.J. PODIPARA, *The Thomas Christians*, 15-18.

[15] P.J. PODIPARA, *The Thomas Christians and their Syriac Treasures*, 46.

[16] T. ELAVANAL, *The Memorial Celebration*, 26.

[17] L. BOUYER, «The Different Forms», 159; J.M. NEALE, *A History of the Holy Eastern Church*, I, 321.

[18] R.J GALVIN, «Addai and Mari Revisited», 386; G. DIX, *The Shape of the Liturgy*, 221.

[19] F.E. BRIGHTMAN, *Liturgies Eastern and Western*, I, 252.

[20] T. ELAVANAL, *The Memorial Celebration*, 28.

[21] B.H. JONES «The History of Nestorian Liturgy», 157.

The earliest manuscripts of the anaphora were written in Syriac. Different opinions exist even today about the original structure of the anaphora. According to some, there are sufficient reasons to think that initially it was a simple hymn of praise, to which a *Sanctus*, intercessory prayers, an epiclesis and an account of the words of institution were later added[22]. Yet, it is more generally accepted that the epiclesis was contained in the original text, whereas the institution narrative was not[23].

Before analyzing the theology of the anaphora, one should treat the problem arising from the absence of the institution narrative in the early manuscripts. A few scholars would argue for the existence of the institution narrative in the original text on the grounds that an anamnesis exists in the anaphora. This theory is based on the principle that there could not have been an anamnesis without an institution narrative[24]. On the other hand, a number of theologians think that the early manuscripts did not include the institution narrative[25].

How can one explain this specific characteristic of the anaphora of *Addai and Mari*? Since it reflected a primitive Eucharistic liturgy, the institution narrative could have served as an introduction to the rite of communion, rather than as a component of the prayers preceding such a rite[26]. Another view is that the absence of the institution narrative was intended, so as to give more importance to the epiclesis[27]. Yet another explanation for the absence in question is that it was eliminated by Mar Iso'yabh II when he shortened the anaphora[28].

It seems probable that the institution narrative was inserted into the anaphora at a later stage. In the Chaldean missal of 1767, the words of institution are placed just before the fraction[29]. In the Syro-Malabar Missal, the institution narrative was at first added after the rite of fraction, but later it was moved and placed just before it, the usage which remained unchanged until 1960[30]. In the present Syro-Malabar Missal the words of insti-

---

[22] E.C. RATCLIFF, «The Original Form», 23-29.

[23] G. DIX, *The Shape of the Liturgy*, 178-187.

[24] H. ENGBERDING, «Zum anaphorischen Fürbittgebet», 117.

[25] E.C. RATCLIFF, «The Original Form», 30; H.W. CODRINGTON, «The Chaldean Liturgy», 204; E.J. CUTRONE, «The Anaphora of the Apostles», 642.

[26] A.G. FUENTE, *Visione liturgica*, 93.

[27] J.A. JUNGMANN, *The Early Liturgy*, 69.

[28] W.F. MACOMBER, «A History of the Chaldean Mass», 113.

[29] T. ELAVANAL, *The Memorial Celebration*, 136.

[30] P. PODIPARA, «The Present Syro-Malabar Liturgy», 319.

tution are found immediately after the *post-Sanctus* prayer, thus bringing the anaphora in line with the other East-Syrian Eucharistic prayers[31]. Parecattil held firmly to the conviction that the institution narrative is an indispensable element of the Eucharistic liturgy, since the former continues «the solemn words proceeding from the lips of Our Lord, which however, thank God, have found a place in our Anaphora[32], though at one time they were conspicuously absent from it»[33].

The theological themes of the anaphora are various. The anamnesis, or the act of commemoration, is meant to obey the command of the Lord «Do this in memory of me» (Lk 22,19). At the Eucharistic service the participants recall and re-present the salvific events of the passion, death and resurrection which undergird the new covenant. This re-presentation makes the historically past events efficaciously present here and now[34]. Through this re-presentation the participants become mystical contemporaries of the Saviour, in the sense that the salvation he inaugurated becomes their own[35]. The anamnetic prayer also commemorates the Last Supper as the definitive foundation of the present celebration.

Yet other key themes, such as that of praise and thanksgiving, are found in the anaphora in question, as the text itself makes evident: God is worthy of praise and thanksgiving; praise to the Trinity; thanksgiving for creation and for the gift of redemption. The introductory prayer to the *Sanctus* is especially marked by these themes: You are «worthy of praise from every mouth and thanksgiving from every tongue»[36].

The epiclesis comprises an important part of the anaphora. The simplicity of the wording of the invocation as well as its position lead many to maintain that its plea for the «coming» of the Holy Spirit represents an earlier form than those others similar to it which implore Christ «to send» the Spirit. The words «May there come, O Lord»[37] are in form quite reminiscent of the *maranatha* prayer recorded by St. Paul (1Cor 16, 22). It is noteworthy that the epiclesis is addressed to Christ[38]. This can be attributed to

---

[31] T. ELAVANAL, *The Memorial Celebration*, 136.

[32] Here, the reference is to the *Anaphora of Addai and Mari* as used in the Syro-Malabar Missal.

[33] J. PARECATTIL, «Liturgical Reform», 55.

[34] B. NEUNHEUSER, «Mystery Presence», 120-127.

[35] J.D. CRICHTON, «A Theology of Worship», 13-14.

[36] T. ELAVANAL, *The Memorial Celebration*, 81.

[37] T. ELAVANAL, *The Memorial Celebration*, 163.

[38] B.D. SPINKS, «The Consecratory Epiclesis», 27; G. DIX, *The Shape of the Liturgy*, 184.260.

the theological experience of the early Christians for whom the Lord became the life-giving Spirit and the divine Pneuma became the Spirit of Jesus[39]. The anaphora invokes Christ to send the Holy Spirit so that he «dwell», in the oblation, and sanctify it.

The epiclesis is also meant to implore the Spirit to sanctify those who receive the body and blood of Christ[40]. This occurs, because the forgiveness of sins is considered one of the primary effects of Eucharistic communion, which is the pledge of Christian resurrection and eternal life. The epiclesis is also marked by the hope that the Spirit render the reception of the Eucharist an occasion in which the assembled Christians are granted new life in the kingdom of heaven. These truths led Parecattil to affirm that the «invocation of the Spirit given in the *Anaphora of Addai and Mari* is a communion epiclesis [...]»[41].

Noteworthy is the fact that, since the *Anaphora of Addai and Mari* was originally a prayer of praise and thanksgiving, it does not stress the sacrificial nature of the Eucharist[42]. However, it does view the «memorial» of the Cross of the Lord as a symbolic re-presentation of his sacrificial death and glorious resurrection[43]. The Eucharist is qualified as an oblation when, at the epiclesis, the Spirit is invoked on the gifts. The pre-anamnetic prayer also makes reference to an act of offering[44]. Hence, although there is no clear mention of the Eucharist as a sacrifice, the anaphora implies that it indeed is of such a nature.

The second Eucharistic Prayer of the East-Syrian liturgy is that of Theodore of Mopsuestia, who was born at Antioch in A.D. 350. He joined the monastery of Diodore of Tarsus, and was consecrated to the See of Mopsuestia in 392. During his lifetime, he was not greatly impeded by doctrinal controversies and he died towards the end of the year A.D. 428. His orthodoxy was never seriously doubted until after his death, when the Second Council of Constantinople A.D. 553 pronounced an anathema against him[45].

---

[39] J.D.G. DUNN, «Jesus-Flesh and Spirit», 67.

[40] E.G.C.F. ATCHLEY, *On the Epiclesis*, 117-118; J.H. McKENNA, *Eucharist and Holy Spirit*, 188.

[41] J. PARECATTIL, «Liturgical Reform», 55.

[42] E.C. RATCLIFF, «The Original Form», 30.

[43] T. ELAVANAL, *The Memorial Celebration*, 33.

[44] T. ELAVANAL, *The Memorial Celebration*, 34.

[45] ND 621; DS 434.

The prominent themes of the *Anaphora of Theodore of Mopsuestia* are: a) praise and thanksgiving; b) petition; and c) the economy of salvation. The appropriate way to give praise and thanks consists in confessing that all glorification is due to the Holy Trinity. The first, fourth and fifth *qanone*[46] deal with praise and thanksgiving to the Trinity. In the anaphora, the term «name» is used to denote both the Trinity in general and the Father in particular. The second *g'hanta*[47] states: «it is just, right and fitting to give thanks to Your holy name»[48]. Praise and thanksgiving are offered to God for his infinite and ineffable gifts of creation and providence (second *g'hanta*) and of salvation (fourth *g'hanta*)[49]. Thanks are offered, too, for the gift of the priest who is made worthy to offer the Eucharistic sacrifice for the salvation of humankind (fourth *g'hanta*)[50].

Prayers of petition are found in the *kusapa*[51], the first *g'hanta* prayer, at the exchange of peace, and particularly in the formal intercessory prayers[52]. The petitionary prayers are offered for various intentions. In the first *kusapa*, the intercession is for the grace of worthily celebrating the Eucharistic sacrifice. The priests pray God not to regard their sins and to make them worthy to celebrate the Eucharist. They also pray for the Church in general and for the Eucharistic assembly in particular. The prayers of intercession are found in the fourth *kusapa* and in the fourth *g'hanta*.

Theodore explains how the different ceremonies of the Eucharistic service represent the various aspects of Christ's work of redemption. The offertory procession is Christ's being led into his passion and death. The linen clothes spread on the altar represent the burial clothes. The ceremony of fanning the air above the sacrificial elements reminds Christians of the custom of performing the same rite over the dead body of an important person. All these ceremonies are conducted without words, so as to call to mind the silence and fear of the apostles at the death of Christ[53]. The breaking of

---

[46] In the liturgy, *qanone* signifies a liturgical hymn. Cf. G.W. LAMPE, *A Patristic Greek Lexicon*, 120.

[47] The word *g'hanta* stands for the part of the liturgy spoken only by the priest. While reciting the prayer, he bends forward (Cf. C. BROCKELMANN, *Lexicon Syriacum*, 106).

[48] Cf. J. VADAKKEL, *The East Syrian Anaphora*, 135.

[49] R.H. CONNOLLY, *The Liturgical Homilies of Narsai*, Cambridge 1909, 18.

[50] G. MOOKEN, *The Liturgy of the Holy Apostles*, 21.

[51] The word *kusapa* means supplication or intercession (Cf. C. BROCKELMANN, *Lexicon Syriacum*, 350).

[52] J. VADAKKEL, *The East Syrian Anaphora*, 143.

[53] Cf. F.J. REINE, *The Eucharistic Doctrine*, 60-61.

the bread is the remembrance of the appearance of Christ to his apostles after his resurrection[54].

According to this anaphora, the salvation of humankind is the work of the Trinity. Each of the three divine Persons has a unique role to fulfil, apart from cooperation in that which the other two Persons effect. The Eucharistic celebration is the re-enacting of the redemptive act of the Trinity[55]. The first and the second *g'hanta* speak of the role of the Father as creator, sustainer and rewarder of all creatures. He exercises these functions through the Son and the Spirit. The first four *g'hanta* prayers deal with the Christology of the anaphora. The Eucharistic sacrifice is the commemoration of the unique sacrifice of Jesus, in that it re-actualizes his passion, death, and resurrection, and thus the apex of the whole economy of salvation. The Eucharist is the real symbol of Christ's sacrifice, because it is its «remembrance» and «likeness». Each day, in and through the sacramental symbols, Christ is immolated again for the sake of mankind[56].

In this context, it is worthwhile to treat Theodore's Christological views. In the early centuries, the main problem regarding Christ was how to define the relation between his divine and human natures[57]. Theodore's Christological doctrines were said to have influenced Nestorius who studied under him[58]. For many, there is no evident difference between the teachings of Theodore and those of Nestorius[59]. Theodore recognized both the divine and the human natures in Christ and the unity of his person. The one person has as intrinsic elements the nature of the Word and the nature of humanity, each in its entirety. Theodore held that the two elements remain separate and distinct since, strictly speaking, there was for him only a moral union between them. He was later interpreted to have maintained that there were two sons, and thus two persons, in Jesus Christ[60]. Although the storm of controversy concerning the title *Theotokos* was yet to start, one of Theodore's sermons on this subject was offensive to many. He immediately retracted his statements, and therefore observed moderation. But his sermon

---

[54] Cf. A. MINGANA, *Commentary of Theodore of Mopsuestia*, 105.

[55] P. PODIPARA, «Interpretation of the Offices», 100.

[56] A. MINGANA, *Commentary of Theodore of Mopsuestia*, 55.

[57] J.N.D. KELLY, *Early Christian Doctrines*, 138.

[58] P.T. CAMELOT, «Nestorianism», 348.

[59] F.A. SULLIVAN, *The Christology of Theodore of Mopsuestia*, 6.

[60] J.F. BETHUNE-BAKER, *An Introduction to the Early History*, 260.

was considered to be a public denial of the privileged status of the Blessed Virgin[61].

In the anaphora, the first and the second *g'hanta* mention Christ's participation in creation. The third speaks of the history of salvation as centred in Christ. He is described as the mediator between God and humanity in the fourth *g'hanta*. The main Christological titles used in the Eucharistic prayer are: «The Only Begotten Son», «God the Word» and «Lord Jesus Christ». The Christological themes found are: the incarnation, the institution of the Eucharist, the passion, the death, the resurrection and the second coming. The incarnation is mentioned in the first, third and fourth *g'hanta*. The institution narrative is found in the third *g'hanta*. The latter also speaks of Christ's passion, death and resurrection. The second coming at the last judgement is referred to in the fourth *g'hanta*.

Theodore teaches the real presence of Christ in the Eucharist; the body and blood of Jesus Christ are really present under the appearances of bread and wine. He bases this truth on the texts of the Gospel which record Jesus as saying «This is my body», and not «This is the symbol of my body»[62].

Theodore attributes great importance to the epiclesis. The *g'hanta* prayers in fact contain the pneumatology of the anaphora. The first *g'hanta* implores the assistance of the Holy Spirit in the offering of the Eucharistic sacrifice. In the second *g'hanta*, the Holy Spirit is said to sanctify the faithful. The third and the fourth *g'hanta* refer to the role of the Holy Spirit in the incarnation and resurrection of Christ respectively. The central point of the pneumatology is the epiclesis, in which the Holy Spirit is invoked to rest upon the bread and wine and to transform them into the body and blood of Christ. Theodore strongly asserts that the consecration of the elements is effected by the coming of the Holy Spirit upon them. He goes far beyond the views of other theologians of his time, such as St. Cyril of Jerusalem and St. John Chrysostom, regarding the consecratory power of the epiclesis. Theologians are generally of the opinion that Cyril and John proposed a synthetic theory, that is, the position that the anamnesis effects the consecration, while the epiclesis perfects the sacrifice[63].

On the other hand, Theodore ignores the words of institution, giving consecratory power solely to the epiclesis[64]. He reasons in the following

---

[61] L. PATTERSON, *Theodore of Mopsuestia*, 4.

[62] A. MINGANA, *Commentary of Theodore of Mopsuestia*, 9.

[63] F. PROBST, «Die antiochenische Messe», 291.

[64] F.J REINE, *The Eucharistic Doctrine*, 18.

way: the body which the Son of God assumed did not receive the gift of immortality until its resurrection from the dead; just as the Holy Spirit raised the body of Jesus from the dead and made it immortal, so now in the Eucharist the Holy Spirit changes the bread and wine and makes them spiritual food and drink. When Theodore states that «from the offertory procession to the epiclesis, Christ lies slain and buried on the altar»[65], he means that the bread and wine, over which solely the institutional words are pronounced, comprise only the dead body of Christ before the resurrection, and are not able to grant Christians a share in his immortality. But, at the epiclesis of the Holy Spirit, the bread and wine become the resurrected body of Christ which is immortal[66].

Joseph Parecattil did not agree with the thought of Theodore concerning the inferior importance of the institution narrative to the epiclesis. Instead he held that the transubstantiation takes place with the recital of the institution words preceded by the first epiclesis. He noted a difference between the *Anaphora of Addai and Mari* and the *Anaphora of Theodore of Mopsuestia*: in the former «the words of institution, not preceded by the invocation of the Holy Spirit, are apparently narratory, not consecratory»[67]. In the latter, however, the Holy Spirit is invoked to convert the bread and wine into the body and blood of Christ[68].

Theodore asserted that there exit both a common and a ministerial form of priesthood. All the baptized offer the Eucharistic sacrifice together with the ordained who serve as the tongue for the whole body. They offer the sacrifice both for themselves and for the people. At the same time, they represent Christ the true High Priest, who offers himself to the Father.

For Theodore, the sacrament of the Eucharist is the nourishment of the soul and the food of immortality. Since it has its source in the death and resurrection of Christ, it is thus a participation in the pneumatic body of the crucified Lord. Theodore makes a distinction between the real food of immortality, that is, the grace of the Holy Spirit, and the symbolic or sacramental food of immortality, that is, the Eucharist[69]. Whereas Theodore affirms that divine grace makes the faithful immortal, he claims that the sacramental food will cease at the eschaton[70].

---

[65] A. MINGANA, *Commentary of Theodore of Mopsuestia*, 25.

[66] F.J. REINE, *The Eucharistic Doctrine*, 22.

[67] J. PARECATTIL, «Liturgical Reform», 55.

[68] J. PARECATTIL, «Liturgical Reform», 55.

[69] F. REINE, *The Eucharistic Doctrine*, 29.

[70] A. MINGANA, *Commentary of Theodore of Mopsuestia*, 30.

Theodore's central insight is that, since through the Baptismal symbol Christians begin to enjoy immortal life, so the Eucharist symbolically or sacramentally provides them the foretaste of future glory[71]. Theodore thus designates the Eucharist as the spiritual food in signs and symbols. The symbols of bread and wine are suitable to the present time: both to the natural life received at birth and to the new life received at the second birth of Baptism. Theodore also considers the Eucharist to be the sign of the unity of Christ with Christians, and of Christians among themselves. The Eucharist strengthens the ecclesial body of Christ, because through the sacrament all the members become more united to their Head.

As the commemoration of the historical sacrifice of Christ, the Eucharist represents his offering the heavenly sacrifice to the Father. At the same time, those who are present at the Eucharistic celebration of the Church also participate in the heavenly sacrifice[72]. The holy celebration of the Eucharist is thus enacted on earth and fulfilled in heaven. Since the full attainment of redemption takes place only in heaven, the participants in the Eucharist are granted a symbolical representation of glory; and in the Eucharist the second coming of Christ is sacramentally made present to them[73].

Apart from spiritual nourishment and ecclesial unity, Theodore regards personal holiness and the remission of venial sins as other effects of the Eucharist. The venial sins which arise from human weakness do not deter the faithful from receiving the Holy Sacrament. He instructs the people to receive Holy Communion in order to advance in the holiness which has been already granted to them in Baptism. The communicants must be holy, in order to receive the sacrament, because the Eucharistic body and blood of Christ are holy and immortal. Having received them, the faithful should offer adoration to the sacrament, press it to their eyes, kiss it and pray to Christ who is present.

The third Eucharistic Prayer of the East-Syrian liturgy is the *Anaphora of Nestorius*. A native of Germanica, Nestorius became a member of the monastery of Euprepius near Antioch, from which he was called to the See of Constantinople. Later he involved himself in doctrinal controversies, was charged with heretical teachings, removed from his bishopric, excommunic-

---

[71] J.M. DEWART, *Theology of Grace*, 107.

[72] A. MINGANA, *Commentary of Theodore of Mopsuestia*, 55.

[73] F.J. REINE, *The Eucharistic Doctrine*, 63.

ated, and banished to the deserts of Egypt where he died in exile[74]. In 431, the Council of Ephesus officially condemned him[75].

The *Anaphora of Nestorius* is similar to the Eucharistic prayer of St. James. But in general, there is a closer parallel between the *Anaphora of Nestorius* and that of St. Chrysostom and of St. Basil[76]. The structural pattern of the anaphora is determined by three main divisions: thanksgiving for the creation and the preservation of humanity; the redemption; and the Great Oblation. In the first part, thanksgiving is offered to God for having fashioned the physical universe, and for having sustained humankind. In the second part, Nestorius includes the words of institution as an integral part of the account of the redemption. In the third part, the Great Oblation, he inserts an intercession after which follows the epiclesis, the climax of the whole action[77].

In the first *g'hanta*, there are three references to thanksgiving and praise. In the first, the celebrants thank God for making them and the assembly worthy of offering the sacrifice. In the second, thanks and praise are offered to the Trinity for all the works of creation and, in the third, the participants thank God for the gift of the Eucharist. The second *g'hanta*, following the *Sanctus*, gives praise for the salvific acts of Christ[78].

The anaphora includes the theme of commemoration, since it recalls the command of Christ to eat and drink the Eucharist in his memory until he comes again. Through the anamnesis, the faithful may attain the remission of sins, and have the hope of being raised to eternal life[79]. The second *g'hanta*, which follows the *Sanctus*, qualifies the Eucharist as the commemoration of the body and the blood of Christ: «He left us the commemoration of our salvation, this mystery which we offer before You»[80].

The Eucharist is viewed as a sacrifice. Christ delivered himself up to be betrayed, and endured pain and crucifixion for our sins. He sacrificed himself that we might live; he pardoned our sins and reconciled us to the Father through the shedding of his blood. Since it is impossible that the

---

[74] J.F. BETHUNE-BAKER, *Nestorius and His Teaching*, 1.

[75] ND 604-605; DS 250-251.

[76] B.H. JONES, «The Formation of the Nestorian Liturgy», 278.

[77] B.H. JONES, «The Liturgy of Nestorius», 405.

[78] B.D. SPINKS, «Eucharistic Offering», 347-371.

[79] P. YOUSIF, «Divine Liturgy», 222.

[80] Cf. B.D. SPINKS, «Eucharistic Offering», 359-360.

atoning sacrifice of Christ be identically repeated[81], it is commemorated
on the altar where he is sacrificed every day sacramentally.

In this context, it is helpful to present briefly the Christology of Nestorius
on which his Eucharistic theology depends. His Christological views led
him into doctrinal controversies with his chief opponent, Cyril of Alexand-
ria, who charged that he was denying the unity of Christ's person. Cyril
held that, by advocating two *hypostases*, Nestorius presupposed two persons
and two sons, as if the divine *hypostasis* spoke and acted at one moment,
and the human at another[82]. Although Nestorius sought to preserve a close
union between the divinity and the humanity of Christ, his premises admitted only a union in the experimental order, and not in the metaphysical
order[83]. Rather than arriving at a synthesis of the natures of the Word and
of humankind, Nestorius proposed the notion of «indwelling»[84] by which
to express the unity found in Christ. His humanity was considered the
temple, the garment, or the instrument of the divinity. In contrast to the use
of «union» or «unity» by the Alexandrines, Nestorius spoke of the «conjunction» of two natures. Jesus the man, not Jesus the Word, was born of
Mary, and was a human person in whom the Spirit of the Word of God was
present. Nestorius declined to attribute to Mary the title *Theotokos*, and
preferred instead to call her *Christotokos*[85].

Cyril opposed the Nestorian doctrine precisely because of its implications
relative to the doctrine of the Eucharist. He insisted that the Logos and the
flesh are inseparable. When the flesh is united to the Logos, the former is
transformed and becomes the body of the latter receiving all of its powers;
hence it is far more than the body of any common person on earth[86]. In
the Eucharist, the bread and wine are transformed into the body and blood
of Christ so that, by partaking in them, the faithful receive the life-giving
and sanctifying power of Christ. As the Church celebrates the Eucharist,
Christ comes into its midst both invisibly and visibly: invisibly as God and
visibly as sacrament, because every Eucharist is a symbolic re-incarnation
of the Logos. Cyril considered that only the concept «hypostatic union»
could render the flesh of Jesus contained in the Eucharist capable of
communicating divine power to the faithful. Hence, he accused Nestorius

---

[81] G.P. BADGER, *The Nestorians*, 176.

[82] J. QUASTEN, *Patrology*, III, 138.514.

[83] M.J. COSTELLOE, «Nestorian Church», 344.

[84] ND 606/11; DS 262.

[85] J. QUASTEN, *Patrology*, III, 514.

[86] H. CHADWICK, «Eucharist and Christology», 154.

of viewing the flesh of Jesus as that of an ordinary man, and of denying the resurrection of this same flesh, thereby falsely understanding the Eucharist as an act of cannibalism[87].

There was also a protracted debate between Nestorius and Superianus, the spokesman of Cyril, concerning the doctrine of the Eucharist[88]. Superianus attacked Nestorius for claiming that the body and blood of Jesus Christ were merely those of a man, and not of one substance with the Word of God. In response, Nestorius claimed that the body and blood of Jesus, by which the faithful are sanctified, is of one substance with their body and blood; that is, Christians are in solidarity with Christ through their common humanity, for they can have no solidarity with the Logos. In the Eucharist the participants receive the body and blood of Jesus which are of one substance with those of human beings, so that thereby they are made to share in his resurrection and immortality. For Superianus, following Cyril's doctrine, the union of the Logos with the flesh of Jesus is parallel to the union of the Eucharistic bread with his flesh. But Nestorius thought that Cyril's doctrine implied that the humanity of the Logos was transformed into his divinity, that is, that his body ceased to be such, and his humanity no longer had any solidarity with that of the faithful. He accused Cyril of believing the body of Jesus to be of one substance with the Logos[89]. Nestorius pointed out that, since our Lord called the bread his body, he implied that his human nature, with its *ousia*, was real and did not simply exist as an idea. He criticized Cyril for making the existence of the human nature of Christ merely a notion by which to support his doctrine of the unification of the natures[90]. Nestorius was of the opinion that, although the bread and wine become the body and blood of Christ, they retain their own *ousia*. And inasmuch as their *ousia* is the same as that of the human nature of Christ, they are his body and Blood. It is because Jesus really has a human *ousia* that the faithful who are human can be his brothers and sisters; thus, the bread and wine become true means of union with him. On the other hand, Cyril's doctrine centred on the concept of transformation by stating that, when the *ousia* of the bread and wine becomes the *ousia* of the Word of God, the elements cease to exist as such. Nestorius concluded that this doctrine, which denies the reality of the bread and the wine, transmutes the

---

[87] H. CHADWICK, «Eucharist and Christology», 156.
[88] J.F. BETHUNE-BAKER, *Nestorius and His Teaching*, 141-147.
[89] H. CHADWICK, «Eucharist and Christology», 157.
[90] H. CHADWICK, «Eucharist and Christology», 157.

human *ousia* of our Lord, and thus annihilates the reality of the Incarnation[91].

As in the other Eastern Eucharistic Prayers, the epiclesis is the climax of the Nestorian anaphora too. Nestorius believed that the elements are changed, not by the power of the officiating minister, or by the repetition of the words of institution alone, but by the mysterious and all-sanctifying power of the Holy Spirit who is solemnly invoked[92]. According to him, the epiclesis typifies the resurrection of Christ; the people need to prostrate themselves and rise before it in order to symbolize their adoration to the risen Lord[93]. Parecattil could not agree with the Nestorian theory regarding the consecratory effect of the epiclesis. Instead, he held that the real change in the Eucharistic elements takes place at the recital of the words of institution[94].

In concluding these brief reflections, one could state that the three anaphorae had determinative influence on the Syro-Malabar Church. The East-Syrian Eucharistic theology, and its concomitant spirituality, came to the Church mainly through these Eucharistic prayers. The theological insights of these anaphorae were determinative of the teaching of the Church at the beginning of the twentieth century, even though those of Theodore and Nestorius were prohibited. This influence naturally affected the thought-pattern of Parecattil, even if he considered the relation of the East-Syrian to the Syro-Malabar Church as one of «Chaldean domination, both juridically and liturgically»[95] which resulted in a «liturgical colonialism»[96].

2. The Post-Tridentine and Neo-Thomistic Eucharistic Theology and Spirituality

Many would consider Joseph Parecattil a churchman who pointed the way into the next century, for he analyzed with theological acumen the issues of his time for the benefit of the Church of tomorrow. At the same time, however, he was loyal to the traditional teachings of the Catholic Church. As regards the theology and liturgy of the Eucharist, he held fast to the

---

[91] J.F. BETHUNE-BAKER, *Nestorius and His Teaching*, 147.

[92] G.P. BADGER, *The Nestorians*, 232.

[93] P. YOUSIF, «Divine Liturgy», 225.

[94] J. PARECATTIL, «Liturgical Reform», 55.

[95] J. PARECATTIL, «Liturgical Reform», 48.

[96] J. PARECATTIL, «Liturgical Reform», 49.

precisely articulated doctrines developed in the Post-Tridentine period, and reinforced during the Neo-Thomistic revival. He became acquainted with these doctrine in two ways. In his youth, the Syro-Malabar Eucharistic theology was already influenced by Western traditions, and presented it consistently to the people[97]. Moreover, in 1935, Parecattil entered the Papal Seminary in Kandy to begin his priestly formation, which was based on a systematic exposition of Western theology.

The important doctrinal concepts of the post-Tridentine theology are the sacrificial nature of the Eucharist, and the real presence by means of the transubstantiation of the bread and wine. Most Reformers considered the Mass solely as a fraternal meal, and thus denied the sacrificial character of the Eucharist[98]. They were convinced that if they did not deny this they would have to hold that Christ is cruelly put to death each day in innumerable places[99]. In response, the Fathers at the Council of Trent affirmed that at Mass the faithful share both in the «Lord's Supper» and in the «sacrifice of his body and blood»[100]. The Lord is present among his followers under the form of bread and wine to be consumed by them, which fact underlines the meal aspect of the Eucharist. At the same time the Eucharist is the unbloody commemoration of the bloody sacrifice of the Lord on the Cross. In short, responding to the command of Jesus, the Church celebrates in each generation the memorial of the Last Supper which is also the sacramental re-actualization of the sacrifice on the Cross[101].

Some papal pronouncements of the twentieth century also reiterate these specific Catholic teachings on the Eucharist. In his encyclical letter *Mystici Corporis* of 1943, Pope Pius XII explains how the divine Redeemer, as the head of the Church, offers all his mystical members to the Father through the sacrifice on the Cross[102]. Another encyclical of the same Pope,

---

[97] The fifteenth century opened a new chapter with the influence of the Portuguese on the Syro-Malabar Church which was so far governed by the Chaldean Church. They tried to eliminate the power of the East-Syrians and bring the Syro-Malabar Church under the *Padroado*. Archbishop Menezes of Goa convened a Synod at Diamper in 1599. In the Synod, he asked the Syrians to condemn the Chaldean patriarch Simon IX Denha and commanded them not to accept any bishop who was not sent directly by the Pope. The Synod brought about significant changes in the laws and customs of the Indian Christians with effects on their spirituality, theology and the liturgy, of the Syro-Malabar Church (Cf. A. M. MUNDADAN, *Indian Christians' Search*, 31).

[98] A. McDONALD, *The Sacrifice of the Mass*, 27.

[99] F. CLARK, *Eucharistic Sacrifice*, 435.

[100] ND 1546, 1556; DS 1740, 1752; A. McDONALD, *The Sacrifice of the Mass*, 27.

[101] D.N. POWER, *The Sacrifice We Offer*, 59.

[102] ND 1564.

Mediator Dei of 1947, reconfirms the pronouncements of the Council of Trent by stating that the fruits of the bloody sacrifice on the Cross are received in abundance through the unbloody oblation of the Mass[103]. Hence, the Mass is offered for the satisfaction of the sins not only of the living but also of the dead in purgatory[104]. This encyclical also developed the theology of the Council of Trent by affirming that the faithful also offer the Mass through and with the priest[105]. Since the priest offers the sacrifice in the name both of Christ and of the faithful, the rite has a public and social character. The Mass, even if celebrated privately, is offered by the entire Church[106]. Since the rite of communion is an integral part of the sacrifice, it is obligatory for the celebrant to receive the consecrated species while it is only highly recommended that the faithful do so[107].

Joseph Parecattil adhered to the doctrine that Eucharist is both the «Lord's Supper» and the sacramental re-actualization of the sacrifice of Christ on the cross[108]. He stated: «the sacrifice on the Cross is the same which was offered by Christ at the Last Supper»[109]. The relevance of this statement becomes clear when he affirmed: «the Eucharist is the sacrifice began at the Last Supper and completed on the Cross»[110]. Moreover, he considered the Eucharist as the sacrifice of Christ offered through the hands of the priest to the Eternal Father. He often pointed out that all Christians are priests through their baptismal character, and thus can offer the sacrifice together with the priest[111]. The Council of Trent rejected the position of Ulrich Zwingli regarding the presence of Christ in the Eucharist only «in sign», and restated the true, real and substantial presence of Jesus Christ, true God and true man in this sacrament[112]. In response to Philip Melanchton, the Council insisted that Christ is present in the sacrament prior to its consumption, and remains until the elements are consumed[113]. Opposing the view of Martin Luther, who held that the substance of the

---

[103] ND 1566; DS 3848.
[104] ND 1548; DS 1743.
[105] ND 1567, 1568; DS 1734, 1735-1736.
[106] ND 1569; DS 3853.
[107] ND 1570; 3854.
[108] J. PARECATTIL, *Liturgy As I See It*, 268.
[109] J. PARECATTIL, «Sacrifice of the Mass», 12.
[110] J. PARECATTIL, *Letters to Children*, 42.
[111] J. PARECATTIL, «How to View the Mass», 268.
[112] ND 1513-1515, 1526; DS 1636-1638, 1651.
[113] ND 1516, 1529; DS 1639, 1654.

bread and wine subsist together with that of the body and blood of Christ, the Council maintained that the bread and wine are substantially changed into the body and blood of Christ, and that only their outward appearances remain after the consecration[114].

The doctrines of real presence and of transubstantiation continued to be the prominent features of Catholic Eucharistic theology in the twentieth century, as is evident in *Mediator Dei*, where it is underlined that in the Eucharistic species «both the body and blood of Christ are rendered really present»[115]. In the encyclical *Humani Generis* of 1950, Pius XII defended the doctrine of transubstantiation against attempts on the part of some theologians to reduce the presence of Christ in the Eucharist to a symbolic one[116]. Parecattil strongly affirmed that the Eucharist contains the real presence of Christ[117], and that this is effected through the changing of «bread into the body of Our Lord, and wine into his blood [...] which in theology we call transubstantiation»[118].

Leading Catholic thinkers of the twentieth century proposed a return to genuine Scholastic ideas by means of an intellectual quest termed Neo-Thomism. At the beginning of the century, Jacques Maritain attempted to reconcile the teachings of Thomas Aquinas with the tenets of modern philosophy. He advocated an «open Thomism» which was on the one hand traditional, by basing itself on the original texts, and on the other progressive, by seeking to assimilate the insights of modern philosophy and science. Maritain played a leading role in revitalizing Thomistic insights by purifying them of later, rather decadent, Scholastic accretions, and by restating them in existential language more intelligible to contemporary human beings[119].

Similarly, Etienne Gilson sought to decipher the essence of Thomism through accurate historical studies, so as to highlight its fundamentally theological rather than philosophical framework. Gilson envisaged a vital Thomistic theology that could interpret, criticize and put in order the expressions of Catholicism which had been erroneously formulated in purely static metaphysical terms since the late Middle Ages[120].

---

[114] ND 1519, 1527; DS 1642, 1652.

[115] ND 1566; DS 3848.

[116] ND 1571; DS 3891.

[117] J. PARECATTIL, *Letters to Priests*, 106.

[118] J. PARECATTIL, *Liturgy As I See It*, 269.

[119] D.A. GALLAGER, «Jacques Maritain», 135-137.

[120] A. MAURER, «Etienne Gilson», 137-138.

This initial revival of the thought of Thomas Aquinas stimulated the emergence of transcendental Thomism by leading theologians such as Joseph Maréchal, Karl Rahner and Emerich Coreth. Transcendental Thomism stresses the universal search for God through existential acts of intelligence springing from the love of the transcendent. All of creation is viewed as oriented toward God, and every act of knowing and loving toward the attaintment of the beatific vision. For example, Rahner holds that every human person grasps God in an unthematic and pre-conceptual way as the absolute mystery permeating the search for truth and love. The believer, unable to demonstrate the existence of God directly, can do so by interpreting each common experience as a manifestation of the gratuitous grace of God in Jesus Christ and in the Holy Spirit[121].

With regard to the Eucharist, Rahner highlights the experience of Jesus in the Cenacle as both a universal search for an authentic way to stand before the mysterious Father and before beloved friends in the solitude, darkness and anguish of death, and as a unique and definitive act of salvation for humankind. Jesus chooses to make a radical gift of himself to the Father and to his friends at table with him for the last time. Rather than isolation, despair or violence, Jesus breaks the bread and shares the cup, so as to symbolise and grant solidarity, hope and love to all suffering people. As the Word of God in the flesh, Jesus institutes the unique ritual of Christianity, offering himself for the salvation of the world in the real symbols of bread broken and wine poured out. Each time Christians gather in faith and love to re-enact his gesture of self giving in the Cenacle and on the Calvary, they associate their own sufferings with those of Jesus present among them, and find hope in the definitive joy they will one day share with him and all others in the kingdom of God. As a student in the major seminary in Kandy and later as a priest and bishop, Parecattil was inclined to express and develop his theological insights according this Neo-Thomistic pattern[122].

Eucharistic devotions also evolved in the Post-Tridentine and Neo-Thomistic periods. By the beginning of the twentieth century they became the main source of spiritual nourishment for the faithful. The Council of Trent encouraged a Christocentric spirituality through veneration of the Blessed Sacrament and solemn celebrations and processions[123]. Thus, devotion to the Eucharist outside the Mass became popular, and the number

---

[121] W. J. HILL, «Thomism», 452.
[122] J. PARECATTIL, *As I See Myself*, I, 256.
[123] ND 1520, 1531; DS 1643, 1656.

of the private Masses increased. And even at public Masses the adoration of the elevated sacred species was fostered as «communion through the eyes», a saving contact with Christ by simply gazing at him[124]. The Council of Trent also defended the feast of Corpus Christi against the Reformers, interpreting it as a most fitting external way of announcing the triumphant victory of Christ over sin and death. All these practices contributed to the intensification of devotion to the Eucharist, while safeguarding the importance of participating in the Mass[125].

In the twentieth century, besides the developments in Eucharistic theology, there were many attempts to renew the liturgy of this sacrament through the use of the vernacular, the emphasis on hearing the Word, and the encouragement of the active role of the participants at the Mass[126]. There also emerged efforts to adapt the liturgy to the culture and daily experience of the people, and thus to emphasise the communal dimension of the Eucharistic celebration[127]. The pastoral function of the Eucharistic liturgy was articulated in the decrees of Pius X which encouraged more frequent reception of communion by the people. In *Tra le sollecitudini*, the pope called for the active participation of the faithful in the Mass, based on the principle that more fruit could be culled from the sacrament in this way. Thus, Pius X held that the renewed involvement of the congregation in the sacred mysteries, and in the public devotions of the Church, would regenerate Christian life[128]. In the decree *Sacra Tridentina* of 1905, the pope encouraged even daily communion and indicated that, while the Eucharist exercises its effects *ex opere operato*, these depend also on the dispositions of the recipients, or the *ex opere operantis* dimension of grace[129].

The liturgical renewal of the twentieth century was inaugurated by Dom Lambert Beauduin in Belgium, and later spread to Germany, Austria and France[130]. Some of the Papal pronouncements during and after World War II also gave impetus to the reform of the liturgy. The encyclical of Pius XII, *Mystici Corporis* of 1943 and *Mediator Dei* of 1947 attributed to the Eucharist a prominent place in the life of the Church, since it defined the liturgy as a participation by the faithful in the priestly activity of Christ the head

---

[124] J.H. EMMINGHAUS, *The Eucharist*, 81.
[125] J. JUNGMANN, *The Mass*, 80.81.
[126] J.H. EMMINGHAUS, *The Eucharist*, 92.
[127] J.H. EMMINGHAUS, *The Eucharist*, xxiii, xxiv.
[128] ND 1208; DS 3379, 3382.
[129] ND 1209.
[130] L. BOUYER, *Eucharist*, 446.

of the Mystical Body. With these encyclicals the movements in favour of the reformation of the liturgy were furthered, and the conscious participation of the community increased[131].

One of the main themes of the Eucharistic theology of Joseph Parecattil is that the proper disposition and active participation in the Eucharistic celebration by the faithful are necessary «in order to attain the maximum benefit from the Mass»[132]. Moreover, he argued for the use of the vernacular in the liturgy so that such a disposition and participation on the part of the faithful would be possible[133].

As has already been mentioned, the Syro-Malabar Church was influenced by Western theology with the arrival of European missionaries in the fifteenth century. Particularly the Eucharistic theology, spirituality and devotional practices of the West were assimilated into the East-Syrian liturgical tradition. Hence, Parecattil became acquainted with the Post-Tridentine and Neo-Thomistic theologies of the Eucharist, which dominated the Latin Church, both from his family and from his formation, and he adapted them as the basis of his own reflections. He was especially inspired by the liturgical renewal of the twentieth century, and tried to promote the reform of the Syro-Malabar liturgy, for example, by advocating the introduction of the vernacular so as to enhance the participation of the faithful[134].

The spiritual life of Joseph Parecattil was decidedly Eucharistic-centred, as is evident not only in his faithfulness to daily Mass, but also in the significant time he devoted to adoration of the Eucharistic Lord[135]. As a young man he made an oath that, if he completed his philosophical studies successfully, he would spend an hour before the Blessed Sacrament for two weeks. He fulfilled this promise, and then as a theology student determined to continue this practice throughout his life, so as to gain strength and courage from the Eucharist[136]. He regarded daily Holy Communion as the lighted lamp sustaining him at times of trial, of criticism and of suffering[137].

Furthermore, the Eucharistic-centred spiritual life of Parecattil was particularly marked by his intense devotion to the Sacred Heart. He was

---

[131] J.H. EMMINGHAUS, *The Eucharist*, 95.
[132] J. PARECATTIL, *Letters to the People*, 113.
[133] J. PARECATTIL, *Liturgy As I See It*, 32.
[134] J. PARECATTIL, «Liturgical Reform», 63.
[135] J. PARECATTIL, *As I See Myself*, I, 281.
[136] J. PARECATTIL, *As I See Myself*, I, 282.
[137] J. PARECATTIL, *As I See Myself*, I, 134.

introduced to this devotion by his mother who dedicated her family to the Sacred Heart of Jesus, as is the common practice in Kerala. He recalls that this ceremony of dedication was conducted in a more solemn manner before he began his studies at the major seminary[138]. He considered the self-consuming love of the Sacred Heart as the source of the grace he was given to withstand the tribulations of his priestly life, especially after he became bishop. In the memoir written on the occasion of his priestly ordination he states that he prayed: «Lord, keep your servant in your Sacred Heart»[139], because he was convinced that the love of Christ had inspired his vocation.

3. The Religious and Social Context of India: The Need of Eucharistic-Centred Social Action

Christians in India must preach the Good News of Jesus Christ in a complex multi-religious and socio-political atmosphere. In order to do so effectively, they are now aware that they must adopt a way of proclaiming the Gospel which is sensitive to the religious and philosophical language and thought-pattern of Indian society, and follow methods meaningful to the people. In the first half of the twentieth century, however, Christianity did not manifest much openness to the non-Christian religions which were generally considered as pagan. In the allocution *Singulari Quadam*, Pope Pius IX re-stated the classical position that no one can be saved outside the apostolic Roman Church. Yet, in the same document the pope held that those who are ignorant of the true religion through no fault of their own are not to be regarded as guilty before the Lord[140]. Moreover, the statement issued by *The First Plenary Council of India*, which was approved by Pope Pius XII in 1951, affirms that there exist truth and goodness outside the Christian religion, since the human soul is naturally drawn towards the one true God[141].

Such magisterial statements induced Parecattil to develop a positive attitude towards the different religious traditions of India, and specially towards Hinduism, which he considered as a natural religion containing «vestiges of the primitive revelation»[142]. Hinduism advocates the attain-

---

[138] J. PARECATTIL, *As I See Myself*, I, 63.

[139] J. PARECATTIL, *As I See Myself*, I, 298.

[140] ND 1010.

[141] ND 1017.

[142] J. PARECATTIL, «Indigenisation and Evangelization», 1.

ment of salvation by all people[143], «either through knowledge or through holy work»[144]. It teaches the *dharma* which leads to *Moksa*, or spiritual freedom, the ultimate goal of human life[145]. Joseph Parecattil was a Catholic prelate who was convinced that «a Christian cannot be blind to the spiritual earnestness, sincerity and work of God's grace in those who profess a faith different from his own»[146]. On the basis of this truth, he felt justified in incorporating elements from the Hindu religion into the Eucharistic liturgy[147].

In the nineteenth and twentieth centuries, mainly due to the spread of Western ideas, there emerged and grew a revival movement in Hinduism which is termed «Hindu renaissance»[148]. Ram Mohan Roy was one of the prominent early reformers whose search for truth led him to study the doctrines of Hinduism, Buddhism, Islam and Christianity. In particular, he tried to unite the ethical principles of Christianity with the philosophical tenets of the *Upaniṣads*[149]. He excoriated Hindu idolatry and such other abuses like *Sati*, or the caste system, polygamy and female infanticide[150]. He advocated the improvement of the social status of women, by stressing the responsibility of males in their regard[151]. In 1828 he founded *Brahmo Samaj*, a reformed religious group, of which Devendranath Tagore later became the head. Tagore played a courageous role in reforming Hinduism through the advocacy of tolerance and rational discourse[152]. In retrospect Parecattil noted that «for about a half a century (Devendranath) Tagore's works interpreted in a unique manner the true spirit of Indian culture and civilization, adding a new dimension to patriotic thoughts»[153].

Then, in 1867, Dr. Atmaram Pandurang founded the *Prarthana Samaj* whose aims were rational worship and social reform. Its members were involved in fostering adult education, in setting up orphanages for

---

[143] *Brh. Up.*, I, 3:28.

[144] *Sat. Brahm.*, X. 4. 3. 9; *Gītā, IV. 33.*

[145] J. NEUNER, «Problems of Teaching Theology», 221; H. RAZA, *The Cultural Role of India*, 45.

[146] J. PARECATTIL, «Foreword» to Z. PARANILAM, *Christian Openness*, xii-xiii.

[147] J. PARECATTIL, *Liturgy As I See It*, 285.

[148] K. SINGH, «The Hindu Renaissance», 1.

[149] A.S. MENON, *Indian History*, 190.

[150] V.A. SMITH, *The Oxford History of India*, 652.

[151] A.S MENON, *Indian History*, 190-191.

[152] V.A. SMITH, *The Oxford History of India*, 730.

[153] J. PARECATTIL, «Be at the Service of Bhārata Māta», 3.

abandoned children, especially in Maharashtra[154]. Bipin Chandra Pal, a Bengali revivalist, was of opinion that the most perilous danger facing India was that the people separated spiritual enlightenment from social welfare[155]. He thus tried to link these two concerns through writings which employed theological terms[156]. In 1875 *Swamy Dayananda* founded *Arya Samaj*, a revival society which concentrated on fostering a Hindu nationalism marked by religious and social unity[157]. The society denounced idolatry, polygamy, and the caste system, and propagated the simplicity and austerity of Vedic rituals and manners[158]. Under the leadership of Mrs. Annie Besant «The Theosophical Society», originally founded in 1875 by Madame Blavatsky, became very influential in India. Its religious syncretism was wholeheartedly accepted by those wanted to remain faithful Hindus in the wake of modern criticism, and its Pseudo-intellectualism attracted those who were repelled by the emotionalism of Ramakrishna[159]. The most notable contribution of the society was the establishment of Benares Hindu University. In his own writings Parecattil praised the attempts of other reformers such as M.G. Ranade, Dr. R.G. Bhandarkar, Gopalakrishna Gokhale and B.G. Thilak who sought to rediscover and re-interpret the ancient past of India[160].

Another reknown personality of this era was Ramakrishna Paramahamsa who sought to attain to God through *Bhakti mārga*, or the path of loving devotion. He preached the virtues of self-sacrifice and concern for social welfare[161]. His illustrious disciple was Swami Vivekananda who advocated that social service be added to traditional Hindu devotion. Vivekananda's teachings inspired in Hindus a sense of pride for their culture and religion, and thus provided considerable stimulus to the national revival of India[162]. He founded the Ramakrishna Mission which promoted the virtues of generosity and tolerance towards other religions, for the reason that all of them are in the end the same[163]. Parecattil once had occasion to remark: «I am

---

[154] A.S. MENON, *Indian History*, 191.
[155] C.H. HEIMSATH, *Indian Nationalism*, 323-327.
[156] W.K. ANDERSEN – S.D. DAMLE, *The Brotherhood in Saffron*, 15.
[157] W.K. ANDERSEN – S.D. DAMLE, *The Brotherhood in Saffron*, 18.
[158] V.A. SMITH, *The Oxford History of India*, 731.
[159] V.A. SMITH, *The Oxford History of India*, 732.
[160] J. PARECATTIL, «Be at the Service of Bhārata Māta», 3.
[161] A.S. MENON, *Indian History*, 192.
[162] A.S. MENON, *Indian History*, 192.
[163] V.A. SMITH, *The Oxford History of India*, 731.

an admirer of Swami Vivekananda and his writings and, as and when I get time, I pore over the pages of his complete works, which often supply me with fresh ideas and new insights. I have noted that Swami Vivekananda has drawn largely on Christian sources; a fact that speaks volumes for his broad-mindedness and ecumenical perspective»[164].

No doubt, the most revered religious and social reformer of India in the early twentieth century was Mohandas Karamchand Gandhi. He was a man of God who tried to improve the living conditions of the Indian people by making them self-reliant through a spiritually oriented socio-economic reform. The Indian political situation at the beginning of this century was in turmoil, because of the independence struggle against the colonial British power. Gandhi led the protest to victory in 1947, when India attained political independence.

Gandhi's life was an inexhaustible experiment with truth which was at the same time a genuine search for God. To him, God is only One without a second[165], whether God is found through the *Koran*, the *Bible*, the *Zend-Avesta*, the *Talmud* or the *Gitā*[166]. Prayer had an important role in his life, because he viewed it as a means to reach out to God and to people[167]. He held that a person may live without eating for days, but may not remain without worshipping God for a single minute[168]. Gandhi espoused the integration of prayer and work, on the basis that it is one's duty to keep repeating God's name, whether one is busy in the fields or taking meals[169]. After he had visited a Trappist Monastery at Durban and noticed how the monks prayed silently while working on the farm, he was so impressed that he tried later to integrate prayer and work in all the *āśrams* he founded[170].

Together with silent and vocal forms of worship, Gandhi rated good works done to others as valid prayer, because God dwells in heart of one who serves[171]. In other words, he was of the opinion that to serve the poor was to serve God[172], and that service of neighbour was a religious and not

---

[164] J. PARECATTIL, <«A Friendly Approach to Religions»>, 303-304.

[165] *CW* 25 (1924-1925) 178.

[166] *CW* 21 (1921) 466.

[167] J.F. BACKIANADAN, *Love in the Life and Works*, 20.

[168] *CW*, 31 (1926) 102.

[169] *CW* 12 (1913-1914) 559.

[170] J.F. BACKIANADAN, *Love in the Life and Works*, 21.

[171] *CW* 28 (1925) 209; M. K. GANDHI, *An Autobiography*, 132.

[172] *CW* 28 (1925) 384; *CW* 31 (1926) 430.

a worldly act[173]. He interpreted the *yajña* (sacrifice) in *Gita* not as the offerings of animals or other material goods but as physical work[174]. The rules of *āśram* life which he formulated were intended to instil in the members the spirit of altruistic service. He remarked that serving a human being in need is serving the Lord crying in distress[175]. Moreover, Gandhi wanted to help the poor to earn their food by becoming self-reliant[176]. He concentrated his attention on strengthening the *khadi*, or the art of hand-spinning cloth, and thus on uplifting the economic production of village life[177].

In 1936, Gandhi decided to live among the ordinary people, so as to experience the hardships of their life and to determine how to free their villages from disease, superstition and oppression[178]. He also propagated the education of the common people in order to improve their standard of living[179]. He openly admitted that his developmental programmes were oriented to the complete economic independence of India[180]. Gandhi worked actively for the removal of *untouchability*, an off-shoot of the caste system of the Hindu religion which determines a particular person's social status, living standard, educational possibilities, rights and responsibilities[181]. During Gandhi's life-time the untouchables were not allowed to come near or touch the *Brāhmins*, lest they be excommunicated from the temples[182]. In a public speech delivered at the Leonard Theological College at Jubbulpore in 1933, Gandhi invited Christians to cooperate in the eradication of untouchability, but also challenged them to recognize the Hindu religion as a gift of God rather than a work of Satan, and to avoid

---

[173] *CW* 11 (1911-1913) 274.

[174] *CW* 32 (1926-1927) 505.

[175] *CW* 32 (1926-1927) 222.

[176] *CW* 25 (1924) 61; *CW* 20 (1921) 471; 444-445.

[177] I. JESUDASAN, *A Gandhian Theology*, 1984, 31; *CW* 32 (1926-1927) 539.

[178] I. JESUDASAN, *A Gandhian Theology*, 37.

[179] *CW* 7 (1907) 45.

[180] *CW* 8 (1908) 529.

[181] *CW* 25 (1924-1925) 514; *Caste* or *Varna*, the Sanskrit equivalent designates the different divisions of Indian society based on birth, occupation, social status and colour. Traditionally there are four main castes, each associated with a specified occupation: 1. *Brāhmins* (priests); 2. *Kshatriyas* (the warriors); 3. *Vaisyas* (agriculturalists and traders and merchants); 4. *Sudras* (Menials and domestic workers) (Cf. J.A DUBOIS ABBE, *Hindu Manners*, 14; A.T. EMBREE, *The Hindu Tradition*, 80).

[182] K.N. PANIKKAR, «Land Control», 65.

religious propaganda and proselytizing[183]. In 1936, he succeeded in having the temples opened to the untouchables for worship[184].

The socio-economic conditions of India made Parecattil an admirer of Gandhi, conscious the need of the Church to promote human progress[185]. He firmly maintained that Christians could not «pretend to be dumb and blind before the sad plight of the destitute»[186]. He tried in his own way to foster a spiritually oriented program of reform. He urged the priests, sisters and laity to be involved in the service of their neighbour, and to do so motivated by sacramental grace, for he believed that «for any kind of work whether manual or intellectual the strength needs to come from the Eucharist»[187]. The approach to social reform advocated by Parecattil was multi-faceted, and included agrarian development, provision of safe water supplies, and adequate sewerage systems and shelters for the homeless, the lepers and the unwanted who were the special objects of his love[188].

Gandhi applied his spiritual method in the field of politics as well. The weapons he used to resist the British were *satyāgraha* (non-cooperation) and *ahimsā* (non-violence)[189]. In 1917, Gandhi began his political career in India with a *satyāgraha* in Bihar, whose aim was to bring government officials to eliminate poverty among the plantation workers[190]. In 1918, he organized the non-violent campaign of textile workers at Ahmedbad for just wages[191]. Then, in 1919, he held a public meeting in Bombay at

---

[183] *CW* 56 (1933-1934) 336.

[184] *CW* 64 (1936-1937) 242.

[185] T. CHAKIATH «The Social Vision», 101.

[186] J. PARECATTIL, «Hard Work for Better Life», 56.

[187] J. PARECATTIL, *Letters to Sisters*, 168.

[188] T. CHAKIATH, «The Social Vision», 110.

[189] The word *Satyāgraha* is coined from *Satya* (truth) and *āgraha* (firmness or insistence). It was a means of passive resistance or non-cooperation in order to make the violater of truth aware of his mistake. About *Satyāgraha* Gandhi said: «Passive resistance is a method of securing rights by personal suffering; it is the reverse of resistance by arms [...] It involves sacrifice of self» (Cf. M.K GANDHI, *Hind Swaraj*, *CW* 10 [1909-1911] 48). This passive resistance is always connected to *ahimsā* or non-violence. This non-violence included both physical non-violence and all forms of anger and hatred. To Gandhi, *ahimsā* signified: «the largest love, the greatest charity [...] and love of my enemy» (Cf. *CW* 13 [1915-1917] 295). Again, «*ahimsā* meant not to hurt any living creature by thought, word or deed, even for the supposed benefit of that creature» (Cf. *CW* 50 [1932] 205). He employed this method of non-violent *Satyāgraha* in his fight for the independence of India.

[190] J.F. BACKIANADAN, *Love in the Life and Works*, 35.

[191] A. THOTTAKARA, *Gandhian Spirituality*, 6.

which he called for civil disobedience against the legislation of the salt monopoly[192], and organized a *hartāl* (strike) against the restrictive laws enacted by the *Rowlatt Act*[193]. After years of non-violent disobedience, Gandhi led a march on March 12, 1930, to the seaport of Dandi where he prepared salt, violating the government's tax regulation on this mineral[194].

Gandhi was convinced that India would be invaded by Japan during World War II because of the British presence. In an effort to prevent such an invasion, the Congress approved the «Quit India» resolution in August 1942, and through acts of non-violent civil disobedience Gandhi coerced the British to accept to leave[195]. Thus, in 1947, the British government announced its intention to transfer administrative power to India, and to appoint Viscount Mountbatten as viceroy so as to facilitate the transfer of authority. On August 15, 1947, India achieved Independence.

In Kerala too, there existed widespread unrest in favour of religious and socio-political reform. The prominent figures who led movements to this end were Chattampi Swamikal, Sri Narayana Guru and Ayyankali. Chattampi Swamikal was a Nair reformist who revolted against the prevailing privileges enjoyed by the Brahmins in Kerala. He worked to improve the social status of his local community with the hope that it would serve as an inspiration to the non-Brahmin castes to champion social change[196]. Sri Narayana Guru was a reformist who worked for the socio-economic betterment of the *Ezhava* community. He constructed shrines for worship for the low castes who were denied entry to the existing temples. Social justice and universal brotherhood were the core points of his teachings[197]. His famous slogan was «One Caste, One Religion, One God for man»[198]. Ayyankali was another noted activist who toiled for social justice in Kerala. He concentrated on efforts to assure that members of the *Pulaya* (one of the lower castes) community could have the right to walk in freedom along the public roads in Travancore[199].

In 1914, Mannath Padhmanabhan founded the Nair Service Society which undertook reforms such as the eradication of the subcastes, and the social

---

[192] I. JESUDASAN, *A Gandhian Theology of Liberation*, 23.

[193] A. THOTTAKARA, *Gandhian Spirituality*, 7.

[194] J.F. BACKIANADAN, *Love in the Life and Works*, 100.

[195] A. THOTTAKARA, *Gandhian Spirituality*, 7.

[196] A.S. MENON, *A Survey of Kerala History*, 324.

[197] K.V. EAPEN, *A Study of Kerala History*, 232.

[198] A.S. MENON, *A Survey of Kerala History*, 324-325.

[199] A.S MENON, *A Survey of Kerala History*, 328; K.V. EAPEN, *A Study of Kerala History*, 238.

improvement of the untouchables. There were some other important events which took place in this period and which furthered the cause of social justice. In 1925, the *Vaikam Satyāgraha* succeeded in opening the temple in Vaikam for Hindus belonging to different castes through the intervention of Gandhi[200]. Another important happening connected with the struggle for the eradication of untouchability was the *Guruvayur Satyāgraha*, led by the Kerala Provincial Congress in 1931-32 in order to guarantee that the Guruvayur temple be open to all Hindus. One of the leaders of the movement, Mr. Kelappan, began an indefinite fast before the temple on September 21, 1932, but gave up it at Gandhi's request.

Joseph Parecattil was thoroughly committed to national freedom, social betterment and economic progress. The attempts at religious revival and political change that took place in India, and especially in Kerala, left a lasting impression on him. He was influenced very much by the personality of Gandhi and by his ideals of *Satyam* (truth) and *Ahimsā* (non-violence). He urged Christians to follow these principles in building up the nation and in maintaining its integrity. Speaking as a citizen of India and as a churchman, he stated that the hard-won freedom would be preserved «only if we walk along the Gandhian way, holding fast to *Satyam* and *Ahimsā*»[201].

By way of conclusion, it can be stated that the liturgical, spiritual and social influences of Parecattil provided him diverse sources from which he could formulate his Eucharistic thought. His family life was steeped in the Syro-Malabar religious tradition; his seminary education provided exposure to the Western theological heritage and its development; and Church leadership necessitated acquaintance with the rapidly changing religio-social life of India. Thus, having been educated during the first half of the twentieth century exerted a significant and lasting influence on Parecattil. Such an education explains why he later believed that theology and liturgy should take into consideration the actual thought-patterns, ideals and living conditions of the Christian people. Hence, he was to be firmly committed to formulating a theology and to devising a liturgy which reflected the context of India. As the Eucharist is the centre of Christian life, this truth ought to be reflected in the very form of the liturgy itself.

---

[200] A.S. MENON, *A Survey of Kerala History*, 326-327; K.V. EAPEN, *A Study of Kerala History*, 235.

[201] J. PARECATTIL, «Satyam and Ahimsā», 49.

CHAPTER II

**Various Prospects on the Eucharist
Proposed by Vatican II:
Their Impact on Joseph Parecattil**

Vatican II has undoubtedly been the epoch-making event in twentieth-century Catholicism. The subsequent history of the Church after this major event has been both vibrant and turbulent, since for some the renewal intended by it has produced welcome innovations in various fields of ecclesial activity, while for others the waves of the reform have been deemed too sudden and destructive of internal Church unity. Joseph Parecattil found the Council envigorating. He was an active participant in the four sessions of the Council and, deeply inspired by its stimulus to the renewal of the Church life, spared no effort in the post-conciliar years to initiate and direct it in the Indian context. His hope was to foster a general reform of the Syro-Malabar Church, especially through the inculturation of its liturgy.

Spurred on by the momentum created by the Council, Parecattil set about implementing the norms on the liturgy, especially concerning the celebration of the Eucharist. He was guided by the Constitution of the Council on the liturgy, *Sacrosanctum Concilium*, which proposes a three-dimensional reform of extant texts through restoration, revision, and adaptation. Parecattil stressed the combined restoration, revision and adaptation of the liturgical texts with a view to promoting the more active participation of the people. These reform measures were also to facilitate a more intense Eucharistic spirituality, which in turn would animate Christ-centred initiatives with regard to socio-economic betterment.

This chapter contains three separate sections which deal both with the perspectives on the Eucharist proposed by the Council and with their effect on Parecattil. The first section is devoted to the teaching of the Council on

encouraging more mature participation by the people in a restored, revised and adapted liturgy. The Council decreed that there should be a restoration of the substantial elements of the liturgy, if these had been lost with the passage of time. Yet, the restoration was to be such that it did not prescind from the varying spiritual needs and social circumstances of the local Church. Similarly, the adaptation of the liturgy aimed at giving due importance to the religious and cultural heritages of the place in which it is celebrated. In keeping with these Conciliar directions, Parecattil was courageous in renewing the Eucharistic texts of the Syro-Malabar Church, no matter what opposition he eventually encountered.

The second section delineates the post-conciliar emergence of a Eucharistic spirituality based on the adaptation of the Syro-Malabar liturgical texts according to indigenous Indian spirituality. The Council had taken a decidedly positive stance regarding the salvific elements in the non-Christian religions of the world, and called for a dialogue with their representatives. In India, this dialogue was begun particularly with the leaders of the Hindu religion. The members of the hierarchy, along with Christian scholars devised experiments with forms of Christian spirituality in which Hindu elements had been assimilated. Parecattil was solidly in favour of such a development.

The third section stresses the theological connection made by Vatican II between the Eucharist and Christian innovations in social transformation. Eucharistic spirituality should bear fruit in civil life, because those who are nourished spiritually at Mass should be eager to give witness to grace by doing charitable works. Christ not only entrusted his followers with the mission to promote the betterment of the poor, but also gave them an example by his own prophetic words and deeds. The Church continues this option for the poor and finds strength to be faithful to it through the grace of God bestowed through sincere participation in the Eucharistic liturgy. Although Parecattil was trained according to a mystical and interior piety with regard to the Blessed Sacrament, he willingly complemented it with a more social and public one.

1. Active Participation of the Laity in the Eucharist: Facilitated by Restoration, Revision and Adaptation of the Missals

That all Christians should view themselves as having an important role in the Eucharistic liturgy is a clear message of *Sacrosanctum Concilium*. The common priesthood of all the baptized is presented as the theological basis for such participation. The bishops at Vatican II, relying on earlier teachings of the Church, confirmed that the «royal priesthood» of the faithful entitles them to offer spiritual sacrifices to the glory of God:

Christ the Lord [...] made the new people « a kingdom of priests to God, his Father» [...] The baptized, by generation and the anointing of the Holy Spirit, are consecrated to be a spiritual house and a holy priesthood, that through all the works of Christian believers they may offer spiritual sacrifices [...] Therefore all the disciples of Christ, persevering in prayer and praising God (Cf. Acts 2, 42-47), should present themselves as a sacrifice, living, holy and pleasing to God [...][1].

Here it is stated that the basis of the common priesthood is the anointing with the Spirit given in the sacrament of Baptism[2]. Moreover, with the reception of Confirmation, the faithful attain the full dignity of being members of a holy priesthood, and are thus enabled to offer spiritual sacrifices in various ways[3]. In particular, the Eucharistic liturgy is the celebration of the entire body of the faithful organized around the unifying figures of the bishops[4]. By envisaging a «full, conscious and active participation»[5] in the liturgy by the faithful, the bishops at Vatican II wanted them to be «conscious of what they are doing with devotion and full collaboration and not as strangers or silent spectators»[6]. If this is done at the Eucharist, the faithful will understand that they are also to exercise their priestly function after the Mass by the witness of a holy life and by active charity[7].

Since the Scholastic and Tridentine theologies had placed an almost excessive emphasis on the objective efficacy of the sacraments, by the time of Vatican II it became clear that the subjective efficacy and the active participation by the people needed to be addressed[8]. Hence, the Council in its recommendation regarding reforms of the Eucharist concentrated on the involvement of the faithful in offering the divine victim to God and themselves along with him[9]. Thus, the Eucharist entails not only the action

---

[1] LG 10.

[2] J.A. JUNGMANN, «Constitution on the Sacred Liturgy», 17.

[3] J.H. EMMINGHAUS, *The Eucharist*, xviii.

[4] A. GRILLMEIER, «The People of God», 157; J.A. JUNGMANN, «Constitution on the Sacred Liturgy», 17; P.R. ROCHA, «The Principal Manifestation», 5.

[5] SC 14.

[6] SC 48.

[7] LG 10.

[8] J.H. EMMINGHAUS, *The Eucharist*, xxiii.

[9] LG 11; SC 48; IO 46.

of the celebrant but also that of the assembled people of God[10]. Through the reception of Holy communion the faithful further deepen their union with God and their relationship with one another: «Strengthened by the body of Christ in the Eucharistic communion, they manifest in a concrete way that unity of the People of God which this holy sacrament aptly signifies and admirably realizes»[11]. Therefore, through involvement both in the offering and in Holy Communion, the baptized have their own indispensable part to play in the liturgical action[12].

Furthermore, the Council stipulates concrete means and offers spiritual motives for the active participation of the faithful in the Eucharist. By means of acclamations, hymns and gestures the personal devotion of the faithful gathered in assembly is expressed. The Mass, even if conducted with profound devotion by the celebrants, does not fully manifest the intention of the Church if the baptized members of the congregation remain silent[13]. Besides devotion, joy and hope result from the involvement of the faithful in the rites. This is fitting, since the earthly liturgy provides a true foretaste of the heavenly worship which is celebrated by the Lamb and the saints in the Holy City of Jerusalem. Even now the faithful anticipate in hope the coming of Our Lord Jesus Christ, until he appears in glory[14]. Hence, by participating in the Eucharist with joy and hope, the faithful receive the spiritual strength to contribute to the Kingdom of God through their public witness to divine charity.

The bishops at Vatican II also desired that the liturgy be renewed through restoration, revision and adaptation of the liturgical texts. This process would greatly facilitate the spiritual enrichment of the faithful[15]. The reform of the liturgy was to be undertaken above all because it is the primary source of animating the life and mission of the Church[16]. Parecattil was fully in accord with this three-dimensional undertaking of the renewal of the liturgy. He laboured consistently to revitalize the Eucharistic liturgy of the Syro-Malabar Church in all three respects, since he was of the opinion that «in any liturgical reform based upon ancient texts, restoration,

---

[10] P.R. ROCHA, «The Principal Manifestation», 8.

[11] LG 11.

[12] LG 11.

[13] J.D. CRICHTON, *The Church's Worship*, 68.69.

[14] SC 8; J. A. JUNGMANN, «Constitution on the Sacred Liturgy», 14.

[15] SC 14.

[16] J.D. CRICHTON, *The Church's Worship*, 13.68.

revision and adaptation should be accomplished together [...]»[17]. He carefully chose the wording «accomplished together», because he was convinced that this would be to the spiritual advantage of the people of Kerala. Thus, when he reflected on the following Conciliar text, he centred on the phrases «with little advantage» and «seem useful or necessary»:

> Parts which with the passage of time came to be duplicated, or were added with little advantage, are to be omitted. Other parts which suffered loss through accidents of history are to be restored to the vigour they had in the days of the holy Fathers, as may seem useful or necessary[18].

This pivotal text led Parecattil to strive for the vigour which is mentioned by assuring that the renewed liturgy be to the advantage of the spiritual lives of the people, and that all that was useful and necessary to this end be done with courage.

Moreover, when the bishops at Vatican II addressed the liturgy of the Eastern Churches, they underlined the principle of organic development:

> All members of the Eastern Churches should be firmly convinced that they can and ought always preserve their own legitimate liturgical rites and ways of life, and that changes are to be introduced only to forward their own organic development [...] They are to aim always at a more perfect knowledge and practice of their rites, and if they have fallen away due to circumstances of times or persons, they are to strive to return to their ancestral traditions[19].

Here, the Council confirms and approves the ancient discipline concerning the sacraments which exists in the Eastern Churches, and also the rituals observed at their celebration. It also stipulates that these be restored, if they have been obfuscated[20]. The process of renewal, therefore, should assure that established liturgical rites and ways of life not be changed in a way that is against their organic development. Furthermore, no elements foreign to the ancient rites should be imposed[21].

As regards the restoration of the liturgical texts, the Council distinguishes between changeable and unchangeable elements:

> the liturgy is made up of unchangeable elements divinely instituted, and of elements subject to change. These latter not only may be changed but ought to

---

[17] J. PARECATTIL, «Liturgical Reform», 61.

[18] SC 50.

[19] OE 6.

[20] OE 12.

[21] J. M. HOECK, «Decree on Eastern Catholic Churches», 318.

be changed with the passage of time, if they have suffered from the intrusion of anything out of harmony with the inner nature of the liturgy or have become less suitable[22].

On the basis of this text, Parecattil argued that proper restoration entails an «up-dating» of the changeable elements, and that this principle should be applied in the restoration of the Syro-Malabar liturgical texts[23]. This means the «reinstating of Indian thought-patterns, gestures, postures and symbols»[24], and not the reiterating of the Chaldean tradition which «does not deserve the name Syro-Malabar, because there is nothing of Malabar in it»[25]. He insisted on the revision and the adaptation, along with the restoration, of the liturgical texts that had existed in the Syro-Malabar Church, since he desired an indianization of the «present Chaldean liturgy as far as it is possible»[26].

In fact, a different kind of restoration of the Syro-Malabar liturgy had already been initiated before the advent of the Council. In 1957, Rome decided that the *Chaldean Pontifical* was to be restored in the Syro-Malabar Church[27]. Referring to its rubrics relative to the ordination ceremony Parecattil had this to say: «their uncouth gestures, frequent prostrations and shallow ideas, failed to impress the priests, religious and people who were acquainted with the beautiful and impressive ordination ceremonies of the Latin rite»[28].

This criticism of the restoration as it was carried out in the *1962 Text* rested on his conviction, that it did not reflect the insights of Vatican II:

---

[22] SC 21.

[23] J. PARECATTIL, «Liturgical Reform», 66.

[24] J. PARECATTIL, «Liturgical Reform», 49.

[25] J. PARECATTIL, «Reply to Archbishop», 9.

[26] J. PARECATTIL, «Reply to Archbishop», 7.

[27] At the beginning of this century the Roman Pontifical was in use in the Latin language. For the Ordination ceremony, both the Latin text of the Pontifical and the Syrian Text of the Mass were used, a conflation which resulted in confusion. The Syro-Malabar bishops requested the approval of Rome for a Syriac translation of the Latin Pontifical. After a study on this matter, Rome decided to restore the Chaldean Pontifical instead of the Latin one. This decision was not wholeheartedly welcomed (Cf. J. PARE-CATTIL, *Liturgy As I See It*, 37-39).

[28] J. PARECATTIL, «Liturgical Reform», 52.

The so-called «restored» Missal of 1962 is a pre-Vatican one. Reportedly it got the approval of Pope Pius XII in 1957, but there is no evidence that it had the approval of His Holiness Pope John XXIII, gloriously reigning in 1962[29].

Regardless, Parecattil had an important part to play in having the Syriac text translated into Malayalam for the restored Missal of 1962[30]. A significant reason for his collaboration was the assurance given to him by the members of the Liturgical Committee that the bishops of the Syro-Malabar Church would be able to revise and adapt the text at a later stage. But he eventually became disillusioned, «since the very same Committee stood in the way of revision and adaptation [...]»[31].

In its guidelines the Council stated clearly that the restoration of the texts must be such that the content and spirit can be easily grasped by the people, so that their communal participation be made possible:

In this restoration of both texts and rites should be drawn up so as to express more clearly the holy things which they signify. The Christian people, as far

---

[29] J. PARECATTIL, «Liturgical Reform», 52; in 1954, a Liturgical Commission was set up in Rome with the purpose of restoring the Chaldean liturgy in the Syro-Malabar Church. Cardinal Tisserant, the Prefect of the Congregation for the Oriental Churches, wrote a letter to the Syro-Malabar Bishops on May 6, 1954 informing them of the appointment of the Commission. According to the letter, the Syro-Malabar liturgy was to be restored to the original Chaldean Rite which existed at an earlier period. The Rite as in use at the time of the letter was considered by Cardinal Tisserant to be «in a mutilated and highly westernized form» (Cf. T. MANNOORAMPARAMPIL, *The Historical Background*, 303). Most of the bishops did not appreciate the draft prepared by the Commission, since they did not want the pure Chaldean liturgy to be restored in the Syro-Malabar Church. The letter of Archbishop Augustine Kandathil of Ernakulam to Cardinal Tisserant dated June 6, 1955 is entitled «Chaldean Liturgy not to be Restored» in which he said that the Syro-Malabar rite is different from the pure Chaldean rite and it has been «established and recognized by the Roman Pontiffs as an independent and unique rite [...] Therefore we want to keep up the independence and the specific character of our rite by all means» (Cf. «Historical Documents», *EM* 43 [1973] 68). About the reform of the liturgy the letter said «we want a reformation in our liturgy that will help it be living, dynamic and progressive [...]» (Cf. «Historical Documents», *EM* 43 [1973] 69). The letters written to the Holy See by Archbishop Kavukkat of Changnancherry on July 25, 1955; bishop Tharayil of Kottayam on May 25, 1955; bishop Valloppilly of Tellicherry on July 31, 1955; bishop Vayalil of Palai on July 7, 1955 and bishop Parecattil on July 10, 1955 proposed the same idea. The Draft was again discussed in the «Plenary session» and was promulgated on January 20, 1962 through the letter *De Ritu Sacrificii Eucharistici Instaurtatio* (Cf. «Historical Documents», *EM* 43 [1973] 70-71).

[30] J. PARECATTIL, «Liturgical Reform», 53.

[31] J. PARECATTIL, «Liturgical Reform», 53.

as is possible, should be able to understand them with ease and take part in them fully, actively, and as a community[32].

Parecattil was very much impressed by this proposal of Vatican II as such, but he shared in the widespread dissatisfaction among the faithful as regards the 1962 Text, which comprised a complete restoration of the Chaldean liturgy said to have existed before the sixteenth century, and did not heed to the importance of the principles of revision and adaptation.[33] The Syro-Malabar Bishops' Conference under the presidency of Archbishop Parecattil requested Rome for the renewal of the Mass Text. On his visit to Kerala in 1968, Cardinal Maximilian de Furstenberg, the Prefect of the Congregation for the Oriental Churches, could gather direct information about the reactions against the 1962 Text. Later, he wrote a letter to Archbishop Parecattil in which he directed him to prepare a new revised Mass Text. This was officially approved on August 9, 1968[34] and its use initiated *ad experimentum*. This approval was renewed in 1971[35].

The Council did not intend to impose a strict uniformity in liturgical worship, instead it wanted to adapt Eucharistic celebration to the living and cultural heritages of the local people:

> Even in the liturgy the Church does not wish to impose a rigid uniformity in matters which do not involve the faith or the good of the whole community. Rather does she respect and foster the qualities and talents of the various races and nations. Anything in these people's way of life which is not indissolubly bound up with superstition and error she studies with sympathy, and, if possible, preserves intact. She sometimes even admits such things into the liturgy itself, provided they harmonize with its true and authentic spirit[36].

In this way the bishops at the Council intended to foster the adaptation of the celebration of the Eucharist to the cultural environment of the place where they are used[37]. In the Indian Church, some concrete steps were

---

[32] SC 21.

[33] Msgr. L.J. Chittor, Vicar General of the Archdiocese of Changanacherry, wrote a letter on August 9, 1962 to all the Syro-Malabar bishops requesting them to shorten the Mass Text, and expressing the dissatisfaction over the Calendar and the selection of the readings (Cf. «Historical Documents», *EM* 47 [1977] 104-105). Bishop Tharayil of Kottayam sent a letter to Archbishop Parecattil on August 12, 1962 requesting the same (Cf. «Historical Documents», *EM* 47 [1977] 106].

[34] «Historical Documents», *EM* 43 (1973) 221.

[35] «Historical Documents», *EM* 43 (1973) 222.

[36] SC 37.

[37] P.R. ROCHA, «The Principal Manifestation», 7.

taken towards liturgical adaptation. The C.B.C.I. appointed a Commission for Liturgy which, in collaboration with the N.B.C.L.C., drew up plans for liturgical adaptations. The hierarchy desired that symbols and gestures familiar to the people should render the liturgy intelligible to them. Liturgical adaptations concentrated on using symbols drawn from the daily life of the faithful[38]. The guidelines prepared by *The Church in India Seminar*[39] were ratified by the C.B.C.I. in 1972[40].

The instruction *Concilium ad exseqendam Constitutionem de Sacra Liturgia* of April 25, 1969 approved the following adaptations in the Indian Eucharistic liturgy as regards symbols, gestures and forms of homage:

1) The posture during Mass, both for the priests and the faithful, may be adapted to the local usage, that is, sitting on the floor[41], standing and the like; footwear may be removed also[42].

2) Genuflections may be replaced by the profound bow with the *añjali hasta*[43].

3) A *pañjānga pranām*[44] by both priests and faithful can take place before the liturgy of the Word, as part of the penitential rite, and at the conclusion of the anaphora.

4) Kissing of objects may be adapted to local custom, that is, touching the object with one's fingers or palm of one's hand and bringing the hands to one's eyes or forehead[45].

---

[38] D.S. AMALORPAVADASS, *Towards Indigenisation*, 21-22.

[39] The Seminar conducted in 1969 in Bangalore had representatives of the three Rites of the Catholic Church: the Syro-Malabar, Syro-Malankara and the Latin Rites. *Sacrosanctum Concilium* was the main focus of the Seminar in regard to the adaptation of the liturgy.

[40] D.S. AMALORPAVADASS, *Towards Indigenisation*, 151-163.

[41] In India, though the use of chairs is spreading, the fact remains that in large assemblies and conventions, and especially in places of worship, the prevalent custom is to squat on the floor on mats or carpets. In village parishes it is a common sight that people sit on the floor in churches.

[42] No religion allows a worshipper in India to enter a place of worship with covered feet. Visitors entering temples and mosques are asked to remove their footwear. Non-Christians are shocked to see the Christians entering churches with shoes on.

[43] *Añjali hasta* means folded hands; salutation with *añjali hasta* is a respectful way of greeting. When followed by a profound bow, it is a gesture of adoration.

[44] The *pañjanga pranām* consists of kneeling and touching the floor with one's forehead and either both palms or the hands joined in the gesture of the *añjali hasta*.

[45] Indians consider kissing as an excessive familiarity lacking reverence. The traditional Indian rite of veneration is done by touching the object with one's fingers or palm of one's hand and bringing the hands to one's eyes or forehead.

5) The kiss of peace could be given by the exchange of the *añjali hasta*/or the placing of the hands of the giver between the hands of the recipient[46].

6) Incense could be made use of more regularly in liturgical services. The receptacle could be the simple incense bowl with handle[47].

7) The corporal could be replaced by a tray of fitting material.

8) The vestments should be simplified. A single tunic-type chasuble with a stole could replace the traditional vestments of the Roman rite[48].

9) Oil lamps could be used instead of candles[49].

10) The preparatory rite of the Mass may include: a) the presentation of gifts; b) the welcome of the celebrant in an Indian way, for example, with a single *ārati*[50], washing of hands[51] and so on; the lighting of the lamp; d) the greetings of peace among the faithful in a sign of mutual reconciliation.

11) In the *Oratio fidelium* some spontaneity may be permitted both with regard to its structure and the formulation of the intentions. The universal aspect of the Church, however, should not be left in oblivion.

12) In the offertory rite, and at the conclusion of the anaphora, the Indian form of worship may be integrated, that is, double or triple *ārati* of flowers, and/or incense, and/or light[52].

Liturgical adaptation took concrete form with the preparation of two important Eucharistic texts: 1) *An Order of the Mass for the Indian Church* and 2) *An Order of the Mass for India*.

An Order of the Mass for the Indian Church, a Missal prepared at Dharmaram College, and published in May 1969, corresponded to the directives of Vatican II by adapting the liturgy to the Indian situation. The Missal was first used during *The Church in India Today Seminar*. Therea-

---

[46] These are the usual ways of greetings in the country.

[47] Such a receptacle is very common in places of worship.

[48] Since India is a tropical country, hot weather prevails in the land almost all year round. The custom of using four layer vestments in the Roman and Syrian Rites causes much perspiration throughout the lengthy ceremonies. Hence, the simplification of vestments is appropriate.

[49] Since oil is a material used in worship, Indians are familiar with oil lamps. Moreover, the wax candles are difficult to obtain.

[50] The celebrant represents Christ. This is recognized by the welcome given to him by the assembly which stands up to receive him, and which through its delegates offers *ārati* to him. *Ārati* is a profound gesture of respect normally performed with incense.

[51] At home, important persons are received by giving water to wash their feet and hands. For practical reasons the priest washes only his hands.

[52] *Ārati* can be performed in three ways or with three elements: 1) homage of flowers (*puspārati*); homage of incense (*dhupārati*); 3) homage of light (*deepārati*). The quoted passages of twelve points are from the original document approved by the *Roman Consilium* and reproduced in D.S. AMALORPAVADASS, *Towards Indigenization*, 31-33.

fter, the text was republished with modifications under the title *Bharatiya Pūjārpaṇam*[53] (Indian Mass). The introduction to the text describes it in the following words:

> As a response to the call of the Vatican II and based on the Christian vision that is rooted in the Indian culture, philosophy, and liturgy, it is the first step in an attempt to Indianise the liturgy in its theology, structure, symbolism and prayer methods[54].

The theological vision behind the Indian Mass is significant, since it integrates the goal of religious sacrifice in Hinduism into that of Christianity. In Hindu thought, *yajña* is aimed at the protection and completion of the universe, and in Christian thought the sacrifice of Christ seeks the full establishment of justice and love in the cosmic order. Through the daily celebration of the Eucharistic sacrifice, Christ can be said to lead all humankind to the ever greater realization that God is the ultimate end of human life and of the cosmos in which it is situated[55]. This concept of «God realization» is viewed as the aim of both the Christian and Hindu spiritual life.

The *Order of the Mass for the Indian Church* served as a basic form of worship which could be further adapted according to the concrete situations of different local churches. This flexibility took into consideration the three Rites of the Catholic Church in India: Syro-Malabar, Syro-Malankara and Latin. The *Missal* followed the basic structure of the Christian Eucharistic liturgy from its origin. What is novel is the introduction of Indian spiritual and cultural elements. The general structure of the Mass is divided into eight parts: i) Preparation of the altar; ii) Preparation of the faithful for a sincere participation in the rite: a) Lighting the lamp to represent Christ the light; b) Recitation of a Psalm; c) Rite of Repentance and Thanksgiving; d) Listening to the Word of God, e) Offertory; iii) Blessing the altar in accordance with the Hindu sacrificial tradition; iv) Anaphora; v) Offering the sacred sacrifice to the Father; vi) Intercessory prayers; vii) Communion; and viii) Concluding rite.

---

[53] For all textual references to this Missal, the study relies on the reproduced original text in F. KANICHIKATTIL, *To Restore or To Reform?*, 177-201.

[54] F. KANICHIKATTIL, *To Restore or To Reform?*, 177.

[55] F. KANICHIKATTIL, *To Restore or To Reform?*, 177.

An Order of the Mass for India[56] was the text of the Mass prepared at Bangalore by the N.B.C.L.C. The Eucharistic liturgy attempts to a great extent to incorporate elements of Indian theology, spirituality and culture. In the introduction to the text it is said:

> The basic structure of the Christian Eucharist, common to all rites, has been preserved [...] Within this general framework, a new Order has been devised, so as to integrate elements from Indian forms of worship[57].

The structure of the Mass consists of four main parts: 1) Introductory rites; 2) Liturgy of the Word; 3) Liturgy of the Eucharist; and 4) Concluding rite. The introductory part includes welcoming gestures of the congregation to the celebrant and vice versa, which are followed by purification rites. An oil lamp is lighted, as the congregation sings a hymn to Christ the Light. In the second part, a reading from Indian Scriptures is introduced into the liturgy of the Word. The third part, the liturgy of the Eucharist, consists in the preparation of the gifts, the recital of the Eucharistic prayer and the rite of communion.

The Eucharistic prayer is unique, since it was composed with the Indian context in mind. It contains the following nine parts: 1) Introductory dialogue which is called as *mangalacaraṇam*[58]; 2) Praise and thanks to God for the acts of creation and of salvation, the climax of which is the Christ-event; 3) First epiclesis in which God is called upon to send the Holy Spirit over the gifts of the Church so as to change them into the body and blood of Christ; 4) Recital of the institution narrative; 5) Anamnesis which consists of the memorial of the Christ-event; 6) Acclamation of the death, resurrection and parousia of the Lord Jesus Christ; 7) Second epiclesis in which the Holy Spirit is invoked so as to empower the participants to reflect the image of Christ and his just and loving deeds; 8) Intercessory Prayers for all the Christian Churches, the pastors, the faithful and all people in need; and 9) Trinitarian doxology.

The structure of the communion rite is as follows: 1) Invitation: the celebrant invites the faithful to communion and pronounces a prayer; 2) Common recitation of the «Our Father» with folded hands; 3) Breaking of the

---

[56] For all textual reference the study depends on the original text reproduced in D. S. AMALORPAVADASS, *Towards Indigenisation*, 59-102.

[57] D. S. AMALORPAVADASS, *Towards Indigenisation in the Liturgy*, 59.

[58] *Mangalacaraṇam* is a prayer for God's blessing on a religious rite. God is called upon to help the believers so that their action may be rightly performed. This seems to be the most appropriate way of relating the introductory dialogue to the Indian context.

bread with a prayer; 4) Participation in the sacred meal; and 5) Recitation of the *Mānasa Pūjā*, a prayer asking that the participants interiorize their union with Christ through the sacred banquet.

The last part of the *An Order of the Mass for India* is the concluding rite in which the celebrant imparts the solemn blessing with *abhayamudra*[59] and *varadamudra*[60]. This prayer of blessing refers to the Persons of the Trinity.

Inspired by these two experiments to integrate aspects of Indian spirituality into the Mass, Parecattil encouraged the composition of a special text for the celebration of the Syro-Malabar Eucharistic liturgy. As a result, in 1974 the Liturgical Centre of the Archdiocese of Ernakulam published a Missal called *Bhāratiya Pūjā* (Indian Mass)[61]. This text printed «pro-manuscripto» was used on important occasions at a few centres as an experiment, and was very much appreciated by the faithful[62]. The anaphora of the Missal is an adaptation of the one prepared by the N.B.C.L.C. and used in *An Order of the Mass for India*. Some hymns are taken from the *Bhāratiya pūjārpaṇam*[63]. Referring to the text, he stated «it is in line with the principle of "organic development" enunciated by Vatican II in Art. 6 of *Orientalium Ecclesiarum*[64] and Art. 23 of *Sacrosanctum Concilium*»[65].

---

[59] *Abhayamudra* is made by holding the right hand lifted up to the shoulder with the palm turned to the people.

[60] *Varadamudra* is made by keeping the left palm with fingers joined and pointing to the ground.

[61] All textual references are from the exact reproduction of the Missal in F. KANICHI-KATTIL, *To Restore or To Reform?*, 202-227; J. PARECATTIL, *Liturgy As I See It*, 82.

[62] J. PARECATTIL, «Liturgical Reform», 71.

[63] F. KANICHIKATTIL, *To Restore or To Reform?*, 202; J. PARECATTIL, *Liturgy As I See It*, 82-83.

[64] The Article reads:
All members of the Eastern Churches should be firmly convinced that they can and ought always preserve their own legitimate liturgical rites and ways of life, and that changes are to be introduced only to forward their own organic development. They themselves are to carry out all these prescriptions with the greatest fidelity. They are to aim always at a more perfect knowledge and practice of their rites, and if they have fallen away due to circumstances of times or persons, they are to strive to return to their ancestral traditions [...]

[65] J. PARECATTIL, «Liturgical Reform», 70. The Article reads:
In order that sound tradition be retained, and yet the way remain open to legitimate progress, a careful investigation — theological, historical, and pastoral — should always be made into each part of the liturgy which is to be revised. Furthermore the general laws governing the structure and meaning of the liturgy must be studied in conjunction with the experience derived from recent liturgical reforms and from the indults granted to various places.

He was inspired to produce the Indian Mass, because the cultural identity of the members of the Syro-Malabar Church is not Chaldean, and a foreign identity should not be imposed on them[66].

Adaptation of the Eucharistic liturgy in accordance with the spiritual traits of the Indian culture sought to encourage the Christians of the Syro-Malabar Church to relate their faith to their surroundings. Hence, a Eucharistic liturgy characterised by symbols commonly used in India, and particularly by Hindus, was attempted with a view to stimulate communal participation, according to the teachings of Vatican II. For the same reason, Parecattil wanted to revise the 1968 Text further, and played an important role in preparing a «Short Mass»[67]. About the abbreviated Missal he wrote: «It only leaves out a few «useless repetitions» in accordance with Art. 34 of the *Constitution on the Sacred Liturgy*»[68].

Attempts were made to finalize the Missal of the Syro-Malabar Eucharistic liturgy after a long period of experimentation. A sub-committee was set up in 1974 for this task, and it presented a Draft in 1978 which made an attempt to go back to the 1962 Text. On January 3, 1977 the Congregation for the Oriental Churches sent a letter to all the bishops of the rite which was entitled «Report on the State of Liturgical Reform in the Syro-Malabar Church» and which renewed the prohibition against the new liturgical texts, because they lacked both the authorization of the Conference and the approval of the Holy see. The letter pointed out the Indian Mass and the Short Mass as examples of such non-approved forms. As Parecattil judged that the document was «based upon some false or distorted reports

---

conjunction with the experience derived from recent liturgical reforms and from the indults granted to various places.

Finally, there must be no innovations unless the good of the Church genuinely and certainly requires them, and care must be taken that any new forms adopted should in some way grow organically from forms already existing.

[66] J. PARECATTIL, «Liturgical Reform», 72.

[67] With an aim to shorten the Text of 1968, The Central Liturgical Committee of the Syro-Malabar Bishops' Conference gave guidelines to prepare the Mass Text on November 29, 1973. The Text was printed *pro-manuscripto* and its use was restricted to the experimental centres of the Archdiocese of Ernakulam. It removed the repetitive prayers, and used «The Anaphora of Mar Addai and Mar Mari» discovered by W. Macomber in 1966 (Cf. J. PARECATTIL, «Liturgical Reform», 72-74).

[68] J. PARECATTIL, «Liturgical Reform», 72. The Article reads:

The rites should be distinguished by a noble simplicity. They should be short, clear, and free from useless repetitions. They should be within the people's powers of comprehension, and normally should not require much explanation.

the Congregation on February 7, 1977. The letter bore the title «Comments on the "Report on the State of Liturgical Reform in the Syro-Malabar Church", sent to All the Bishops of the Rite *'sub secreto pontificio'*»[70].

Then, in October 1981, at the direction of the Congregation for the Oriental Churches, Parecattil, the President of the Syro-Malabar Bishops Conference, submitted a revised text of the Mass[71]. On receiving this, the Congregation sent a letter entitled «Observations on the Order of the Holy Mass of the Syro-Malabar Church 1981» which contained corrections and suggestions. In 1983 the Syro-Malabar Bishops' Conference appointed a committee of five bishops to study the text. On August 16, 1983 the minority group of the bishops sent a reply to the Roman document with the title «Observations on the Directives from the Holy See on the Qurbana Text», supporting the recommendations made by it. The majority group, on the other hand, was not satisfied with the Roman document and in the letter, «A Response to the Observations of the Sacred Congregation for the Oriental Churches», requested clarifications on certain points. The Congregation responded soon thereafter with the letter: «Final Judgement of the S. Congregation for the Oriental Churches concerning the Order of the Syro-Malabar Qurbana»[72]. In 1985, the Bishops' Conference examined the draft text in light of the «Final Judgement» and, at its meeting has «seen»[73] the Text of the Raza and resolved to forward it to the Congregation for necessary action[74]. Finally, the *Raza Text* was approved by the Congregation on December 19, 1985 and was signed by Pope John Paul II on February 9, 1986. The next step was to finalize the *Solemn and Simple Forms* of Mass. On May 5, 1988 the Congregation issued a document with the title «Directives of the Order of the Syro-Malabar Qurbana in Solemn and Simple Forms», containing some practical guidelines. Then the Text was approved and signed on July 3, 1989.

---

[70] Cf. J. PARECATTIL, «Liturgical Reform», 83-88.

[71] Cardinal Rubin, the president of the Congregation for the Oriental Churches asked the Syro-Malabar Bishops' Conference to submit a draft by Easter 1981 together with the reports of the majority and minority groups of the bishops. A committee was entrusted with the task of preparing the draft. The majority group of bishops was in favour of the draft (Cf. J. PARECATTIL, «Liturgical Reform», 132).

[72] For Parecattil's comments on this letter, cf. J. PARECATTIL, «Reply to Archbishop», 3-31).

[73] J. PARECATTIL, *Liturgy As I See It*, 132. The use of the word «seen» means that the bishops only have seen the text and not wholeheartedly accepted it (Cf. F. KANICHIKATTIL, *To Restore or To Reform?*, 84).

[74] T. MANNOORAMPARAMPIL, *The Historical Background*, 221.

and Simple Forms», containing some practical guidelines. Then the Text
was approved and signed on July 3, 1989.

These attempts at restoration, revision and adaptation of the Syro-Malabar
liturgical texts were intended to promote an active participation by the
people in the liturgy. The restoration aimed at reintroducing the entire
Chaldean tradition. The revision concentrated on making the liturgy simple
and intelligible to the common people. The adaptation sought to integrate
into the Eucharistic liturgy elements of the cultural heritage of India and
of the spiritual depth of Hinduism.

2. The Emergence of a Eucharistic Spirituality in India: Motivated by the Positive Approach of Vatican II towards the Non-Christian Religions

The Eucharist has a commendable influence on the interior lives of
Christians, since it contains the entire spiritual good of the Church[75]. Yet,
the openness which the bishops at Vatican II showed towards the non-
Christian religions stimulated the formation of an Indian Christian
spirituality appreciative of the religious sense found in Hinduism. With
regard to such a religious sense, the Council document *Nostra Aetate* states:

> There is found among different peoples a certain awareness of a hidden power,
> which lies behind the course of nature and the events of human life. At times
> there is present even a recognition of a supreme being, or still more of a
> Father. This awareness and recognition results in a way of life that is imbued
> with a deep religious sense[76].

Furthermore, the reference in the same document to Hinduism is of
particular importance: «in Hinduism men explore the divine mystery and
express it both in the limitless riches of myth and the accurately defined
insights of philosophy»[77]. Yet, while respecting the beliefs of non-Christian
religions and acknowledging what is holy in them, the Church also holds
fast to the principle that it «proclaims and is in duty bound to proclaim
without fail, Christ who is the way, the truth and the life»[78]. Hence, the
Church understands that it is through a genuine dialogue with adherents of
other religions that the needs and concerns of modern men and women can

---

[75] PO 5.
[76] NA 2.
[77] NA 2.
[78] NA 2.

be addressed[79], and that the former teachings of the Church regarding the salvation of humankind can undergo a theological development[80].

The documents of Vatican II encouraged Catholic theologians to fashion an Indian Christian theology that could aid dialogue to take place at three levels: spiritual-contemplative, philosophical-theological and socio-political[81]. The focus of attention here is primarily on the spiritual-contemplative level which deals with religious experience[82]. Hence, it is more personal and existential than essential or conceptual[83]. Christians can appreciate the fact that discovering the Supreme Being, or the Divine Presence, in all realities of life is the prominent feature of Hindu spirituality[84]. They can understand as well that the necessary pre-condition for such a discovery is interiorization, that is, entering into the depth of one's own being, so as to be led to share in the self-realization of the Supreme Being.

The Hindu spiritual systems of *sannyāsa* and *āsram* have been of particular relevance for Christians. A *Sannyāsi* is an ascetic who renounces the world and devotes himself to the search for the Supreme Being. *Sannyāsa* is the way of life which withdraws totally from the things of the world in order to arrive at God-realization[85]. *Sannyāsa* can also be described as the fourth stage of the life of the Brāhmana, the other three being *Brahmacarya* (student), *Gṛahastha* (householder), and *Vānaprastha* (hermitage or forest dweller)[86]. The Indian *Sannyāsa* holds in high esteem the values *Tapas*, *Brahmacarya*, Renunciation and Contemplation[87]. *Tapas*, which literally means «heat» is used in the broad sense of «asceticism» since spiritual power emerges from self-discipline[88]. *Brahmacarya* is the art of gaining control over sensual pleasures in order to attain Brahman as the centre of one's life[89]. Contemplation is a necessity in the life of a *sannyāsi* since it is the most efficacious means of arriving at God-realiza-

---

[79] B. GRIFFITHS, *The Marriage of East and West*, 24-25.

[80] K. RAHNER, *Theological Investigations*, XX, 84.

[81] Cf. A.M. MUNDADAN, «Hindu-Christian Dialogue», 375-394.

[82] R. PANIKKAR, *The Unknown Christ*, 10.

[83] R. PANIKKAR, *The Unknown Christ*, 11.

[84] Cf. J.A.G. GERWIN VAN LEEUWEN, *Fully Indian*, 280-285.

[85] PRASANNABHAI, «Indigenous Forms», 196.

[86] M. MONIER-WILLIAMS, *A Sanskrit-English Dictionary*, 1148.

[87] Cf. JESU RAJAN, *Christian Interpretation*, 67-81.

[88] Manu. XI: 239.

[89] Manu. VI: 49; *Kathaka Upaniṣad*. VI: 14-15; G.M. DHALLA, «Brahmacarya», 484-485.

tion[90]. A *Sannyāsi*, who aspired to attain the principal way to salvation, was originally a wanderer living with the bare necessities of life, but at a later stage, groups of *sannyāsis* began to live together thus giving rise to what is referred to as the *āsram* life[91].

Āsram[92], literally a dwelling place of a seeker of God, refers to a hut in the forest where *sannyāsis* or *ṛṣi* lived. Since the word *āsram* may be derived from «*sram*» which means «to exert», such a centre is characterised by an intensified ascetical life purified of worldly attachments and by an atmosphere of hospitality and of peace[93]. Since these hermitages became the heart of the Hindu society,[94] they are still considered as sources of spiritual strength oriented to social action, because the community of *sannyāsis* lives in solidarity with the poorest people of the society[95]. In short, the dwellers in the *āsram* seek God through prayer, ascetical practices and service of their needy neighbours.

Āsram is the best meeting place of the East and West, because this Indian institution has many things in common with Christian monasticism[96]. Most forms of Christian monastic life in India have recently been influenced by the *āsram* style, that is, they reflect materially, mentally and spiritually Indian traditions, while they preserve their Christian identity[97]. For Christian *sannyāsa*, the Eucharist stands at the centre of the *āsram*, because it is the source and summit of Christian life[98]. The Christian *sannyāsi* through renunciation and contemplation seeks to attain fuller incorporation into the Jesus-experience. This experience is most intense in the Eucharistic liturgy in which Jesus invites his followers to join with him in offering

---

[90] D. ACHARUPARAMBIL, «Monasticism in Hindu Tradition», 453.

[91] VANDANA, *Gurus, Ashrams and Christians*, 44-45.

[92] *Āsram* also refers to the four stages of life.

[93] VANDANA, *Gurus, Ashrams and Christians*, 45.

[94] Cf. F. MAHIEU, «Monasticism in India», 45-47.

[95] VANDANA, *Gurus, Ashrams and Christians*, 46-59.

[96] Cf. A.J. MONCHANIN and H. LE SAUX, *A Benedictine Ashram*, 26-27.

[97] ABISHIKTANANDA, *The Eyes of Light*, 75-76; A.J. MONCHANIN and H. LE SAUX, *A Benedictine Ashram*, 36. It is true that there is a radical difference between Hindu *sannyāsa* and Christian religious life. Indian *sannyāsa* and *āsram* life are modes of lifestyle, while the Eucharist is a cultic act. It is a sacrament of the unique sacrifice of Jesus Christ on Calvary. Hence, it would have been more correct to compare the Christian concept of sacrifice with the Hindu one (*yajña*). However, in this text, an extended sense of sacrifice is referred to. The Eucharist re-presents the sacrifice of Jesus. The self-emptying aspect of sacrifice is also exemplified in Hindu *sannyāsa* and *āsram* life.

[98] PO 2, 5, 6.

himself to the Father. The Christian *gurus* (spiritual guides) have therefore attempted to integrate spiritual elements more familiar to the Indian people into the Christian Eucharistic liturgy, in order to facilitate arriving at the Jesus-experience.

Among these Christian *gurus*, Abishiktanada is one of the more prominent, since he regarded Hindu-Christian dialogue as facilitating a union of two God experiences: the Jesus-experience of Christianity and the divine self-experience of Hinduism[99]. By adopting the experiential approach to religion, Abhishiktananda wanted to inculturate the person, message, prayer and values of Jesus in the Indian traditions and realities[100]. He was of the opinion that the Indian Christian *sannyāsis* who wear the same garb and follow the same regime as the traditional Indian monks, carry out their consecration in a manner faithful both to the teachings of Christianity and to the principles of the Hindu religion[101]. Hence, by adopting the *āśram* style of life, where Christian *sannyāsis* create an ecclesial atmosphere suited to the Indian cultural, theological and social situation. Assisted by Swami Parama Arubi Anandam[102], Abhishiktananda founded a Christian *āśram* on March 21, 1950 named *Saccidānada Āśram*[103].

Abhishiktananda desired to construct a bridge between Christianity and Hinduism through the manner of celebrating the Eucharistic liturgy in India. He could easily immerse himself in the presence of the Supreme Being meditating over the Hindu symbols, and he often celebrated the Eucharist in a long ceremony in which, seated on the floor, he read the Bible, *Upaniṣadic* (Hindu sacred scripture) passages, sang the «Our Father» in Sanskrit and recited *OM*[104]. He considered the Eucharist as the sacrament which descends to the deepest level of the *advaita*[105] of being[106]. Once he celebrated a cosmic liturgy with a fellow priest at Gangotri, by the

---

[99] Cf. ABHISHIKTANANDA, «The Depth-Dimension», 214-215.

[100] J. STUART, *Swami Abhishiktananda*, 19.

[101] Cf. ABISHIIKTANANDA, *The Eyes of Light*, 75-76.

[102] He received the Indian name *Parama Arubi Anandam* (Bliss of the Supreme Formless One).

[103] *SAT* (being), *CIT* (thought), and *ĀNANDA* (bliss). It is a hermitage of the Most Holy Trinity. *SAT* signifies the Father the «Principleless» Principle, *CIT* signifies the eternal Son and *ĀNANDA* stands for the Holy Spirit (Cf. A.J. MONCHANIN and H. LE SAUX, *A Benedictine Ashram*, 77-78).

[104] Sacred Syllable signifying God.

[105] «Not two»; the doctrine and experience of «non-duality».

[106] ABHISHIKTANANDA, *Guru and Disciple*, 171-172.

Ganges. At the beginning, both of them took a ceremonial bath. This signified both a return to the source of Being and a recommitment to the promises of Baptism. They celebrated Mass with the water from the Ganges and with *chapāttis* (a special kind of baked bread common in India). The rays of the sun served as the candles, and a stone as the altar[107].

As prophetic and suggestive as these actions of Abhishiktananda may have been, and as influential as they may have eventually proven to be in determining more moderate forms of inculturating the liturgy in a Hindu context, the theological investigations which he doubtlessly caused to be made have had a more lasting effect on an Indian-Christian form of thought. The positive attitude of the Vatican II encouraged many Catholic theologians also to interpret Christian doctrines in terms of the multi-religious beliefs of India, and especially those of Hinduism. Jacques Dupuis, Michael Amaladoss, M.M. Thomas, Bede Griffiths, and Raimundo Panikkar have been the most prominent among them. Their main theological concern is to affirm the uniqueness of the role of Jesus Christ in the history of salvation, and the universal necessity of being incorporated into him through faith and Baptism[108]. Yet, they admit that there is a universal salvific will of God in which the revelation of Jesus Christ, the second person of the Trinity is a qualitative not quantitative one[109]. Therefore, according to J. Dupuis, there is the possibility that God also reveals himself in other religions[110]. For M. Amaladoss, the saving divine plan is identical with the «mystery of Christ» which includes not only the historical Jesus but all the genuine manifestations of the being and value of God in the world[111]. According to M. M. Thomas, Jesus Christ is the revelation of God manifested in the new life which arises from his incarnation, life, death and resurrection[112]. However, since Jesus Christ transcends all religions, this truth necessitates Christian openness to all other forms of belief[113]. B. Griffiths, maintains that a distinction can be made between two modes of revelation, namely, 1) the cosmic mode which is God's revelation in creation and in all religions;

---

[107] ABHISHIKTANANDA, *Guru and Disciple*, 173-174. It is to be noted that this «cosmic liturgy» of Abhishiktananda remained an experiment and was never accepted in India as a usual practice.

[108] Cf. J. DUPUIS, *Jesus Christ*, 108-110.

[109] J. DUPUIS, *Jesus Christ and His Spirit*, 235.

[110] J. DUPUIS, *Jesus Christ*, 174.

[111] M. AMALADOSS, «New Wine and Old Bottles», 44; ID., *Making All Things New*, 258.

[112] M. M. THOMAS, *Risking Christ*, 3.

[113] M.M. THOMAS, «Significance of Marxist and Barthian Insights», 65.

and 2) the historical mode which is centred in Jesus Christ alone[114]. In R. Panikkar's view, all human search for God tends to find its ultimate validity in Christ who is present in an unknown or hidden way in other authentic religions[115].

While spiritual sages and theologians were making variously formulated attempts at integrating Hindu religious belief into Christian spirituality, the hierarchy of the Church contributed its share to the inculturation of faith through documents treating its theological, liturgical and spiritual aspects[116]. The C.B.C.I, which includes all the bishops from the three Rites, took the initiative in 1974 to appoint a Commission for Dialogue, and thereby stated: «dialogue is a mutual communication and sharing of religious experiences, of spiritual and moral values, enriching both the partners [...]»[117]. The Conference declared that in the field of spirituality, experiments in Hindu-Christian dialogue were particularly fruitful, and that Christian *sannyāsi* can attest to the Gospel by assimilating Indian cultural elements into their lifestyle[118]. At its meeting in 1988, the C.B.C.I. promoted interreligious prayer meetings and joint celebrations of national feasts[119].

3. The Connection between the Eucharist and Social Involvement: Sharing in the Grief of All the Children of God

An aspect of Eucharistic spirituality is its function as a connecting link between the liturgical celebration of the sacrament itself and the social activities which flow from its sanctifying grace. Active participation in the Eucharistic liturgy is directed towards a spirituality rooted in self-giving which in turn is oriented towards the practice of social love. A full and mature participation in the celebration of the Eucharist not only nourishes the faithful interiorly, but also activates their concern for those in their environment who are suffering. The Eucharist is the celebration of Jesus' self-giving love through real symbols of his body and blood which leads his followers to greater orthodoxy and orthopraxis. Together with the sacramental sacrifice of Christ, the participants offer themselves to the Father at the

---

[114] B. GRIFFITHS, *Return to the Centre*, 76; ID., *Christ in India*, 69.

[115] R. PANIKKAR, «Hinduism and Christ», 120-121; ID., *The Unknown Christ*, 27.

[116] C.B.C.I., *All-India Seminar*, 257.

[117] C.B.C.I., *Report of the General Meeting 1974*, 140.

[118] C.B.C.I., *Report of the General Meeting 1974*, 146.

[119] C.B.C.I., *Report of the General Meeting 1988*, 168-171.

liturgy and in their day-to-day situations[120]. A Eucharistic spirituality which fosters concern for the neediest in society gives living witness to Jesus of Nazareth who in his life time always aligned himself with the poor[121]. Yet, to ensure this form of spirituality, the Eucharistic liturgy itself must reflect to the social context in which the Church exists, so that the contrast between constant divine love and changing human generosity can be brought into clear light[122].

The documents of Vatican II state that the faithful, through sincere participation in the liturgy, receive the divine grace to become Christ's leaven and salt of the earth, and to manifest this by devoting themselves to the service of their neighbours[123]. Every ministry of the Church is linked with the Eucharist and is directed towards it since, enriched by heavenly food and drink, all members of the Church are constituted and organized as a society in the present world by Christ[124].

As such a society, the early Christians linked the «agape» to the Eucharistic supper, and in doing so showed themselves to be one body united to Christ and to each other by the bond of charity[125]. This moral authenticity of the first Christians reiterated the importance of the practico-social dimension of the Eucharistic liturgy.

In order to accentuate the practico-social aspect of Eucharistic grace, the documents of Vatican II direct the bishops to form the people into one family who live in communion and act out of charity. The bishops are to motivate the faithful to find ways to alleviate the sufferings of others in the concrete circumstances in which they live[126]. Besides attending to the spiritual and moral needs of their people, the bishops must also address the demographic, economic and political areas of life, promoting progress and prosperity based on justice and charity[127]. Pastors are encouraged to give moral and spiritual help to those who labour for the renewal of the temporal order in Christ. Guided by the light of the Gospel and the mind of the Church, and prompted by Christian love, the laity have an important role

---

[120] D. S. AMALORPAVADASS, *Towards Indigenisation*, 20.
[121] J.A.G. GERWIN VAN LEEUWEN, «Liturgy, the Struggle for Relevance», 31.
[122] M. AMALADOSS, *Becoming Indian*, 69.
[123] IO 8.
[124] PO 5.
[125] AA 8.
[126] CD 16.
[127] CD 17, 19.

to fulfil in the renewal of the temporal order[128]. Mercy to the poor and the sick, and charitable works to meet basic human needs, are some eloquent expressions of Gospel values, and are thus held in special honour by the Church[129]. Those lacking food, clothing, housing, medicine, education or work are to be comforted with devoted care[130].

Parecattil believed that the Eucharist is the driving force of all Christian apostolates[131]. Motivated by this sacrament, those Christians who dedicate themselves to social service make their work a prayer[132]. He also believed that authentic contemplation should lead to activities directed to the well-being of humanity. Contemplation without action, and action without contemplation, were alien to his understanding of the Christian life[133].

Thus, Vatican II confirmed the social vision of Parecattil, and gave him courage in reading the signs of the time and in addressing the problems faced by his contemporaries. He therefore instructed the religious women of the diocese to visit the houses in their neighbourhood, and in this way to become aware of the means to help families both spiritually and materially.[134] Parecattil sincerely considered the efforts to eliminate the poverty and misery of those who lived in small huts and slums to be pleasing to the Lord Jesus[135]. He desired that the priests strive to imitate Christ in doing good for the poor so as to liberate them from their anxieties. For him, the priests of the Church should be men for others who find in Christ every reason to involve themselves in humanitarian activities[136].

Furthermore, Parecattil put into practice the teachings of Vatican II concerning social service. A main thrust of his social work was economic progress through: i) development of the agrarian sector in order to provide the basic need of food; ii) beginning small scale industries so as to combat unemployment; and iii) organizing housing projects for the homeless[137]. He undertook the latter in the Archdiocese of Ernakulam as early as 1961, the year when thousands of families lost their homes because of a devasta-

---

[128] AA 7.

[129] AA 8.

[130] AA 9.

[131] J. PARECATTIL, «The Eucharistic Sacrifice», 106.

[132] J. PARECATTIL, «Offering through Suffering», 83.

[133] J. PARECATTIL, *As I See Myself*, III, 454.

[134] J. PARECATTIL, *As I See Myself*, III, 453-454.

[135] J. PARECATTIL, *Letters to Sisters*, 90.

[136] J. PARECATTIL, «Decree on the Ministry», 17.

[137] T. CHAKIATH, «The Social Vision», 104.

ting flood. He personally visited flood-ridden villagers to assess their sufferings[138]. Without distinction of caste or creed, several poor families benefitted from his relief project.

Health care and sanitation were other areas which attracted the attention of Parecattil. The concrete results of his interest are, among others, the «Lisie Hospital», Ernakulam[139] and «Little Flower Hospital», Angamaly[140], the two most respected hospitals in Kerala. He also resolved to labour for the eradication of leprosy[141]. Yet another aim of the social work of Parecattil was to reduce alcoholism[142]. His efforts to engage the Church in the field of education is also worth mentioning, since in Indian society the education of the poor was essential to attain moral progress and social equilibrium[143]. «Bharata Mata College», Trikkakara, «Kothavara College», Vaikom and the «Ernakulam Archdiocesan Education Trust» are among his more famous legacies[144]. Another area of his social involvement was his prophetic witness on behalf of the rights of women. He understood that India would never make serious progress unless women were treated with dignity[145]. He asked the women religious of the diocese to work for this cause, and he established an organization called «Women Welfare Services»[146].

In these impressive ways Parecattil tried to channel the spiritual force of the people of the diocese, derived mainly from the sacrament of the Eucharist, to active involvement on behalf of social betterment. He viewed such involvement as an intrinsic dimension of the spiritual growth of the faithful. Well aware of his episcopal responsibility for such growth, he challenged the priests, sisters and lay people to devote themselves to charitable works and social development programmes. It is clear that, adopting both a comprehensive and concrete approach to pressing problems, Parecattil worked tirelessly for the spiritual and social welfare of the people. In effect, Parecattil thereby lived according to the following statement of Vatican II on the practico-social aspect of the Mass: «This Eucharistic

---

[138] J. PARECATTIL, *As I See Myself*, III, 456.

[139] J. PARECATTIL, *As I See Myself*, III, 400-420.

[140] J. PARECATTIL, *As I See Myself*, III , 420-422.

[141] J. PARECATTIL, *As I See Myself*, III, 480-483.

[142] J. PARECATTIL, *As I See Myself*, III, 582.

[143] T.K.N. UNNITHAN, *Gandhi and Social Change*, 76.

[144] J. PARECATTIL, *As I See Myself*, III, 424-430; 433-434; 477-479.

[145] V.B. KHER, *Social Service*, 22.

[146] J. PARECATTIL, *As I See Myself*, III, 471.

celebration, to be full and sincere, ought to lead on the one hand to the various works of charity and mutual help, and on the other hand to missionary activity and the various forms of Christian witness»[147].

The chapter has made it clear that Vatican II inaugurated an unprecedented reform of the Eucharistic worship through restoration, revision and adaptation of the liturgical texts. It proposed the restoration of the pristine form of the Missal, if in the course of time unchangeable elements had been altered or omitted. It also decreed that in this process a revision of the changeable elements should be undertaken, so as to render them more intelligible for the people. Moreover, the adaptation of the liturgy to the cultural and spiritual traditions of the local church was an imperative. Parecattil was very much influenced by the proposals of the Council, and concentrated his efforts on the revision and adaptation of the Syro-Malabar Missal. He collaborated in the preparation of the 1962 Text, and oversaw with great interest its revision which became the 1968 Text. Inspired by the directives of Vatican II and in accordance with the experiments already undertaken elsewhere in India, Parecattil assumed the responsibility of preparing the *Bharatiya Pūja*. His aim in this work was to facilitate the active participation of the people through the use of spiritual and cultural elements familiar to them so that they could grasp the correlation between faith and experience.

His main goal in adapting the liturgical texts, was to promote an Eucharist-centred spirituality. He was convinced that Syro-Malabar Christians, being of Indian origin, ought to express such a spirituality by means of the thought patterns and symbols of their culture. In this understanding, Parecattil was motivated by the open approach of Vatican II to the true religious sense found in non-Christian religions, and by the strongly stated encouragement to initiate dialogue with them. In India, Christian sages, theologians and members of the hierarchy engaged in a sincere and profound dialogue with Hindu scholars especially concerning religious experience and contemplative prayer. As a result, many elements of Hindu spirituality and of Indian culture were incorporated into the Eucharistic liturgy, with the hope that such adaptations could benefit collaboration in facing the problems and aspirations of the land.

Parecattil was also adamant in asserting that Eucharistic spirituality has an effect on the social involvement of Christians. A mature participation in the Eucharistic celebration leads to the spiritual nourishment of the people so that, motivated by the self-giving love of Jesus, they can devote

---

[147] PO 6.

themselves to the service of their neighbours, and especially the poor. He was, therefore, a champion of social reform, requesting that priests, sisters and people take up various activities on behalf of social betterment. He himself initiated housing schemes, efforts to upgrade education and health-oriented projects. He was a deeply spiritual bishop whose moral strength was derived from the Eucharist and was directed toward the reform of society. He thus could credibly challenge his people to direct their energies along a similar path, for he himself felt bound by the teaching of Vatican II that «Although priests owe service to everybody, the poor and the weaker ones have been committed to their care in a special way. It was with these that the Lord himself associated, and the preaching of the Gospel to them is given as a sign of his messianic mission»[148].

---

[148] PO 6.

PART TWO

EXPOSITION OF THE EUCHARISTIC WRITINGS
OF JOSEPH PARECATTIL

CHAPTER III

The Eucharistic Writings of Joseph Parecattil
in the Pre-Vatican II Period

The present chapter, which is divided into three parts, studies the reflections of Joseph Parecattil on the role of the Eucharist in the spiritual and social life of the Church, based on his works composed prior to Vatican II. In the first part, Parecattil's view on the active participation of the faithful in the Eucharistic liturgy is treated. According to him, the Mass is a sacramental sacrifice offered by both Christ and the people to the Father. The baptismal character consecrates all the faithful into the priestly people of God, and renders them worthy of offering the Eucharistic sacrifice. All the same, there is a clear difference between the common and the ministerial form of Christian priesthood, the latter being a necessary prerogative for the participation of the former in the celebration of the Mass. Yet, a sincere and mature involvement in the Eucharist presupposes an interior and an exterior disposition on the part of all. Towards this aim, Parecattil thought it was necessary to explain three dimensions of the sacrificial nature of the Eucharist: the Last Supper, the Cross and the Altar. The three sacrifices are one and the same, and yet can be distinguished, since Jesus' immolation on the cross was prefigured in the Last Supper and is re-actualized in the Eucharist.

The second part deals with the views of Joseph Parecattil concerning the existential worship of the triune God in the Eucharistic celebration as a primary means by which the Church derives grace for its spiritual life. He also explained that adoration of the Blessed Sacrament and devotion to the Sacred Heart enable the Eucharist to foster the virtues of love and unity among the faithful, along with the strength to bear the trials of life.

The third part interprets the role played by Eucharistic grace in the social ministries of the Church. Parecattil maintained that an intense participation in the Eucharistic liturgy permeates the social witness of Christians with a spirit of generosity. He held that the Eucharistic Lord is the model for the social involvement of the Church since he personifies love of neighbour, which is its basis. Parecattil suggested various fields of social activity in which the Church, as a Eucharistic community, must engage itself: family life, welfare schemes and politics.

1. Active Participation of the Baptized in the Eucharistic Liturgy: Joining Christian Life to the Self-sacrifice of Jesus

The Eucharistic liturgy is a community act, since all the participants have an active part in its celebration because of their baptism and confirmation. Thus, Parecattil constantly affirmed the priestly role of all the faithful:

> In one sense, all Christians are priests. All share in the priesthood of the Messiah. Therefore, St. Peter says: «be yourselves [...] to be a holy priesthood, to offer spiritual sacrifices acceptable to God through Jesus Christ [...] But, you are a chosen race, a royal priesthood, a holy nation, God's own people [...]» (1Pet 2, 5-9)[1].

In order to substantiate his argument, Parecattil referred to the encyclical *Miserentissimus Redemptor* of Pope Pius XI in which it is stated that not only the ministers chosen by Jesus Christ, in order to celebrate the holy sacrifice, are active participants, but also all the Christians share in his priesthood[2]. Parecattil noted that «all Christians have the baptismal character through which they become the members of the mystical body of Christ and the partakers of the priesthood of Christ. The ordained priest offers sacrifice as a member of the mystical body»[3].

The congregation of the faithful is constituted not only of the ordained priests but also of the Christians who received the priestly character through baptism and confirmation. All join with Christ in the celebration of the sacrifice, but according to their distinct roles. In this context, Parecattil treated the relationships and the differences between the ministerial and the common form of the Christian priesthood:

> in order to offer a public and official sacrifice, the priestly character is necessary. It is given to only those who have received the sacrament of ordination. Therefore, only they can pronounce the words of consecration

---

[1] J. PARECATTIL, «A Course of Instruction», 14.

[2] J. PARECATTIL, «A Course of Instruction», 14.

[3] J. PARECATTIL, «How to View the Mass», 6.

which effect the transformation of the bread and wine into the body and blood. But, all those gathered in the church, together with the priest, can offer the public sacrifice. In this way, they also participate in the Eucharistic sacrifice.[4]

Well before Vatican II, therefore, Parecattil clearly affirmed that the ministerial priest must understand that he offers the bread and wine as a representative of the universal Church and of the faithful, especially those present in the church[5]. In order to convince the faithful of their part in the priesthood of Christ, Parecattil invariably gave due importance to both the common and the ministerial modes of priesthood: «It is true that the priest plays the important role in the celebration of the Eucharist, all the same, the entire body of the faithful together offer the sacrifice»[6]. He believed that all the faithful across the world participate in each Mass, because the latter is offered by the priest and the people in the name of the Church[7]. He pointed out that at any moment, there are thousands of priests celebrating the Mass in different parts of the globe and that all the Christians receive a spiritual benefit from each of them[8].

The baptized and the ordained join with Christ in re-actualizing the sacrifice which he enacted at the Last Supper and on the Calvary. In the Mass, Christ is both the offerer and the offering, and his people offer themselves along with him to the Father:

On the Cross, Jesus sacrificed himself for us. Today, he re-presents his self-offering through us, so that, we may offer ourselves with him. The earthly life of Jesus was a sacrifice. He desired that we, the members of his body, also become sacrificial matter [...] [9].

On another occasion, Parecattil repeated the same idea when he said that, in the daily Mass, the Lord Jesus offers himself sacramentally to the eternal Father[10].

Along with the proper disposition Parecattil was thus adamant in asserting that a proper grasp of the theology of the Eucharist enables the faithful to reap the maximum benefit from participating in it actively. Hence, it is

---

[4] J. PARECATTIL, «A Course of Instruction», 14.

[5] J. PARECATTIL, «How to View the Mass», 6.

[6] J. PARECATTIL, «Eucharistic Sacrifice,» 1.

[7] J. PARECATTIL, «Domenica Infra Octavae Nativitatis», 1; ID., *Letters to the People*, 113.

[8] J. PARECATTIL, «How to View the Mass», 6.

[9] J. PARECATTIL, «A Course of Instruction», 17.

[10] J. PARECATTIL, *Letters to the People*, 113.

necessary to transmit to the people a clear knowledge of the theology and liturgy of the Eucharist, in order to assure that they view themselves as joining their sufferings to the sacrifice of Jesus, and thus find them meaningful.

Joseph Parecattil point out that, although the sacrifice of Christ is always the one and the same, it is understood in three different ways. Thus, he explained that the forms of sacrifice accomplished at the Last Supper, on Calvary and in the Mass, though different, are inextricably connected:

> The sacrifice on the cross is the same which was offered by Jesus at the Last Supper and is re-actualized at the altar by the priest today. Christ submitted himself to death at the Last Supper, saying «This is my body given for you and this is my blood poured out for you». It was a looking forward to the sacrifice on the cross. In the Mass, we look backward to the cross[11].

Parecattil interpreted these three forms of sacrifice both as «numerically different», and as «one and the same» self-giving of Christ[12]. Through the words of institution spoken in the Cenacle, the body and blood of Christ were made present in the bread and wine, so as to anticipate his imminent death on the cross. When the ordained pronounces the words used by Jesus at the Last Supper, the sacrifice present on the altar is the same as that offered on the cross[13]. Yet, it is evident that Parecattil understood the sacrifice of Jesus as more than an offering of flesh and blood to the Father.

Parecattil pointed out that before going to the Father, Jesus had decided to establish the Eucharist as a sign of the eternal love[14]. It was this love to his beloved people that made Jesus to «perform a miracle which marvel-led all other wonders he worked»[15]. «Eucharist is the excellent discovery of Jesus to remain with his people eternally»[16].

Parecattil frequently reflected on the fact that Jesus instituted the Holy Eucharist in the Cenacle after making it clear through words and deeds that it was necessary to have an attitude of love coupled with service and humility in order to participate in the sacrament of his self-giving[17]. He viewed

---

[11] J. PARECATTIL, «A Course of Instruction», 12.

[12] J. PARECATTIL, «A Course of Instruction», 11.

[13] J. PARECATTIL, «A Course of Instruction», 8-9.

[14] J. PARECATTIL, «The Eucharist is the Bond of Charity», 2.

[15] J. PARECATTIL, <«The Last Supper»>, 2.

[16] J. PARECATTIL, «Corpus Christi», 3-4.

[17] J. PARECATTIL, «The Eucharist is the Bond of Charity», 3.

the sacrifice initiated in the Cenacle as the same one which was to be completed on the cross:

> The same sacrifice (on the cross) was offered at the Last Supper in the form of bread and wine without shedding blood [...] The words Jesus used at the institution of the Eucharist prove that it is a sacrifice [...] : «This is my body which is given for you [...] This cup which is poured out for you is the new covenant in my blood» (Lk 22, 19-20.). These words signify a true sacrifice. In the OT, to shed blood for the remission of sins meant to offer a sacrifice. The main ceremony of the sacrifice was to kill the sheep or oxen and to sprinkle the blood over the altar [...] Hence, at the Last Supper Christ was offering sacrifice [...] The sacrifice on the cross is the same that is offered at the Last Supper[18].

Parecattil further affirmed the unity of the sacrifice of the Last supper and of the Calvary by noting that both events entailed that the body and blood of Jesus were separated, either through his words or through his dying. What theologians call a «sacramental separation» or a «mystical immolation» or a «sacrifice»,[19] is based on the assumption that the words of Jesus «This is my body» and «This is my blood» brought about a symbolic yet real division of his body and blood in the upper Room[20]. In this context, Parecattil gave special attention to the significance of blood in the Bible. Just as it was necessary to seal the exodus covenant with blood (Ex 24, 8), so the blood offered by Jesus at the Last Supper is also called the «blood of the new covenant». Therefore, what Jesus offered at the Last supper and what he underwent on Calvary are aspects of one and the same sacrifice[21].

It follows that the Mass is a continuation of the Last Supper and of Golgotha, since the risen Jesus continues to offer the same sacrifice in a sacramental form:

> Again, the Eucharist is the re-presentation of the sacrifice on the cross. «For as often as you eat this bread and drink the cup, you proclaim the Lord's death until he comes» (1Cor 11, 26). Therefore, each altar is a Golgotha. We see the death of Jesus in each Mass[22].

Parecattil pointed out that the sacrifice offered by Jesus on the cross, nineteen centuries ago is the same sacrifice offered at the altar: «The

---

[18] J. PARECATTIL, «A Course of Instruction», 8-9.

[19] J. PARECATTIL, «A Course of Instruction», 9.

[20] J. PARECATTIL, «The Eucharist is the Life of the Church», 11.

[21] J. PARECATTIL, «A Course of Instruction», 10.

[22] J. PARECATTIL, «The Eucharist is the Bond of Charity», 6.

Eucharist is the sacrifice began at the Last Supper and completed on the cross»[23]. Regarding the difference between the varying forms which the one sacrifice of Jesus takes on the cross and on the altar, Parecattil referred to the teaching of the Council of Trent: On Golgotha there was shedding of blood and in the Eucharist there is an unbloody act, but the sacrificial matter is the same[24]. On the cross Jesus sacrificed himself, whereas on the altar he does so through the words and gestures of the priests[25]. Parecattil thus stated that, at the pronouncement of the words of institution, Jesus Christ is really present in the Eucharist[26]. In a sermon on the precious blood of Christ, he pointed out that, when the faithful participate in the Eucharist, they should be aware that «in the form of wine, blood of the Lord is really [...] present»[27].

Parecattil often explained that the real presence is effected through a change or transformation of the bread and wine into the body and blood of Jesus:

> He receives our offerings (bread and wine) and makes them his body and blood [...] The Messiah brings about a great change in the offerings. As the institution words: «this is my body» and «this is my blood» are uttered, the Messiah transforms the bread and wine into his body and blood. Therefore, the pronouncement of the words of institution is the most important part of the Mass. This is the climax of the Mass[28].

Parecattil called the attention of the faithful to the fact that the Eucharistic words proceeded, at first, from the mouth of Jesus Christ. Since even today he pronounces these words through his representative, the priest, they are vital words capable of transforming the bread into his body and the wine into his blood[29]. Parecattil looked into the relationship between the substance and the accidents of the bread and wine before and after the consecration. Before it, the substance of the bread supports its accidents, such as the colour, shape, and taste; after the consecration the substance of the body and blood of Jesus supports these visible qualities[30]. Parecattil ad-

[23] J. PARECATTIL, *Letters to Children*, 42.

[24] Cf. ND 1743; DS 1548.

[25] J. PARECATTIL, «Echaristic Sacrifice», 1.

[26] J. PARECATTIL, «A Course of Instruction», 16.

[27] J. PARECATTIL, «The Precious Blood of Jesus», 4.

[28] J. PARECATTIL, «A Course of Instruction», 16.

[29] J. PARECATTIL, «The Eucharist is the Life of the Church», 11.

[30] J. PARECATTIL, «The Eucharist is the Bond of Charity», 8.

mitted the limitation of the human mind in attempting to comprehend the mystery that at the Mass transubstantiation takes place, for one knows this is true only through faith[31]. He stated that at the recital of the Eucharistic words, the transubstantiation which takes place, though not visible to the physical eye, was comprehensible to the interior eye.

Parecattil, compared the three important parts of the Mass, namely, the Offertory, the Consecration and the Communion, to the different parts of moments of a sacrifice[32]. The people have a significant role to play in offertory because, as the priest holds up the bread and wine, the people join with him in remembering their relationship with God:

> At the time of offertory, we see the priest holding the chalice and the patten in the shape of a cross and raising eyes to heaven offer the bread and wine to God. What is the meaning of this? When we present something to a person we express respect and love towards him [...] When we give a gift to somebody greater than we, the action normally has two intentions: firstly, it expresses the submission and love that we have towards the recipient. Secondly, we request love and help from him. The offertory of the Mass is a similar action. God is our Father. We are obliged to adore and love him. We need his protection, help and love. Therefore, when we present the gifts at the offertory, it signifies the relationship between God and us[33].

In this context, Parecattil also spoke of the necessity which the faithful should feel of offering themselves with the bread and wine, since they are the sacrificial matter of the interior and spiritual gift made to God[34]. Thus, Parecattil interpreted the offering of the faithful as a self-surrender to God: «at the time of the offertory, the sacrificial matter is offered to God. Since it is a sign of the offer of our self, the sacrifice is a self-surrender [...] In reality, we offer ourselves in the patten as we offer the sacrificial matter»[35].

At the consecration, Jesus Christ consecrates the offering and converts them into his body and blood:

> The essence of the sacrifice consists not in our sacrifice, instead, [...] in his receiving our offering and converting them into his body and blood. The prayer at the offertory points to this: «May the Lord, who sacrificed himself for our

---

[31] J. PARECATTIL, «The Feast of Corpus Christi», 1.

[32] J. PARECATTIL, «A Course of Instruction», 13.

[33] J. PARECATTIL, «How to View the Mass», 5.

[34] J. PARECATTIL, «A Course of Instruction», 14.

[35] J. PARECATTIL, «A Course of Instruction», 16.

salvation, and ordered to celebrate the commemoration of his suffering, death, burial and resurrection, receive this sacrifice with mercy and blessing». We can only offer the sacrificial matter. With that we express our desire to offer the sacrifice [...] Then the Lord changes the sacrificial matter [...] [36].

Parecattil maintained that, after Christ converts the bread and wine, «we offer his body and blood to God»[37]. In this way, the faithful present to the eternal Father the same sacrifice which was offered by Jesus Christ on the cross. In the Mass, Christ presents himself to the Father through the faithful. Therefore, at the consecration various mysteries coincide[38].

In any sacrifice, the sacrificial matter is consumed by those who make the offer. Then, the Mass reaches its culmination in the Holy communion:

> We should understand that Holy Communion is a part of the sacrifice. It could be called a «sacrificial banquet». In the past, after offering oxen or goats to God, the meat was eaten by the priest and the people. Therefore, eating the sacrificial matter is part of the sacrifice. Hence, Holy Communion is an important part of the Mass[39].

Parecattil instructs all the faithful to participate in the Mass by receiving Holy Communion[40]. He pointed out that there was no Mass without Holy Communion. At least the priest receives it[41]. He stated that the most perfect way to return love to the Lord, is to receive Holy communion frequently[42]. Parecattil held that it is enough to receive the Eucharist in one species though it exists in two: «it is necessary to consecrate the bread and wine separately since the sacrifice has to signify the death of Christ. But, in Holy Communion one species is enough because, in both the species the Lord is present fully»[43]. Parecattil further explained that in each consecrated host the Lord is fully present, and thus even if the host is broken into pieces, in each particle there is the complete presence[44].

---

[36] J. PARECATTIL, «A Course of Instruction», 16.
[37] J. PARECATTIL, «A Course of Instruction», 17.
[38] J. PARECATTIL, «A Course of Instruction», 17.
[39] J. PARECATTIL, «A Course of Instruction», 19.
[40] J. PARECATTIL, «A Course of Instruction», 19.
[41] J. PARECATTIL, Letters to the People, 114.
[42] J. PARECATTIL, «Corpus Christi», 6.
[43] J. PARECATTIL, «A Course of Instruction», 20.
[44] J. PARECATTIL, «The Feast of Corpus Christi», 3.

After having explained in detail the three main parts of the Mass, Parecattil often stressed the theme «the Eucharist is a strength to us»[45], since he desired that the people join the cross of their life to that of Jesus and offer it to him in the Mass. He considered it a fortune to be able to share in the suffering of Christ, since this helped everyone to lead a good Christian life[46]. The faithful should therefore believe that sufferings which come from God have a part in his plan to their life. Hence, they ought to accept all the difficulties and all pains of life as the will of God, and do so in a good spirit[47]. If the Lord, who was sinless and did good to all, was crucified as a sinner, it is not surprising that his followers have to face sufferings and humiliations because the servants are not greater than the master[48].

2. Eucharistic-Centred Spirituality: Existential Worship of God in all the Activities of the Faithful

Parecattil often pointed out that the celebration of the Eucharist occupies the key position in Christian worship, and is greater than all other private prayer and pious practice[49]. According to him, the fruits it imparts to the members of the Church are invaluable. Therefore, the sign of the authentic Christian spirit is devotion towards the Eucharist[50]. Concerning Eucharistic grace, Parecattil made the following comment:

> There is no other powerful or easier way than this (Eucharist) to receive grace. In order to offer praise and adoration to God in the way he deserves and to give thanks to him in the manner proper to him, there is no better means than the celebration of the Eucharist[51].

Parecattil was convinced that the followers of Christ share in his life through Grace: «It is no longer I who live, but Christ who lives in me [...]» (Gal 2, 20). Although Christ begins to abide in the Christian souls through Baptism, his life in them becomes a more profound reality through the reception of holy Eucharist[52]. He maintained that the interior offer of

---

[45] J. PARECATTIL, «A Course of Instruction», 17-18.

[46] J. PARECATTIL, *Letters to the People*, 132.

[47] J. PARECATTIL, «How to View the Mass», 7.

[48] J. PARECATTIL, *Letters to People*, 129.

[49] J. PARECATTIL, «The Eucharist is the Life of the Church», 18.

[50] J. PARECATTIL, «The Eucharist is the Life of the Church», 12.

[51] J. PARECATTIL, «A Course of Instruction», 12-13.

[52] J. PARECATTIL, «A Course of Instruction», 20.

themselves which the faithful make at the offertory reaches its fullness at Holy Communion, because the Lord truly presented along with his self-offering on the cross comes to them and helps them to perfect their personal surrender[53]. Thus Parecattil often, stressed the incomparable role of the Eucharist in the spiritual life of Christians. He also pointed out that, in order to receive abundant grace, Christians should receive the Holy Communion frequently[54]. He understood that the Eucharist was instituted so that the followers of Christ may have a share in divine life: «I came that they may have life, and have it abundantly» (Jn 10, 10). According to Parecattil this life is received mainly through the Eucharist[55].

For Parecattil, the Eucharist is the very life-beat of the Church, because it forms it into a community that lives from divine grace:

> What is the power resource which supports the existence of the Church? It is nothing else than Eucharist [...] Eucharist is the life of the Church [...] In the beginning, in the garden of Eden there was a «tree of life» (Gen 1, 9). It provided eternity. In the NT, there is a garden which is more beautiful than the garden of Eden and is the object of the special care of God. It is nothing but the Catholic Church. The tree of life in the centre of that garden is the Eucharist. It gives the food of eternity. The Lord Says: «This is the bread which came down from heaven, not such as the fathers ate and died; he who eats this bread will live for ever» (Jn 6, 59). Therefore, more than anything else, it is the Eucharist that has kept alive the life of the Church. This sacrament is the main source which causes the flow of grace, that gives eternal life, to the members of the Church[56].

Referring to St. Paul, Parecattil said that the Church is a living organism: «the head of the body is the Messiah and the faithful are the members. The Eucharist which is the heavenly *Manna* nourishes the body»[57]. On another occasion Parecattil remarked that it is no exaggeration to say that Catholic Church without the Holy Eucharist would lose its stamina[58].

Mindful of the divisions in the Church, Parecattil viewed the Eucharist as the sacrament of the unity among Christians:

---

[53] J. PARECATTIL, «A Course of Instruction», 21.

[54] J. PARECATTIL, «The Eucharist is the Life of the Church», 20.

[55] J. PARECATTIL, *Letters to Children*, 13.

[56] J. PARECATTIL, «The Eucharist is the Life of the Church», 5-6.

[57] J. PARECATTIL, «The Eucharist is the Life of the Church», 7.

[58] J. PARECATTIL, «The Eucharist is the Life of the Church», 18.

The bread and wine that we use in the Mass signify the unity created among [...] us through this sacrament. St. Paul says: «[...] The bread which we break, is it not a participation in the body of Christ? Because there is one bread, we who are many are one body, for we all partake of the one bread» (1Cor 10, 16-17) [...] We become one in Christ. The priest who celebrates the Mass and the people who participate in it are one body, and a community. Since, the Eucharist unites us, are not all those participate in it — the priests who offer sacrifices among themselves, the faithful among themselves and the priests and the people together-obliged to live in unity? We are not worthy to receive the body of the Lord so long as quarrels and divisions exist among us[59].

Parecattil underlined the necessity of unity among Christians, since it is not enough that the faithful go to Mass daily, fast twice a week, and pray much. If after doing all these things, they did not love their neighbour, they are not walking on the path of Jesus Christ[60]. Quoting a well known scriptural passage, Parecattil stressed the need of fraternal love which is the basis of Christian unity: «If any one says, "I love God", and hates his brother, he is a liar; for he who does not love his brother whom he has seen, cannot love God whom he has not seen» (1Jn 4, 20). Furthermore, according to Parecattil, unity among the Christians means the coming together of the members of all Christian denominations. Since all the baptized are the followers of Christ, the Catholic Church hopes that the separated brethren will return one day to its former unity.

Since the Eucharist is fountain of grace for the entire Church and for all its individual members, Parecattil repeatedly instructed the people to offer the Eucharistic sacrifice both for the various intentions of the living and for the repose of the souls of the dead. He once requested the people to participate in the daily Mass, and to pray for India and for the State of Kerala in particular[61]. On the occasion of the Silver Jubilee Celebration of the reunion of the Syro-Malankara Church[62], Parecattil wished to give thanks

---

[59] J. PARECATTIL, «The Eucharist is the Bond of Charity», 7.

[60] J. PARECATTIL, «The Eucharist is the Bond of Charity», 9.

[61] J. PARECATTIL, Letters to the People, 119.

[62] The fifteenth century opened a new chapter in the history of Indian Christianity. The Portuguese under the leadership of Vasco da Gama reached Calicut, Kerala, in 1498 (Cf. A.M. MUNDANDAN, Indian Christians Search, 31). The Indian Christians, at first, were happy to receive the powerful Westerners. Unfortunately, good relations existed between the two only for a while. Tension mounted between them later, and the Portuguese took full control over the Indian Church. In 1653, a revolt broke out against the Portuguese and the Indian Christians were not ready to obey them. However, by the positive interference of Rome, the majority of the Christians remained loyal to the Pope. They are called the Syro-Malabar Christians. All the same, a small group broke away from

to God for the blessings given to the Church of Kerala through the re-union movement by singing the *Te Deum* during solemn Eucharistic benediction in all the parishes of the diocese[63]. In his pastoral letter of November 6, 1958, he stated that he had prayed for Pope John XXIII two days beforehand, on November 4, the day of his coronation, by conducting a solemn Eucharistic benediction and singing the *Te Deum*[64]. At the conclusion of the «Liberation Struggle»[65], he asked the people «to offer as early as possible a High Mass» for the persons killed during it[66]. In these concrete ways, Parecattil re-iterated that the grace flowing from the Eucharist is efficacious both for the living and the dead.

Adoration of the Eucharistic Lord was considered another sublime form of prayer by Parecattil. On the occasion of the Silver Jubilee of his priestly ordination, he wrote the following to the nuns of the archdiocese:

> I am happy to know that you are conducting solemn adoration of the Eucharistic Lord in order to give thanks to him for the blessings he has showered upon me and, through me, on others. Truly, a priest is a minister and servant of the Eucharist. He is consecrated to offer the sacrifice. Hence, priesthood is closely united to the Eucharist. Therefore, the best way to celebrate the jubilee of the priestly ordination is to adore the Eucharistic Lord. Realizing this fact, I try to make one hour adoration every day [...] I pray for the priests, nuns and people of the archdiocese during this time of blessing [...] In this way, if the Eucharistic Lord is glorified through the jubilee of my priestly ordination, what more could I desire?[67].

In this context, one should refer to the close connection that Parecattil perceived between the devotions to the Eucharist and to the Sacred Heart. He mentioned on different occasions that the Sacred Heart of Jesus is present in the Eucharist:

Rome and entered into communion with the West-Syrian Jacobite Church of Antioch. On September 30, 1930, a fraction of this Jacobite Church was reconciled with Rome and is called the Syro-Malankara Church.

[63] J. PARECATTIL, *Letters to the People*, 81.

[64] J. PARECATTIL, *Letters to the People*, 107.

[65] In 1950's the Communists governed the State of Kerala. The Government brought about many regulations which negatively affected the rights of minorities. A state-wide protest was organized at the end of which the ministry fell in 1957. The Struggle against the government is termed as «Liberation Struggle» (*Vimochanasamaram*).

[66] J. PARECATTIL, *Letters to the People*, 158.

[67] J. PARECATTIL, *Letters to Sisters* 75.76.

Remain close to the Eucharistic Lord always. Joined with him fight the spiritual enemies. Then he will protect us in the caves of his Sacred Heart[68].

In this text, Parecattil brings together three themes: the Eucharist, Christ's love and spiritual struggle. No doubt these themes reveal his own inner life as the locus of his strength to carry out mission as a bishop. This speculation confirmed by one of his sermons on Eucharist which is entitled «The Hidden Life of the Sacred Heart in the Blessed Sacrament»[69]. In practical ways as well, Parecattil gave witness to the connection of these pure devotions in his own spirituality. On September 10, 1956 he asked the people to give thanks to the Lord for the various gifts showered up on the archdiocese by reciting the prayer of dedication to the Sacred Heart, during solemn Eucharistic benediction[70]. On another occasion he requested the people to do the very same as they pray that Christian youth survive the dangers of adolescence and early adulthood[71]. By means of the same devotion the people were asked by him also to pray for the members of the government formed in the State of Kerala[72]. All these requests show that Parecattil found the focus of his spirituality in the Sacred Heart who is present in the Eucharist.

Parecattil explained that the Eucharist is the food and drink of the soul, as Jesus himself made clear by choosing to give himself in the form of bread and wine. In the Eucharist, he provided his life to the people as a spiritual nourishment. Their union with the Eucharistic Lord challenges the Christians to live in a new way: «Put off your old nature [...] and put on the new nature, created after the likeness of God in true righteousness and holiness» (Eph 4, 22-24). Thus Parecattil desired that the Lord who is present in the Eucharist help all the Christians to understand the need to live according to love[73]. He thus said that, since the followers of Christ participate in his sacred banquet of love, they have to take up the responsibilities of loving to the Lord who considers his disciples not as mere slaves, but as friends, which means that they must love him in return. Moreover, this friendship with the Eucharistic Christ must be shared among all those who participate in the sacrament, since Jesus himself is offended when his

---

[68] J. PARECATTIL, «The Holy Eucharist», 12.

[69] J. PARECATTIL, «The Hidden Life», 1.

[70] J. PARECATTIL, *Letters to the People*, 28.

[71] J. PARECATTIL, *Letters to the People*, 65.

[72] J. PARECATTIL, *Letters to the People*, 181.

[73] J. PARECATTIL, «An Appendix to "The Holy Eucharist"», 1.

friends quarrel among themselves[74]. The Eucharist is therefore monument of love, that Jesus has for his friends for whom he sacrificed his life. As a response to this love, the Christians should recall that they recovered it from him who was an expiation for their sins. If God so loved them in Christ Jesus, they also ought to love one another (1Jn 4, 10-11).

3. The Social Involvement of the Church in Indian Life: A Eucharistic Interpretation

Joseph Parecattil often stated that the Church calls its members to conduct a Eucharistic life by experiencing the grace they receive from the sacrament in the service of the weakest in their society. He viewed the Eucharist as the principal source of the humanitarian activities of Christians, because it contains the same Jesus who was charitable to others not only during his public ministry, but also in the Cenacle before his death, is present in the sacrament. Therefore, love of the neighbour, a virtue nurtured by the Eucharist, is the basis of the social actions of the faithful:

> When we receive Holy Communion, we share in a common meal. We eat from a single table as did Jesus, seated at the centre, and the disciples around him at the Last Supper. Eating together is always a sign of love and unity. Therefore, how is it possible to share in this meal if enmity and hatredness, among the participants? In order to show that all those who eat from this bread shall have pure, humble and service-minded love, before instituting the Eucharist, Jesus washed the feet of the disciples and said: «[...] If then, I, your Lord and teacher, have washed your feet, you also ought to wash one another's feet» (Jn 13, 14). After the institution of the Eucharist, the Lord said: «A new commandment I give you, that you love one another; even as I have loved you, that you also love one another» (Jn 13, 24) [...] Each time we receive this sacrament, let the commandment of love touch in our minds deeply[75].

In this most forceful text, Parecattil uses the phrase «pure, humble and service-minded love» to describe the practico-social dimension of Eucharistic grace. For he was convinced that the Eucharist changes human relations. It changes a natural love for others into a supernatural one: husband and wife are united in Christ, so too are mother and child, friends and classmates. «All the differences, such as colour, country, status, economic conditions shall be forgotten»[76]. He maintained that the Risen Jesus continues

---

[74] J. PARECATTIL, «The Eucharist is the Bond of Charity», 5-6.

[75] J. PARECATTIL, «A Course of Instruction», 21.

[76] J. PARECATTIL, «The Eucharist is the Bond of Charity», 7.8.

to live among the people in the Eucharist because of his great love towards them[77]. This sacrament always called them to practice this love in their social context[78].

For Parecattil, it is most significant that Jesus showed social concern through his words and deeds. On various occasions, Jesus was moved by compassion, and gave food to the hungry. «Today», Parecattil asserts, «he continues to do so in the Eucharist»:

> Jesus spent his earthly life as a close friend of the poor [...] The same Jesus, who consoled the suffering, is always, present in the altar [...] Many of us are poor and do not have enough to eat. But, remember that Jesus was a friend of the poor. He was born poor, lived poor and died poor. We read how he worked a great miracle to feed the hungry. He cared for the bodily needs of those who came to listen him. When it was evening, the disciples came to him and said, «This is a lonely place, and the day is now over; send the crowds away to go into the villages and buy food for themselves». Jesus said: «They need not go away; you give them something to eat» (Mt 14, 15). Then he multiplied the five loaves and two fish and gave them to them. The same Jesus is present onthe altar. Even though today he does not work a miracle, that is visible to the physical eye, he will not leave those who depend on him. Therefore, those of you who suffer from poverty, visit the Eucharistic Lord and then go to your duties. He will bless your work and your families[79].

In this text, Parecattil clearly implies that the compassion towards one's neighbour that springs from Eucharistic grace is the constant basis of the social action of the Church. He was of opinion that to work for the welfare of one's fellow citizens of India is to practice real love of neighbour, the virtue which characterized the life of Jesus. For Parecattil this is the chief motive which should encourage all Christians to be involved in welfare activities[80]. He noted that the love of neighbour which the Eucharist instils in the faithful has two practical dimensions. On the one hand, it is the absence of hatred and enmity. Looked at from another angle, it consists in good deeds done freely for other persons. Hence, the Eucharist gives Christians the grace to practice many positive forms of social love:

> Forgiving the enemy is only a negative side of love. Love has also a positive side. Therefore, it is not enough that there is no enmity. We are obliged to help

---

[77] J. PARECATTIL, *Letters to the People*, 20.

[78] J. PARECATTIL, «The Eucharist is the Bond of Charity», 12.

[79] J. PARECATTIL, «The Holy Eucharist», 6-7.

[80] J. PARECATTIL, «The Progress of Our Country», 225.

our neighbours as we can. As regards the kind of actions we should be involved in [...], it is necessary to speak about two or three of them in the modern context: «give food to those who are hungry; drink to those who are thirsty; and cloth to those who are naked». Dress and food are two of the fund-amental problems any person is faced with. Nobody can live without them. God has created enough goods that would be sufficient for all. But, these are not distributed properly [...] However, it is not to be forgotten that the rich have the duty to protect the poor [...] We should help those who suffer with an attitude of love of neighbour and with a sense of equality [...] We should abide by the virtues of truth, justice and mercy [...] love of neighbour in all actions [...] Some may question the relevance of these things in a sermon on the occasion of the «forty hour adoration». But, in a Eucharistic life one learns these kinds of practical lessons[81].

This text is most revelatory of the depth of commitment which Joseph Parecattil felt concerning the connection between Eucharistic faith and the duty to help and protect the poor, since at its end he mentions that some of his hearers might be disturbed at being confronted with social issues in a sermon held during a devotion centred on the presence of Christ in the Eucharist. In effect, this text justifies the emphasis placed in this study on the importance of the sacrament of the altar, in the theology, spirituality and social teaching of Parecattil. The phrase, «But in a Eucharistic life one learns these kinds of practical lessons» can be understood as proof that for him the devotion to Christ in this sacrament was a school which provided him the insights by which to guide his people on social matters. If in the following pages little direct reference is made to the Eucharist, it can be presumed that the spiritual energy needed to assume the social commitment which Parecattil asks of the people of the archdiocese is understood by him to flow from the grace of this sacrament.

If Eucharistic grace is the foundation of Christian social involvement, Parecattil urged that Christians be spiritually motivated in all they do for others. In the following text he presents Christian social involvement to religious sisters as the pressing need of the modern age:

We live, today, in a world that is changing and developing day by day. Accordingly, we have to change our views, life and activities, to keep up with the modern trends. It is an urgent necessity of today's circumstances that we give more importance to social involvement. Though the nuns cannot give financial help to the poor and cannot work in the political field, all the same they can contribute much because of their spiritual orientation [...] If you visit

---

[81] J. PARECATTIL, «An Appendix to "The Holy Eucharist"», 2-4.

poor families you will be able to lead many of those who have gone astray to the right path. How many young women in our families suffer and would like to share their problems with persons who are loving and trustworthy[82].

Although no explicit mention of the Eucharist is made in this text it is clear that the challenge to Christianity which Parecattil perceived as coming from the modern age means that all forms of religious commitment including a life dedicated to contemplative prayer, are not immune from the need to reach out to people who suffer silently and to communicate to them through simple human signs, the love and trustworthiness of Christ. Thus, it was edifying for him to see that some religious «coming out of the limited horizons of a mere contemplative life, began to use their talents in social action on behalf of the poor in accordance with modern needs»[83].

With regard to the laity, Parecattil insisted that they abide by Christian moral principles in all their social dealings and business transactions. On November 1, 1961, the ways of comment on the encyclical letter *Mater et Magistra* of Pope John XXIII, he wrote: «The social life will be successful only if it is deeply rooted in truth, justice and love»[84]. He mentioned some of the fields of civil activity where these principles are to be particularly applied. It was unquestionable for him that employers should pay their paid labourers well, and that latter should perform their duties justly. Making profit by not paying the proper bill for goods purchased, exacting enormous prices, buying smuggled goods, using false measurements, and selling adulterated goods were clearly unjust dealings[85]. He was adamant that all in the archdiocese should be mindful of their responsibilities towards God and society[86].

Because of much rampant injustice, the Christians who dedicate themselves to social work require much moral strength in order to accomplish their goals. They need the grace of God especially so as to bear all the trials and sufferings attached to such activities. They may indeed feel at times that they are being crucified for the good they do for others. In such moments, the self-surrender of Jesus, which is symbolised and contained in the Eucharist, will have the power to console them: «Those who engage in social work shall derive the strength and courage from the

---

[82] J. PARECATTIL, *Letters to Sisters*, 18.
[83] J. PARECATTIL, *Letters to Sisters*, 21.
[84] J. PARECATTIL, *Letters to the People*, 232.
[85] J. PARECATTIL, *Letters to the People*, 232.
[86] J. PARECATTIL, *Letters to the People*, 233.

suffering of Jesus. Those who walk in the way of service will surely be criticized and will spoil their names»[87].

Aware of the criticism that Christians are indifferent to the problems of India, Parecattil pointed out that the Church undertakes various charitable projects with the aim to building a better society. These are not against the government, but are done out of good will so as to active the goal of better living standards. On October 10, 1956 Parecattil remarked:

> Nobody can close their eyes to the service the Catholic Church undertakes in the field of social work through hospitals, centres of different kinds, homes for the destitute, and the works of the St. Vincent de Paul Society. We have to be prepared to meet the problems of the modern age [...] Each government works out plans to solve the problems of the farmers and labourers with an aim to raise the standard of life. It is the need of the time that citizens of good will come forward to co-operate with these enterprises and work for the betterment of the society[88].

Parecattil was optimistic regarding the various programmes the field of social action by the Church in India. The Catholic bishops of the sub-continent were in fact attempting to co-ordinate the social works of their dioceses. As a result, an «All India Social Service Centre» was established. Moreover, in order to organize the social programme of the different dioceses of Kerala, a «Malabar Regional Committee» was formed. Parecattil also maintained that it was desirable to organize parish committees under the name «Social Service Centres»[89]. The aim of such centres was to help the poor and the sick and to eradicate unemployment[90]. He was convinced that the economic and social teachings of the Church offered the means to resolve many problems of modern era. By indicating the limitations of the economic policies of corrupt capitalism as well as of atheistic communism, the Church argued both for private ownership which fosters human dignity and industry, and for the proper distribution of wealth[91]. On February 4, 1960, he reminded the people that one of the most important social responsibilities was that people interact among themselves as equals, and work to improve their social status. They should try to help one another by giving financial aid to the needy, employment to the unemployed and the basic

---

[87] J. PARECATTIL, *Letters to the People*, 131.
[88] J. PARECATTIL, *Letters to the People*, 30.
[89] J. PARECATTIL, *Letters to the People*, 31.
[90] J. PARECATTIL, *Letters to the People*, 31.
[91] J. PARECATTIL, *Letters to the People*, 40.

necessities of life to those who were deprived of them[92]. Parecattil compared the situation of the holy family searching a place where Jesus could be born, with that of the homeless of his own time, and noted that providing shelter for them was equal to harbouring Joseph and Mary[93].

Since politics comprises an integral part of the social life of people, Parecattil admitted that Christians involved in social activities have to deal directly or indirectly with it. Although the Church does not enter actively into politics, all the same it must never fail to urge its members to form a responsible political consciousness. Thus, Parecattil instructed the people to love both the Church and the country even though he also foresaw the possibility of that two allegrances would not coincide. In such cases he clearly required them that his people stand by the values of their Christian faith:

> We must have very clear notions about religio-political matters. As Catholics, our most fundamental need is the freedom of conscience and that of public worship: in other words, the freedom to follow our holy religion and to profess it openly, which includes the freedom to put up churches, cemeteries and to preach our religion publicly and gain converts. Secondly, we must have the freedom to conduct our own educational institutions without being subject to any discrimination regarding grants-in-aid or other facilities. Thirdly, we must have our due representation in Government service [...] This is the real hierarchy of values and in judging the merits or defects of a Government or of a party in power all these points are to be considered without over-emphasizing either the one or the other[94].

As regards the relationship which Indian Christians should have towards their country, Parecattil was lucid in stating: «Love God above all, and love the mother-land after God is our motto»[95]. Speaking over the Vatican Radio, on May 10, 1958, he saluted Bharata Mata, Mother India, whom he loved dearly and who by means of the two moral weapons of *Satyam* and *Ahimsa*, truth and non-violence, was marching ahead and making rapid strides of progress, especially after attaining independence[96]. Then he commented that the Catholics of India have been loyal and law-abiding citizens of the land, illustrating by their lives that it is possible to be a devoted Roman Catholic and a patriotic Indian National at one and the same

---

[92] J. PARECATTIL, *Letters to the People*, 181-182.

[93] J. PARECATTIL, <«Homes for the Homeless»>, 190.

[94] J. PARECATTIL, «Clear Thinking», 222.

[95] J. PARECATTIL, «The Progress», 225.

[96] J. PARECATTIL, <«The Church»>, 102.

time[97]. In fact, Parecattil agreed with Gandhi that those who hold the view that religion has no relation with politics do not know the meaning of religion[98].

However, this love of the nation on the part of Christians should not lessen their adherence to Gospel principles. On November 6, 1958, he wrote to his people: «We are not obliged by conscience if any government enacts laws that impede fulfilling our duties towards God or neglect our fundamental rights. On the other hand, we shall protest and resist such laws and procedures»[99]. He also spoke about the supremacy of the divine over the civil authority: there is no power on earth that could call in question God's holy mandates or try to improve on them[100]. Parecattil gave voice to the political philosophy of the Church, namely that any people or country which did not respect God the supreme law-giver would not last long, and would not maintain peace and fraternity.[101] He stated that the hour had come for Catholics to gain expertise in politics, and he encouraged the people to become members of the political parties which were not against Catholic principles. It was clearly his view that those honestly involved in politics served the society and the Church[102].

Since in a democracy, each citizen has the right and duty to be involved in the electoral process, Parecattil wrote in strong terms about the responsibility of the Catholics to utilise their voting power in the proper way and for the benefit of their country:

> As regards the importance of the coming general election, I would like to remind you of certain things. We shall try our best so that the liberation we won from the iron yoke of the communist government, may last long. To this end, what is needed most is that those who have the right to vote exercise their franchise. In a democratic system, it is the citizens who govern. One who does not utilize the noble right to vote, does not participate in the government [...] It is to be said that in the context of Kerala it is a great sin, if one does not utilize his voting power[103].

At the time when the Communist party could come into power, Parecattil urged his people to exercise their right to vote so as to assure the defeat of

---

[97] J. PARECATTIL, «The Church», 102.

[98] J. PARECATTIL, <«The Church and Politics»>, 45.

[99] J. PARECATTIL, *Letters to the People*, 110.

[100] J. PARECATTIL, «The Church», 100.

[101] J. PARECATTIL, «The Church and Politics», 46.

[102] J. PARECATTIL, «Serve in a New Spirit», 66.

[103] J. PARECATTIL, *Letters to the People*, 173.175.

materialistic ideology: «We cannot run the risk of the communists coming into power as a result of our lethargy or want of foresight»[104]. He reminded them that vigorous efforts should be made to get people to the polling stations, since they sometimes prefer to remain idle rather than exercise their right to vote. Yet, on another occasion Parecattil was careful to adhere to the policy of the Church, namely, not to engage directly in politics: «I do not wish to enter into any party politics, but, I would emphasize that we should be objective in our judgements and assessment of facts without being carried away by prejudices or personal grudges»[105].

Parecattil also stated that the success of any government was to be evaluated in relation to its welfare activities, such as ensuring better working conditions, solving the problem of unemployment, producing more food by irrigation schemes and scientific methods of cultivation, increasing transport facilities through the construction of railways, bridges and roads, and removing illiteracy by opening more educational institutions and by allotting adequate pay to teachers[106]. Given these standards, he judged that India had sufficiently well after having attained independence from the British in 1947 without bloodshed and violence[107].

In all these concrete efforts which Parecattil made to assure that Catholics of Kerala practice justice, be engaged in charitable work and take part in the betterment of the country. He was motivated by these to live a Eucharistic life. For, in this sacrament the ideals of Christ and of the Church are embodied and become evident to each generation of believers. The values by which to regulate all social activities are concern for the poor, the hungry and the suffering, and generosity in meeting their needs:

> We should not think that we have fulfilled our duties towards the Eucharist by participating often in the Mass, or by receiving Holy Communion only. We shall live a Eucharistic life through out the year. We can say that we lead a Eucharistic life only when we lead a life in accordance with the ideals shinning in the Eucharist. We shall put into practice the lessons the sacrament teaches us. Let them regulate all our activities[108].

Parecattil often instructed the people about the challenge of leading a Eucharistic-centred Christian life. The people should offer their hard daily

---

104 J. PARECATTIL, «Clear Thinking», 222.
105 J. PARECATTIL, «Look to the Party», 220.
106 J. PARECATTIL, «Look to the Party», 220.
107 J. PARECATTIL, «Look to the Party», 220.
108 J. PARECATTIL, «Eucharist is the Bond of Charity», 1.

work to the Eucharistic Lord, so as to receive the blessings of peace and consolation[109]. He also stated that one can lead a Eucharistic life only when the grace of the sacrament controls, purifies, and renews all one's daily activities[110]. Therefore, all Christians should strive to make their thoughts, words and deeds conform to the will of the Eucharistic Lord by overcoming pride, extravagance, impurity and enmity. Parecattil was convinced that this could be done only if the people grow in Eucharistic devotion day by day[111]. He stated this quite succinctly in the phrase: «If Catholic life is to be kept alive, the Eucharist plays the most important role»[112].

On the basis of this reflection, one can draw certain conclusions regarding the first phase of the Eucharistic theology of Parecattil. The Eucharist is perceived as the core of the Christian worship, since through participation in the Mass, adoration of the Blessed Sacrament and devotion to the Sacred Heart the people encounter the self-sacrificing love of Christ and respond to it by loving him in return. The Christian people are made worthy to offer this sacrifice with the priests by the share in the common priesthood they received at Baptism. An active participation in the Mass on the part of the people is facilitated by an understanding of the Eucharist as the sacramental self-sacrifice of Christ. Along with him, they are to offer themselves and all their sufferings to Father. Since the one and the same sacrifice exists in liturgy in three modes, — the Last Supper the Cross and the Altar —, reception of Holy Communion affords people access to the source of salvation, the self-giving Jesus.

Since Parecattil was convinced that the Eucharist caused a flow of divine grace to inundate the Church, he often proposed that people take part in the celebration of the Eucharistic liturgy in order to pray for the spiritual well-being of the living and the dead. He stated that the virtues of love and unity were deepened by this sacrament, and the strength to surrender oneself to the will of God, was provided. Yet, Parecattil maintained that a Eucharistic life which remained within the spiritual realm, of individual Christians was not complete. The grace received at the Eucharist should lead the people to the practice of love in their society. Parecattil claimed that this mandate came directly from the Eucharistic Christ who is the model of the social work of the Church.

---

[109] J. PARECATTIL, «The Eucharist is the Bond of Charity», 7.

[110] J. PARECATTIL, «An Appendix to the "The Holy Eucharist"», 1.

[111] J. PARECATTIL, «An Appendix to "The Holy Eucharist"», 1; ID., *Letters to the People*, 206.

[112] J. PARECATTIL, *Letters to Children*, 20.

CHAPTER IV

The Application of the Teachings of Vatican II
to the Eucharistic Liturgy, Spirituality,
and Social Action of the Syro-Malabar Church

Like most Christians who lived at the time of Vatican II, Joseph Parecattil was greatly influenced by this major ecclesiastical event. Thereafter he sought to implement the Conciliar documents in the Syro-Malabar Church. The present chapter, which is divided into three parts, analyzes the Eucharistic theology which Parecattil articulated while Vatican II was in session and during the first phase of the post-conciliar period, until he was named a Cardinal in 1969.

The first part treats how Parecattil adhered to the teachings of Vatican II regarding the restoration, revision and adaptation of the liturgical texts. Inspired by this goal Parecattil attempted to support every effort to renew the Syro-Malabar Eucharistic liturgy. In this attempt, his attention was focused on two Missals: the restored text of 1962 and the revised one of 1968. He was not satisfied with the former because of its rigid adherence to the ancient Chaldean traditions without considering the theological and pastoral difficulties which this entailed. All the same, he co-operated in the preparation of the 1962 Text with the hope that it could be revised and adapted in the future. He also played a prominent role in overseeing the publication of the 1968 Mass Book. In his opinion, it proved to be far superior to the preceding text, since it was updated through the revision of the ancient formulas and through the addition of elements from Indian culture.

The second part offers a detailed exposition of the thought of Parecattil with regard to the place of the Eucharist in the spiritual life of Christians. At the celebration they learn from Jesus himself what attitudes should fill their minds and hearts, as they become one body with him as their Head.

Then, with the help of Eucharistic grace, they can participate more fully in the communal life of the Church and its mission. Parecattil also claimed that dialogue with members of other religions should be undertaken, so as appreciate elements of their belief which do not contradict the values of the Eucharistic Christ. However, he did not mean that evangelization, which is the prime responsibility of each Christian, should not be carried on, so that others might come to new and eternal life through Eucharistic grace.

The third part presents the social dimension of the Eucharistic theology of Parecattil. The charitable activities of the Church were viewed by him as the means by which to follow the example of Jesus who is present in the Eucharist. The doctrine of the Mystical Body of the Church urges all Christians to promote the welfare of their brethren. Among the social activities of the Church, Parecattil was specially interested in those which advanced the economic development of the people through such projects as the increase of food production and the construction of houses. As a true son of democratic India, Parecattil called the people to live up to the high ideals of the country, such as those of *Satyam* and *Ahimsā* taught by the Hindu religion and preached and exemplified by Gandhi.

1. The Vatican II Proposals of Restoration, Revision and Adaptation of the Eucharistic Liturgy: Interpreted in the Context of the Syro-Malabar Church

As has been pointed out in the opening part of this study, Parecattil wholeheartedly accepted the teachings of the Council on the need to renew Christian worship. He thus worked tirelessly to include Indian cultural forms into the Syro-Malabar liturgy in the post-conciliar period. Speaking at the «Church in India Seminar» in Alwaye, he remarked:

> I would like to emphasis that a liturgy that will cater to the present needs of the people and will influence their actual lives must be dynamic and not simply static, one that responds to the tastes, aspirations and requirements of contemporary people in the circumstances in which they are placed and not simply one that merely reproduces in stereotyped formulas what was composed by liturgical experts of bygone days for a people of a different clime, country and time. There arises the need for a careful adaptation and healthy Indianisation of the liturgy. This is quite in keeping with the Decrees of the Vatican Council and subsequent documents of the subject[1].

---

[1] J. PARECATTIL, «Concluding Remarks», 20.

Parecattil substantiated his argument for further alterations in the liturgy with an «important axiom that resounded at Vatican II on October 22, 1962: «Liturgy is for the people and not the people for liturgy»[2]. He recollected that this phrase was coined by Cardinal Montini, who later became Pope Paul VI[3]. Writing concretely about the Syro-Malabar Eucharistic liturgy, he mentioned in a letter to the Oriental Congregation that in its meaningful reform the sentiments of the people and the pastoral exigencies of the Church of Kerala were to be taken into account. He pointed out that it was all the more necessary to give importance to local customs, as the national Government and regional leaders considered Christianity a «foreign religion» opposed to the Indian tradition[4]. He further remarked that the liturgists who have accepted the directives of Vatican II recognized the need of brevity, variety and adaptability in divine worship. He noted that the Latin liturgy in India was already making rapid strides toward adaptation along these lines[5]. Parecattil thus argued that, if the Roman Rite can make such changes in the post-Conciliar period without losing the organic identity of its ritual, the Syro-Malabar Rite also had the right to do likewise. He emphasized that to deny this right to the Syro-Malabar Church, «even it be under the influence of the so-called "specialists in liturgy" of the Syro-Malabar Rite itself, would be discrimination and would be against the equality of Rites, so much emphasised by the Vatican Council»[6].

Coming to concrete terms with the Syro-Malabar liturgical renewal, Parecattil considered the Missal of 1962 pre-conciliar, since it was an unabridged restoration of the ancient Chaldean Traditions. He remarked: «the reintroduction of purely Chaldean gestures and the prohibition of Indian gestures betray an anachronistic spirit, diminishing the relevance of the liturgy in the eyes of contemporary people»[7]. He also pointed out the considerable theological confusion in the 1962 Text as regards the use of terms and formulas. Moreover, he lamented the fact that «in the Liturgical Commission which handled the restoration of our liturgy and in the Plenary Session of the Sacred Congregation which took the final decision, the Syro-Malabar Bishops had not even a single representative to explain and defend

---

[2] J. PARECATTIL, «Concluding Remarks», 20.
[3] J. PARECATTIL, <«Our Liturgy»>, 9.
[4] J. PARECATTIL, <«Our Liturgy»>, 5.
[5] J. PARECATTIL, <«Our Liturgy»>, 9.
[6] J. PARECATTIL, «Renewal of an Imaginary Prohibition», 106.
[7] J. PARECATTIL, «Liturgical Reform», 57.

their views»[8]. In *Liturgy As I See It*, Parecattil quoted from a letter composed by Msgr. Cyriac J. Mattathil, the then Vicar General of Kottayam. The following excerpt indicated the questions which the 1962 Text had raised:

> Was the idea of «aggiornamento» taken into consideration while steps were taken to ensure the «pristine purity» of our Rite? For centuries, our Oriental Liturgy was in use in the Middle East; and our Rite in Kerala is distinguished from the other by the special name «Syro-Malabar Rite». Our Liturgy in Kerala should be allowed to be developed, taking into account our milieu, we presume. Was this point of «aggiornamento», in the sense given above, taken into consideration in the restoration of our Liturgy? If not, is it not still possible and desirable to take into account our Indian Culture?[9]

Therefore, for the reason mentioned here, very soon it became clear that the 1962 Text was no longer spiritually or pastorally advantageous, since members of hierarchy and the people themselves expressed strong dissatisfaction with it.

In the eyes of Parecattil, the 1962 Text contained many anomalies and incongruities which he deemed to be un tenable. He remarked that, although these difficulties are found in the original text, they should have been omitted at the time of restoration, especially because in the vernacular their inadequacy becomes more evident. One of the limitations of the text which he singled out concerned the use of the terms «body» and «blood» rather than «bread» and «wine» during the offering rite:

> The main difficulty one encounters in the text is that wine and bread are called «blood» and «body» of Christ right from the time they are brought to the altar. And there is no indication of any real change taking place in them according to the Anaphora now actually in use. This lends itself to the idea of «transignification», rather than to the accepted doctrine of transubstantiation. To quote the relevant text: the priest says while pouring wine into the chalice: «infunditur sanguis pretiosus in calicem Domini nostri Jesu Christi [...]». Regarding the bread it is said: «Et sumit "primogenitum", eumque super discum ponit, dicens: 'Signatur hic discus Corpore sancto Domini nostri Jesu Christi' [...]». This appellation is repeated at the Offertory hymn, when it says: «Corpus Christi et sanguis eius praetiosissimus sunt super altare sanctum [...]»[10].

---

[8] J. PARECATTIL, <«Our Liturgy»>, 6.
[9] For more details of the letter, cf. «Historical Documents», *EM* 54 [1977] 113-115).
[10] J. PARECATTIL, «Liturgical Reform», 53-54.

Parecattil saw a theological problem in calling the bread and wine the body and blood of Christ before the beginning of the Eucharistic prayer[11]. In this way He expressed his concern that the liturgical language could seem to conflict with the defined doctrines of the Church. In other words, there would appear to be a discrepancy between the *lex orandi* and the *lex credendi*. The ritual language employed in the 1962 Text seemed to indicate that no ontological change of the bread and wine occurred at the consecration, since at the offertory the elements are already called the body and blood of Christ. The text could give the impression that the real presence entails only a symbolic change of the bread and wine. Although most proponents of the validity of the term «transignification» would not have held that it denied that of «transubstantiation», but was only a contemporary way of explaining the traditional dogma, Parecattil was not certain that the people would properly grasp such theological subtleties.

Another confusion created by the text concerns the divine Person to whom the Eucharistic sacrifice is offered. According to the 1962 Missal Christ not only offers the sacrifice, but also receives it:

At the offertory the request is made to Christ to accept the *sacrifice*: «Christus, qui immolatus est pro salute nostra et praecepit nobis, ut agamus memoriam passionis eius, mortis, sepulturae et resurrectionis eius, accipiat hoc sacrificium de manibus nostris». In our catechism children are taught that the Eucharist is the sacrifice of Christ offered through the hands of the priest to the Eternal Father. That is quite in accordance with the scripture, for St. Peter says: «You will serve as holy priests to offer spiritual and acceptable sacrifices to God through Jesus Christ» (1Pt 2, 5)[12].

According to Parecattil, Scripture and Tradition hold that the Eucharistic sacrifice is to be offered to the Father the first Person of the Trinity. Since Christ is the offerer and the offering, it is not meaningful to state that he receives it as well[13]. If one insists that it is valid to hold that Christ who receives the Eucharistic offering, Parecattil suggested that it would be better to change the word «sacrifice» to «sacrificial matter»[14]. Similarly in the response of the people, the prayer to receive the sacrifice is addressed to Christ. Parecattil thought this expression would be correct only if Mass is

---

[11] J. PARECATTIL, *Liturgy As I See It*, 72; ID., «Syro-Malabar Church», *Sathyadeepam* 54 (1981 February 11) 3.

[12] J. PARECATTIL, «Liturgical Reform», 54.

[13] J. PARECATTIL, *Liturgy As I See It*, 72.

[14] J. PARECATTIL, «Syro-Malabar Church», *Sathyadeepam* 54 (1981 February 11) 11.

considered as an offering rather than a sacrifice[15]. He was aware that liturgical experts might be able to explain such anomalies but that they were nevertheless confusing to the faithful and could possibly weaken their firm faith in the real presence. Since the constitution of Vatican II, *Sacrosantum Concilium* insists that the liturgical rites «should be within the people's powers of comprehension, and normally should not require much explanation»[16], Parecattil claimed that the restored 1962 Mass is a typical example of a divine liturgy that lacks this quality»[17].

Yet another drawback of the 1962 Text, according to Parecattil is the confusion found in the manner in which the first two Persons of the Trinity are understood:

> Another incongruity that strikes the careful reader of the original text of the restored Mass is the confusion between the Father and the Son of the Holy Trinity. On page 28 of the Latin text it is said that the Son taught us the Eucharistic Sacrifice: «Memoriam facimus, Domine, passionis, Filii tui, quemadmodum *ipse nos docuit.* In illa nocte qua traditus est [...]» But according to what is given on page 30, it is the Father who taught it: «Tu Domine, per misericordiam tuam multam et ineffabilem, suscipe commemorationem bonam et acceptabilem virginis Mariae Deiparae et omnium patrum iustorum et sanctorum qui tibi placuerunt per memoriam corporis et sanguinis Christi tui, quae offerimus tibi super altare tuum purum et sanctum, sicut *edocuisti nos».* The same confusion occurs in the Anamnesis that follows immediately after the words of the Institution. The Anamnesis begins by saying «Nos quoque, Domine, servi tui imbecilles [...], qui, congregati in nomine tuo, stamus coram te hoc tempore, et accepimus per traditionem *exemplum tuum».* That the prayer here is addressed to the Father is evident from what follows: «[...] Confitemus tibi et glorificamus te indesinenter in Ecclesia tua, sanguine pretiosissimo *Christi* tui redempta [...]»[18].

Parecattil certainly viewed a confusion in the text regarding the role of the Father and of the Son in connection with the Eucharistic sacrifice[19]. It

---

[15] J. PARECATTIL, «Syro-Malabar Church», *Sathyadeepam* 54 (1981 February 11) 3; ID., *Liturgy As I See It,* 72.

[16] SC 34.

[17] J. PARECATTIL, «Liturgical Reform», 54-55.

[18] J. PARECATTIL, «Liturgical Reform», 57.

[19] J. PARECATTIL, «Syro-Malabar Church», *Sathyadeepam* 54 (1981 February 11) 3; ID., *Liturgy As I See It,* 72-73. Parecattil pointed out that he held this position in line with Father Van der Ploeg who wrote to him on August 13, 1967. The relevant part of the letter is as follows:

seems that the objection which Parecattil makes in this regard is not only a theological and liturgical but also a spiritual and pastoral one, since confusion about who revealed the sacrifice and who gave the example of self-surrendering love could lessen the devotion which the faithful have to the humanity of Jesus. It is the supreme sign of the love of the Father for human beings that he sent his Son to stand on their side, to teach them how to worship the one he called «Abba» and to show them the way to make a self-surrendering gesture as a fitting response to such condescending love. This interpretation of why Parecattil lists all the technical and theological problems in the 1962 Text is based on the entirety of his Eucharistic reflections, at the core of which is personal reverence for the humanity of Jesus which renders his divinity approachable for Christians, and the basis of their striving to lead a Eucharistic life.

Furthermore, Parecattil maintained that the 1962 Text had assigned the Creed in an appropriate place, and suggested a different and more meaningful one:

> Whatever be the historical reasons for reciting the Creed after the offertory, it does not seem to be the ideal. At the offertory, the celebrant calls to mind the command of Jesus «to commemorate his suffering, death, burial and resurrection». It is not reasonable to recite the Creed just after this prayer. Instead, [...] after confessing the faith in the life and death of the Lord by the reciting Creed and as the expression and commemoration of our faith it becomes more meaningful[20].

Parecattil was of opinion that the Creed should not be recited after the celebrant has entered the altar, made the offertory and stepped down and

---

in the newly restored text of the Syro-Malabar liturgy the text of the prayer *Wap Hanan Mar*, as it stands now, is the result of the combination of two different texts, the second of which being nothing else (*Wal Apai Quolla*) than the end of the epiclesis [...] The combination of the two parts was done in Rome and nowhere else [...] I consulted my colleague who teaches liturgy in our faculty and who is himself a deacon of the Byzantine rite, on the question of the possible transition, in one prayer, of an invocation of the Son to an invocation of the Father. He thought that this kind of transition is not uncommon in ancient prayers, which are not always very logical. But I think, with Your Excellency, that this very unlogical transition should not be permitted in a newly created, or combined prayer.

For more details of the letter, cf. *EM* 35 [1955] 191-192; J. PARECATTIL, *Liturgy As I See It*, 72-73).

[20] J. PARECATTIL, «Syro-Malabar Church», *Sathyadeepam* 54 (1981 February 11) 3.

said a prayer of purification[21]. He held that by placing the Creed before the offertory, the Portuguese had not made an essential change in the Eucharistic liturgy that had long existed in the Syro-Malabar Church[22]. Thus, Parecattil was quite satisfied that, in the Raza, the Creed was recited before the offertory[23].

Another problem with the 1962 Text, in the view of Parecattil was that the *Anaphora of Addai and Mari*, the most ancient Eucharistic prayer, is not comprehensive, because in its original form it lacks, the consecratory epiclesis and of the narration of the Institutional Words:

> There is no indication of any real change taking place in any part of the present Anaphora. The terminology of the Chaldean Mass, particularly of the first Anaphora, would give the impression that the bread and wine are but the symbols of the Body and Blood of Christ. One may argue that, according to Oriental tradition, it is difficult to pinpoint the moment of the conversion of the bread into the Body and of the wine into the Blood of Our Lord and that the whole Anaphora is the consecratory formula, equivalent to the consecratory words — the words of the institution — of the Roman Mass. *Prima facie* the explanation may be acceptable, but when analyzed it is an escapism. For, it is not reasonable to equate a man-made Anaphora with the solemn words proceeding from the lips of Our Lord, which, however, thank God, have found a place in our Anaphora, though at one time they were conspicuously absent from it[24].

Parecattil was ready to accept the *Anaphora of Addai and Mari*, because, it can claim apostolicity. Hence, he supported the idea of keeping the anaphora without making any essential change in it[25]. Yet he did hold that most of the features which contributed to the uniqueness of the Anaphora also manifest its defects[26]. He added: «It is to be remembered that the Anaphora of Addai and Mari was composed for a people of a different nation than India and for a period different than that of today. If they wrote

---

[21] J. PARECATTIL, «Syro-Malabar Church», *Sathyadeepam* 54 (1981 February 11) 3; ID., *Liturgy As I See It*, 73.

[22] Parecattil substantiated his position quoting Fr. Raes, S.J. For more details, cf. RAES, *An Explanations*, 14.24).

[23] Parecattil agreed with Archdale King on this point. For more details, cf. A. KING, «Syro-Malabar Rite», 474-475).

[24] J. PARECATTIL, «Liturgical Reform», 55.

[25] J. PARECATTIL, «Syro-Malabar Church», *Sathyadeepam* 53 (1980 December 17) 10; ID., <«Our Liturgy»>, 3; For more details about the anaphora, cf. W.F. MACOMBER, «The Oldest Known Text», 335-371).

[26] J. PARECATTIL, *Liturgy As I See It*, 76-77.

for the Indians of today they would not have used many of the expressions found in the Anaphora»[27].

To those who proposed the theory that the whole Eucharistic prayer is consecratory, Parecattil answered by analyzing the Anaphorae of Theodore and Nestorius, since both specify the moment of consecration. Yet, at the same time, he rejected both these Eucharistic Prayers because they attribute consecratory value to the epiclesis, while ignore the Words of Institution:

> in the second and third Anaphora, attributed to Theodorus and Nestorius respectively, the Epiclesis consists in an invocation to the Spirit to come down and convert the bread into the Body of Our Lord, and wine into His blood, thus indicating the time and purpose of the conversion which in theology we call transubstantiation. So these two Anaphorae, pinpointing the moment of conversion of bread and wine, are not in keeping with the first Anaphora. And this offsets the argument that the Anaphora as a whole is consecratory[28].

Hence Parecattil argues that it is difficult to accept the contention that the whole anaphora is consecratory, and thus pertifies his opponents to the *Anaphora of Addai and Mari*. All the same, he had reservations about the Eucharistic prayers of Theodore and Nestorius because, according to them, the consecration of the elements is effected by the epiclesis alone. Yet, this invocation of the Holy Spirit is a communion epiclesis and not a consecratory one. Therefore, Parecattil held that if the second and the third anaphorae were translated into Malayalam, they would be unintelligible for the people, who have been taught that the transubstantiation of the elements takes place at the recitation of the Institutional Words. Parecattil considered this issue as well to be more a spiritual and pastoral problem than a theological and liturgical one. Precisely for this reason, he said, the *Sacrosanctum Concilium*, directed that, while the tradition should be retained, due time and attention must be given to a careful investigation of the historical, theological, and pastoral aspects of the liturgy[29]. Parecattil was of opinion that the authors of the 1962 Text had concentrated only on its historical aspect.

Furthermore, they failed to take into account the Indian elements that characterised the liturgy of the Christians of Kerala from the time of the Apostle[30]. In a particularly forceful way Parecattil resisted all attempts to

---

[27] J. PARECATTIL, «Syro-Malabar Church», *Sathyadeepam* 53 (1980 December 17) 10.
[28] J. PARECATTIL, «Liturgical Reform», 55.
[29] SC 23.
[30] J. PARECATTIL, «Liturgical Reform», 56-57.

reintroduce the anaphorae of Theodore and Nestorius into the Syro-Malabar Eucharistic liturgy. Since he was convinced that their theology was heretical, he claimed the use of their anaphorae would damage the legitimate pride of the Syro-Malabar Christians[31]. Instead of restoring these anaphorae, he advocated composing new Eucharistic prayers which would be more in line with Indian thought patterns, and offer more variety, so that the spiritual experience of the people would be enriched[32].

The widespread criticism on the 1962 Text by the hierarchy and the people of the Syro-Malabar Church led Rome officials to grant permission to undertake a new revision. This permission paved the way for the 1968 Missal. Parecattil narrated the well planned process which was followed in preparing the 1968 Text. In his view, the process entailed proper consultation and due representation, with the result that the Missal stressed the pastoral dimension of the liturgy:

> The Central Liturgical Committee, composed of the representatives of all the Dioceses, Major Seminaries and religious congregations of men, has had, reportedly, more than 90 sittings. Controversial issues were decided by a two-third majority of votes. We hear that it is the small minority which did not succeed in imposing its retrogressive views on the majority that subsequently gave the lead in making propaganda against the new text at home and abroad, and in sending complaints to Rome. However, it is a fact that all the necessary steps were really taken to ensure that the priests, religious and people had their say in regard to the new draft of 1968. It was published in Catholic journals and Diocesan bulletins, calling for suggestions, remarks and criticisms. All the comments thus received, numbering more than a thousand, were duly considered while the text was being finalised. A few representatives of the laymen, who had made representations to Rome against the 1962 text were specially called and consulted by the Bishop's Conference[33].

The text and rubrics were finally fixed at the Syro-Malabar Bishops' Conference on May 20, 1968, at which representatives of the Liturgical Committee and of the signatories of the Memoranda were present by special invitation. Parecattil noted: «as a matter of fact, the revised text of 1968 put

---

[31] J. PARECATTIL, <«Our Liturgy»>, 3.

[32] J. PARECATTIL, <«Our Liturgy»>, 3.

[33] J. PARECATTIL, «Liturgical Reform», 59; ID., «Syro-Malabar Church», *Sathyadeepam* 56 (1983 May 25) 3.

a stop to the general unrest among priests and people, that followed in the wake of the re-introduction of the Chaldean liturgy»[34].

According to Parecattil, the 1968 Text had done major advantage in comparison with that of 1962 — it kept a proper balance among the goals of restoration, revision and adaptation:

> The 1968 edition paid attention not only to restoration but also revision and adaptation. It put the Credo in its proper place according to logical sequence and our Syro-Malabar tradition. It did away with a good many repetitions in the prayers and updated some passages, and adopted some new gestures taking into account modern exegetical and liturgical insights [...] The priests and people, who were in general dissatisfied with the cumbersome 1962 text having a Semitic overtone, breathed a sigh of relief, seeing the 1968 text, and welcomed it wholeheartedly. Though there was still freedom to use the former edition, priests relinquished it and gladly took to the latter. Even those who were still using the old post-Diamper Syriac text switched to the new edition which they found attractive in comparison with the 1962 edition[35].

However, what Parecattil considered to be the main advantages of the text were viewed as drawbacks by the supporters of the 1962 Text. The main criticism levelled against the new edition was that it revised the former by introducing Latin elements. Parecattil answered that those elements interpreted as Latin ones, in reality are Indian adaptations: «I am not for Latinization but for Indianization»[36]. He went on to comment on some specific points. One criticism is that the original East-Syrian way of making the sign of the Cross from right to left, reintroduced in the 1962 edition, had been replaced by the accidental way of signing oneself from left to right. Parecattil responded that this change is in keeping with the mentality of Indians who do not write or mark anything from right to the left as do the Chaldeans. He also pointed out that in the Syro-Malankara Church, which jealously guards its Orthodox traditions, the people make the sign of the cross from left to right. According to Parecattil, to brand this change a Latinization is «unwarranted and betrays a lack of understanding of Indian ways»[37]. Moreover, he argued that the Orientals are not prohibited from beginning the Mass with the sign of the Cross, just because the Latins do it in the same way: «the Indian Christians begin any good activity with a

---

[34] J. PARECATTIL, <«Our Liturgy»>, 7-8; ID., «Liturgical Reform», 60; ID., *As I See Myself*, III, 621; ID., «Remarks about the 1968 Edition» 1.

[35] J. PARECATTIL, «Liturgical Reform», 59-60.

[36] J. PARECATTIL, *As I See Myself*, III, 625.

[37] J. PARECATTIL, <«Our Liturgy»>, 10.

sign of the Cross. Therefore, the Mass, the centre of such actions, should commence with the sign of the Cross»[38].

The elevation of the sacred species after the consecration was also singled out as an example of Latinization. However, Parecattil noted that this gesture had already been introduced into the 1962 Text. The only change made in the new version is that, at the time of elevation, the host is held with the fingers rather than remaining on the paten. According to Parecattil, it matters very little whether which rubric is to be employed, once the principle of elevating each of the species after the words of the Institution is accepted[39]. This led him to comment further: «a certain measure of pluralism is not only permissible, but even desirable in this transitional period. But the principle of «the survival of the fittest» will triumph in due course»[40]. However, Parecattil himself introduced a modification, because he deemed it more meaningful than individual elevations to raise both the species together, holding the chalice and the paten in the hands[41]. In this context, he noted that in the first millennium, Oriental liturgy ruled over the Latin Church, and that in the next millennium it happened the other way. Now it is clearly seen as wrong if the Orientals impose their liturgy on the Latins and vice versa[42].

The critics also accused Parecattil of having introduced the Apostles' Creed in the 1968 Missal «on his own accord». He replied by saying that he had sent a circular letter to all the bishops on June 14, 1968, asking their opinion regarding the advisability of printing the Apostles' Creed as well in the Mass book[43]. He added that, if any one had objected to it, it would

---

[38] J. PARECATTIL, «Syro-Malabar Church», *Sathyadeepam* 54 (1981 February 18) 3.

[39] J. PARECATTIL, <«Our Liturgy»>, 10; ID., «Syro-Malabar Church», *Sathyadeepam* 54 (1981 February 18) 3.

[40] J. PARECATTIL, <«Our Liturgy»>, 9.

[41] J. PARECATTIL, «Syro-Malabar Church», *Sathyadeepam* 54 (1981 February 18) 3.

[42] J. PARECATTIL, *As I See Myself*, III, 626.

[43] J. PARECATTIL, *Liturgy As I See It*, 65; The relevant part of the Circular is cited below:

The advisability of substituting the Apostle's Creed for the Niceno-Constantinopolitan Creed in the ordinary low Mass, reserving the latter creed for the High Mass and for other solemn occasions. A similar resolution was passed for the Latins in the Synod of Bishops held in Rome last year. In this ecumenical age uniformity in such matters will be appreciated by our laity. Apart from it, the children may confuse the two Creeds, if they have to recite one at home for the Rosary and another at the church for the Mass. For the same reason the Liturgical Committee opted for the recital of the ordinary Our Father also during Mass. No formal decision was taken in the Litur-

not have appeared in the text as an alternative formula to the Nicene Creed[44]. An option now exists, so that the solemnity of the feast day and the preference of the priests and the people can be taken in to consideration[45]. Referring to the criticism that the Apostles' Creed has no place in any liturgy whatsoever, Parecattil called attention to its long standing use in the Latin liturgy, and to its being more familiar to the people since in their ordinary prayers they recite it[46]. He added that common prayers, such as the creed and the «Our Father», should be said in the form which is most familiar, because the longer and more complicated versions «bring no spiritual advantage to the people»[47]. Moreover, rather than being static the liturgy should be dynamic. Obviously, as regards the Syro-Malabar liturgy, Parecattil played the role of a pioneer and he bore all criticism calmly, since he had discerned that the Eucharistic celebration of the people had to be inspiring if it were to be the basis of their Eucharistic life[48].

2. The Renewal of Christian Spiritual Life Effected by Eucharistic Grace

As already mentioned in the preceding chapter on the thought Parecattil before the Vatican II, he viewed the Eucharist as the primary source of grace for Christian life. After the council he urged the people all the more to reflect on their relationship with the Eucharistic Lord. He often stated that the best way to acquire a spirit of repentance, and thus to maintain spiritual fervour, is attending the Mass with increased sincerity. He referred to some parts of the Eucharistic liturgy so as to show how the grace of this sacrament grands the forgiveness of sin:

> At the elevation of the Sacred Host the words of the priest are most relevant: «For this living and life-giving bread has come down from heaven, and gives life to the whole world; those who eat it do not die; those who receive it are saved by it; their sins are pardoned, and they live for ever». Sin causes eternal death. Thus through the Holy Mass we receive the forgiveness of sins and

---

gical Committee regarding the Credo, though it was just touched in passing. Please let me know your views on the matter as soon as possible [...].

For more details of the Circular, cf. «Historical Documents», *EM* 45 [1975] 70-71).

[44] J. PARECATTIL, «Renewal of an Imaginary Prohibition», 118-119.

[45] J. PARECATTIL, «Malabar Liturgy», 1.

[46] J. PARECATTIL, «Syro-Malabar Church», *Sathyadeepam* 56 (1983 February 25) 3.

[47] J. PARECATTIL, «Syro-Malabar Church», *Sathyadeepam* 56 (1983 February 25) 3.

[48] J. PARECATTIL, «Syro-Malabar Church», *Sathyadeepam* 56 (1983 February 25) 3.

eternal life [...] The priest before receiving the Holy Communion, says: «O Lord, may Your body be to me not unto condemnation, but unto the pardon of offenses and forgiveness of sins [...] Of the same cup, You have given me also, a sinner to drink. Praise be to Your ineffable love, for ever[49].

After citing many more examples of this kind Parecattil instructed the people to ask pardon of the Lord during Mass, because it is the «commemoration of the suffering and death of our Lord who died for our sins»[50]. Parecattil also instructed the people to learn to be forgiving and non-violent after the example of Christ who is present in the Eucharist. The words of the Lord «as sheep in the midst of wolves» (Mt 10, 16) were put into practice by the first Christians, as is evident when St. Paul says: «[...] When reviled, we bless; when persecuted, we endure» (1Cor 4, 12). Whenever Christians grow in peacefulness and non-violence they embark on the path which best pleases the Eucharistic Lord[51].

Referring to the profanation of the Eucharist which took place in Kerala in 1964, Parecattil expressed his great consternation to such an act of disrespect:

the message I have to give you [...] is to have an increased devotion to the Holy Eucharist and to lead a Eucharistic life. The forthcoming International Eucharistic Congress at Bombay — on the soil of India, at our very doors, so to say — provides the greatest incentive for this, and the asecration of churches and the profanation of the Holy Eucharist committed in several localities in our State enhances our duty of reparation[52].

Parecattil called on those whose religious sentiments were offended by the profonation to react peacefully but forcefully in order to show love towards the Eucharistic Lord[53]. And he pointed out that the attacks on the churches and the Blessed Sacrament challenged the Christians to approach the Eucharistic Lord with an attitude of reparation for the disrespect shown to him[54]. Apart from the main theme of reparation to be made to the Eucharistic Lord, another important aspect of the spirituality of Parecattil is alluded to in the phrase «to lead a Eucharistic life.» In fact it can be said that, for him, the encounter with the Lord at the sacramental celebration around the

---

[49] J. PARECATTIL, *Letters to Children*, 54.
[50] J. PARECATTIL, *Letters to Children*, 55.
[51] J. PARECATTIL, <«Devotion to the Sacred Heart»>, 81-84.
[52] J. PARECATTIL, <«Devotion to the Holy Eucharist»>, 2.
[53] J. PARECATTIL, <«Disrespect towards the Eucharist»>, 83.
[54] J. PARECATTIL, *Letters to Priests*, 11.

altar is prolonged at those moments of daily life when Christians put into practice his values of love and non-violence in the home, in the working place and in the neighbourhood.

Parecattil asserted that one of the most tangible fruits of the Eucharist is the unity among Christians of different denominations of Christians:

> As Christians, we partake of the same body of Christ and thus we become one body [...] We become one in Christ through the Holy Eucharist, regardless of the distinctions of colour, nationality or race[55].

For this reason, while preparing for the Thirty-ninth International Eucharistic Congress, Parecattil remarked: «these ceremonies will call to our mind the great principle that we are one in Christ and the Eucharist is symbol and source of this unity»[56]. Furthermore, such unity among Christians must be expressed in terms of solidarity with adherence to other religions, because of their shared faith in the transcendent God and in eternal life. Thus, Parecattil contended that the members of different religions must come together, for the very reason that they are believers in God: «this is the time for not only Christians but also all those believe in God come together and express love and friendship [...] All those who believe in God have the responsibility to protect the eternal values and moral principles»[57]. On another occasion he asserted that at a time when atheism and materialism are such dangers, servants of the Church must exercise great prudence, «preferring to see people remain fervent members of the religion into which they were born, rather than be deprived of religion altogether»[58].

A modern aspect of Christian spirituality, which has become pronounced since Vatican II is respect for the truth found in other religions. Parecattil thus urged the people to practice discernment so that they could recognize the presence of grace wherever it is found:

> If we dive deep and search the gems of truth in the tenets and practices of all religions, we will be able to collect a good many of such precious stones, which we have to respect and value. Though for a Christian, Christ is «the way, the truth and the life» (Jn 14, 6), he must be prepared to recognise and assimilate the elements of truth wherever he finds them. This is not to be misinterpreted as religious indifferentism, but is in reality the correct attitude to Truth, which is God himself. To cite a passage from the Council document:

---

[55] J. PARECATTIL, <«Housing Project»>, 1.

[56] J. PARECATTIL, «Thirty-ninth International Eucharistic Congress», 163.

[57] J. PARECATTIL, <«The Themes of the Synod of Bishops-1967»>, 202.

[58] J. PARECATTIL, «Dialogue with Hindus», 129.

«The Catholic Church rejects nothing of what is true and holy in these religions. She has a high regard for the manner of life and conduct, the precepts and doctrines which, although differing in many ways from her own teaching, nevertheless often reflect a ray of that truth which enlightens all men»[59].

Parecattil pointed out that, although there is need of more detailed investigation of those truths contained in the holy writings of non-Christian religions, it is even more important to acknowledge the invisible action of the Holy Spirit in the hearts of those who adhere to them. And if Christians recognize that God loves all those who sincerely seek Him, they must also realize that there is a basic unity between all people who adore God «in spirit and truth»[60].

From these reflections it seems legitimate to conclude that, after Vatican II Parecattil developed his notion of eucharistic spirituality so that it could include the element of discernment. Just as at the liturgy Christians discern the body and blood of Christ in the Eucharistic species, they must behave afterwards in such a way that they searched for traces of his truth and of his Holy Spirit in the adherents to other religions among whom they live.

At the same time, Parecattil maintained that Eucharistic devotion has a significant part to play in the Christian mandate of spreading the Good News. In 1964 he wrote to his priests about the link between love of the Eucharistic Lord and zeal for evangelical activities:

In order to attain the real missionary fervour we have to approach the Eucharistic Lord. The Lord is humbly present in the tabernacle day and night due to his unfathomable love towards souls and the ardent desire for their redemption. He loves each soul, you and me [...] Are we like the Lord?[61].

Here an important leitmotif of the thought of Parecattil is revealed: those who do not grow in devotion to the Eucharistic Lord will not be proved to be zealous in apostolic work. In this manner of speaking Parecattil reflects one of the major statements on the Eucharist issued by Vatican II: «The Eucharist appears as the source and summit of all preaching of the Gospel»[62]. Since missionary zeal is precisely a forceful impulse to evangelize others, Parecattil links this ministerial quality to devotion to the Eucharistic Christ. This explains why Parecattil instructed the priests of the

---

[59] NA 2; J. PARECATTIL, «Y.M.C.A and Ecumenism», 2.
[60] J. PARECATTIL, «Dialogue with Hindus», 129-130.
[61] J. PARECATTIL, Letters to Priests, 12.
[62] PO 5.

archdiocese to examine their attitude towards mission work as culminating in and being repevenated by the Eucharist[63].

Parecattil frequently reminded the people of the necessity of providing financial assistance to those engaged in missionary activities, for no works of charity are more meritorious than those oriented to saving souls[64].

At the same time, Parecattil reminded the people that they have to do more than support the work of evangelization; they have to lead a «real Christian life» in accordance with the command of the Lord: «Let your light so shine before others, that they may see your good works and give glory to your Father who is in heaven» (Mt 5, 16)[65]. Christians should attract others to Christ by their commitment to living his values of non-violence and love. With these insights, Parecattil gives voice to another important teaching of Vatican II, namely, «The Eucharistic celebration, to be full and sincere, must lead [...] to missionary activity and the various forms of Christian witness»[66]. Thus, when Parecattil states that the laity should regard a «real Christian life» as a form of missionary activity, he is in effect asking them to live the Eucharistic mystery in a full and sincere manner.

3. The Social Mission of the Church: A Means to Extend The Self-lessness of the Eucharistic Lord

In the post Conciliar period, parecattil reiterated in Pauline language his firm conviction that christian social work is an attempt to follow the humanitarian activities of Jesus. As the members whose Head is Christ, Christians have the responsibility to imitate his concern for the welfare of the weakest parts of his body. The assimilation of the concerns of the head takes place most forcefully in the Eucharist.

In the eyes of Parecattil, engaging in social work means assuming the obligations learned from Jesus who is present in Eucharist:

The doctrine of the mystical body of Christ also imposes serious obligations on us. For, as St. Paul remarks, «if one member suffers, all the members suffer with it; or if one member be honoured, all the members rejoice with it» (1Cor 12, 16) We have, therefore, a duty to the weaker and suffering members of the

---

[63] J. PARECATTIL, *Letters to Priests*, 12.

[64] J. PARECATTIL, <«Mary and Evangelization»>, 151; ID., <«Helping the Missions»>, 1-2.

[65] J. PARECATTIL, «Mary and Evangelization», 148-149.

[66] PO, 5.

mystical body of Christ. The Church has always been keenly aware of this, and has been trying to inculcate the idea in the minds of her beloved children[67]

On the basis of this theological principle, Parecattil lauded the many activities of the Church in kerala on behalf of the poor. Such charitable action effectively means that «not even one member of the mystical body of the Christ shall not be devoid of food, cloth, medicine and houses»[68]. He remembered with gratitude the kind gesture of Pope Paul VI to the suffering people of his archdiocese. He stated: «just the other day I got news from Rome that His Holiness has donated the blood pressure apparatus, which was used to take the blood pressure of Pope John XXIII, to our archdiocesan hospital for the lepers at Shertallay»[69].

Referring to the Conciliar *Decree on the Apostolate of Lay People*[70], Parecattil reminded his fellow Christians of their duty to help the poor with food, clothing, housing, medicine, work and education[71]. His own fatherly heart was pained at the misery of the people around him who were devoid of work and food:

> The family life and social situations are upset due to the scarcity of food and unemployment. We who have received the call from Jesus to give food to the hungry and water to the thirsty [...] cannot close our eyes from this painful reality»[72].

Parecattil noted that the Church views unemployment and hunger not only as physical problems but also as spiritual ones. He often said that life on earth should be simple but satisfactory, so that one can grow spiritually. Just as Jesus fed the hungry people with the multiplication of the loaves, so his followers should not remain idle when confronted of poverty and unemployment and hunger[73]. In this context, Parecattil stated that *dharma*, the Indian concept which means «the sum total of man's obligation in his relationship with God and man»[74] necessitates that people be concerned for their

---

[67] J. PARECATTIL, «Housing Project», 1; ID., <«Homes for the Homeless»>, 190-191.

[68] J. PARECATTIL, <«The Role of the Catholic Church»>, 1-2.

[69] J. PARECATTIL, «Housing Project», 1-2.

[70] AA 8.

[71] J. PARECATTIL, <«Catholic Charities»>, 206.

[72] J. PARECATTIL, <«Hard Work for Better Life»>, 52.

[73] J. PARECATTIL, «Hard Work for Better Life», 53.

[74] J. PARECATTIL, <«Dharma»>, 2.

brethren. The observance of *dharma* gives a meaning to one's life so that only a foolish person will disregard it[75].

Although Parecattil depended mainly on priests and sisters to co-ordinate the social activities of the archdiocese in a spirit of service to the people, and of sympathy with them[76], he clearly stated the distinction between what the Church and what the State could do: «our main aim has not been, nor will ever be, to supplant governmental efforts but only to supplement them. In this connection I wish to place on record our deep-felt gratitude for all the help and encouragement we have been receiving from the State and Union Governments»[77]. Moreover, Parecattil believed that among the social activities, priority should be given to bettering the economic standard of the people:

> It is over two decades since our mother country achieved political freedom. As for economic freedom, we have still a long way to go, but we are moving in the right direction. Conferences like this will accelerate our pace towards economic freedom and meetings of this kind will acquaint us with our problems and potentialities. May God help our country to preserve its hard-won freedom[78].

Parecattil regarded it a pity that India had not yet become self-sufficient in consumer commodities. Thus, he called the people to co-operate with the five-year plans of the time which are calculated to increase production in industry and agriculture, to stamp out the causes of disease and to provide better transport facilities.

It should be noted here that to recount how a modern Catholic archbishop spoke about stamping out disease and providing more efficient transport systems is forceful proof of the influence which *Gaudium et Spes*, the Pastoral Constitution on the Church in the Modern World, had on the hierarchy in the years immediately after Vatican II. In effect, Parecattil still advocates the themes of his episcopacy prior to the Council, such as the need to practice a Eucharistic life, and thereby show that Christians are members of the suffering body of Christ at the present time. But, after the Council there is more urgency to his linking together Eucharistic orthodoxy, or proper faith in the real presence of Christ on the altar, and Eucharistic

---

[75] J. PARECATTIL, <«Dharma»>, 3.

[76] J. PARECATTIL, *Letters to Priests*, 17; ID., *Letters to Sisters*, 95.

[77] J. PARECATTIL, <«Reception to Prime Minister»>, 236-237; ID., «Sushila Nayar», 1.

[78] J. PARECATTIL, <«Rubber Plantation»>, 5.

orthopraxy, or proper commitment to the social well-being of one's neighbours.

After speaking about production in general, Parecattil focused on food manufacture in particular. Increase of the output of the food material was an imperative of the time, as the scarcity of such articles was quite alarming:

> I resolve on this occasion to participate in the «battle against hunger». If all try their best to increase food production, our Kerala State will attain self-sufficiency such materials in the near future. Much land remains uncultivated [...] If electricity is supplied, irrigation facilities are improved and modern manures are distributed, the out-put of consumption articles could be increased. In this matter, we have to extend our full co-operation to the Government's undertakings[79].

Parecattil considered the lack of scientific methods of cultivation as the reason for the low agricultural production in the State of Kerala. As a first step towards rectifying this defect, he advised the people to increase the water supply through the Lift Irrigation system. He claimed that for this purpose nearly three hundred water pumps had been distributed through the Ernakulam Archdiocesan Social Welfare Society[80]. Moreover, he called on the government to grant loans so that farmers could buy pump sets and manure. In fact, he believed that the farmers are the back-bone of India, and that the help given to them will not be an excess[81]. He suggested that constructive projects were needed to solve the shortage of food, and that all should work together leaving aside religious or politica¹ differences. He promised his co-operation in this regard and encouraged any attempt to produce more food[82]. On a visit to the «Modern Bread» factory at Edap-pally, he stated: «thus the Kerala Unit undoubtedly opens a new chapter in the history of this region in its fight against hunger and disease»[83].

Parecattil often noted that women have a significant role in building the nation and thus he argued for their equality with men and their co-responsibility in working for the welfare of the people:

> These are days when women have been insistently called upon to occupy their rightful place in society and to contribute their legitimate share to the all round

---

[79] J. PARECATTIL, <«The Office of the Cardinal»>, 3.
[80] J. PARECATTIL, <«The Office of the Cardinal»>, 3.
[81] J. PARECATTIL, «Irrigation and Food Production», 1.
[82] J. PARECATTIL, <«The Office of the Cardinal»>, 4.
[83] J. PARECATTIL, «Modern Bread», 3.

progress of humanity. Since they constitute half of the human race, without their proper co-operation and assistance in shouldering burdens, no country or nation can hope to make headway in the various phases of its development programme. The attainment of independence made the women of India increasingly conscious of their own duties to the nation and made them think in terms of new possibilities and added responsibilities. As a result, they have been willingly casting their lot with men and have been in the mainstream of the political, economic and social life of the country[84].

In his own native town, he noted that «there are now several ladies at Ernakulam in the legal and medical professions rendering efficient service. No less active are the women of the locality in the social field, which, perhaps, is offering the greatest challenge to all men and women of good will»[85]. Nevertheless, he clearly stated that mothers are entrusted with the formation of the future citizens so much so that the fate of the country is in their hands. Thus, he once said «to exchange this primary duty for other forms of activities will not be in the best interest of the nation»[86].

For these reasons, Parecattil predicted that both the Church and the State would make more rapid strides towards social progress if the potentialities of women were properly realized: «the women of India, especially the Catholic women, can prove themselves to be powerful instruments in the hands of God for strengthening that unity and consolidation of the nation's political and social potential by virtue of the dedication and determination that are characteristic of the so-called weaker sex»[87]. Parecattil was of the opinion that the Christians should view the movements against Purdah, the caste system and child marriage as specially worthy of mentioning among the steps to be taken for raising the status of women[88]. He also singled out three service areas in which women could exercise their influence. Welfare activities aimed at relief and rehabilitation measures; health services concerned with the prevention of disease and the care of the sick;[89] and rural improvement by teaching the latest methods of farming, and organizing cottage industries to foster economic progress[90].

---

[84] J. PARECATTIL, <«Mothers' Mercy Trust»>, 238.
[85] J. PARECATTIL, <«Mothers' Mercy Trust»>, 238.
[86] J. PARECATTIL, «The Role of Women», 25.
[87] J. PARECATTIL, «The Role of Women», 27-28.
[88] J. PARECATTIL, «The Role of Women», 24.
[89] J. PARECATTIL, «The Role of Women», 26.
[90] J. PARECATTIL, «The Role of Women», 27.

When parecattil states that especially Catholic women can serve as instruments of God for the unity and consolidation of the social potential of the nation, he seems to be designating the particularly feminine way of living a Eucharistic life in the Indian context. This interpretation seems justified because the two words «unity» and «consolidation» call to mind the effects of Eucharistic grace: to unite the members of the social body of the Church to Christ and to each other, and to create solidarity among them for the sake of intraecclesial harmony and of extraecclesial ministry. Yet, it is also clear that this sacramentally based spirituality is not understood by Parecattil as requiring Catholic women to act apart from all other Indian women engaged in welfare activities, health services and rural improvement programmes. The Eucharistic Christ urges them to be light, salt, leaven and mustard seed precisely in their social ambience, and along with their sisters of other religions.

Parecattil believed that the welfare of the Indian nation depended on the moral unity of its people in safeguarding the exalted principles of democracy and freedom:

> Our country is now facing a crisis, economic and social [...] It is up to us to strengthen the hands of those who hold the reins of Government and ruling party. We are giving this support in the interest of democracy and freedom»[91].

Parecattil implored all the people of the archdiocese to ask what have they done for the welfare of their fellow men, their locality, their community and their country[92]. He urged them to dedicate themselves to the cause of the vast Republic with loyalty and integrity[93], since «in a democracy there must be that sense of security for all citizens irrespective of caste, race or community. Communal prejudices or extra-judicial reasons should not stand in the way of the conscientious discharge of one's duty»[94]. Referring to the independence struggle of the nation which was won by upholding high moral principles, Parecattil pleaded with the future generation to live up to the great ideals of the freedom movement:

> The point I wish to stress on this occasion is that our College being called Bharata Mata, all the inmates of the institution are in duty bound to foster an intense devotion and an abiding loyalty to our motherland and be always on the

---

[91] J. PARECATTIL, «Sushila Nayar», 2-3.

[92] J. PARECATTIL, «Fire Services», 2.

[93] J. PARECATTIL, «Sathyam and Ahimsā», 48.

[94] J. PARECATTIL, <«Felicitations to Justice Isaac»>, 5.

alert to safeguard its integrity sovereignty and freedom. For this it is essential to study and understand the true nature and significance of our national awakening and struggle for freedom, so that we may be alive to the need of conserving the fruits of our hard won independence in the most possible manner, without being lured away by disruptive forces[95].

Parecattil asked the youth to imbibe the spirit of Freedom struggle, which was «a movent against the intellectual domination of the West over Indian thought and culture»[96]. Since the college at which he spoke was called «Bharata Mata» (Motherland), he reminded the students to bring consolation and happiness to their «beloved mother», by their adherence to the principles of truth and non-violence, and by their sincere efforts to ensure peace and harmony at all levels of society, beginning with every home[97].

Parecattil openly proclaimed to be a strong admirer of Gandhi, and to be fascinated by the way he led the freedom movement with the seemingly useless weapons of *Sathyam* and *Ahimsā:*

> The Mahatma did not «wade through slaughter to the throne», as many conquerors have done. On the contrary, without battles and bloodshed, he led the country to victory by the help of two harmless arms, viz. *Sathyam and Ahimsa*, truth and non-violence[98].

In this and in other passges of a well known discourse, Parecattil pointed out that, until Gandhi wielded the moral arms of *Sathyam* and *Ahimsā*, their efficacy and potentiality were unknown to the world. Then he added a most provocative statement: «although he(Gandhi) imbibed these ideas from Christ's Sermon on the Mount, he can still lay claim to originality in harnessing them to efforts for freedom»[99]. This statement is provocative, since Parecattil points out, on the one hand, that Gandhi was influenced by the ideals of Jesus of Nazareth, and on the other that he followed his prophetic message creatively, attempting to apply it to local forms of social sin which need to be overcome so that people gain freedom. It seems clear that parecattil makes this statement, because he intends to challenge his Catholic listeners to ask themselves how they could be prophetic in their present circumstances, as Jesus and Gandhi were in theirs. Since Vatican II affirms that a full and sincere participation in the Eucharist entails being

---

[95] J. PARECATTIL, «Be at the Service of Bharata Mata», 3.

[96] J. PARECATTIL, «Be at the Service of Bharata Mata», 3.

[97] J. PARECATTIL, «Be at the Service of Bharata Mata», 3.

[98] J. PARECATTIL, «Sathyam and Ahimsā», 50.

[99] J. PARECATTIL, «Sathyam and Ahimsā», 48.

engaged in various forms of charity and mutual help, Parecattil would certainly view Gandhi as a stimulus for Catholics to make the connection between being prophetic in society and living fully and sincerely according to the grace received in Holy Communion.

Spiritually troubled by increasing incidents of violence in some parts of the country, Parecattil exhorted the people to heed to the principles of truth and non-violence after the example of Gandhi and his followers:

> But the problem before us Indians is whether we will preserve our hard-won freedom. We will be able to do so only if we walk along the Gandhian way, holding fast to *Sathyam* and *Ahimsā* [...] By swerving itself slowly from the noble ideals of *Sathyam* and *Ahimsā*, India is heading towards a catastrophe. If the Indian Republic were to lose her freedom, it would be the greatest tragedy the world would ever witness. Hence, it is up to us to try might and main to preserve our freedom using the same weapons as those we used for gaining independence [...] Today when we celebrate the Republic Day, our bounden duty is to dedicate and consecrate ourselves to the ideal of *Sathyam* and *Ahimsā*, the tools with which this greatest Republic of the world has been built[100].

In this context Parecattil clarifies the concepts of *sathyam* and *ahimsā*. *sathyam* is an attribute of God, or rather is God himself, since «sath» means being; *sathyam* comprises our duties towards God and others. One who is bound to *sathyam* will be loyal to God, his Lord and Master. It is an essential aspect of truthfulness to acknowledge God's supremacy over human beings, and to give honour to those to whom it is due, because of one's love of truth. Defence of *asathyam* leads to violence, which is degrading of the honour of India and disloyal to the Father of the Nation. Parecattil pointed out that outbursts of violence, which take place here and there in the country, are symptoms of a cancerous disease, slowly but surely eating into the very vitals of the country: «let *sathyam* and *ahimsā* be our watchword in our efforts to protect the honour of our country and safeguard her sovereignty. May be unwittingly, we offer worship to the idols of the false gods *asathyam* and *himsā*, instead of the true images, *sathyam* and *ahimsā* of the true God»[101].

The many themes treated in this chapter call for a few concluding observations. Parecattil was privileged to participate in all the sessions of Vatican II and made interventions in the aula which touched on the need to

---

[100] J. PARECATTIL, «Sathyam and Ahimsā», 49-50.
[101] J. PARECATTIL, «Sathyam and Ahimsā», 50-51.

respect members of other religious groups. He wholeheartedly accepted the call of the Council for ecclesial renewal, and devoted himself to implementing them in the Syro-Malabar Church. In this regard, his first task was to oversee the restoration, revision and adaptation of the Eucharistic liturgy. For him, restoration of the ancient traditions did not mean mere return to the ritual, but entailed their interpretation in the light of current life situations. On their account, he could not agree with the mode of restoration undertaken in the 1962 Missal which, in his view, was simply a reiteration of the ancient Chaldean rite. Later, he played a prominent role in the preparation of the revised Missal of 1968, which included a few adaptations to Indian culture.

Parecattil was convinced that the proper renewal of the Missal aided the people to regard the Eucharist as the source of grace for a courageous Christian life. The Eucharistic Lord nourishes his followers so that they can practice Gospel values. Moreover, Eucharistic grace strengthens the bond of love and friendship among the various denominations of Christians, and enables them all to foster a spirit of solidarity with adherents to other religions. Parecattil pointed out that in the modern era all the followers of different faiths should recognise that common ground as believers in God so that, united by a moral cohesion, they could resist secularism and atheism.

Parecattil firmly maintained that Eucharistic grace has a far-reaching influence in the social life of Christians. Christians learn from their Eucharistic Lord how to carry out their humanitarian works faithfully even if they must face opposition. He believed that, as members of the mystical Body of Christ, they have the unavoidable responsibility to show compassion to the weakest among them. In his view, this obligation is the motivating force of all the social activities of the Church. In the social projects which he furthered, Parecattil gave primary importance to providing of the basic necessities of life such as food and shelter. He hoped that the welfare activities of Catholic men and women would create better living standards for the emarginated. Parecattil called the people of India to preserve and build up the democratic tradition of India, especially through the principles of truth and non-violence taught by Gandhi.

CHAPTER V

An Indian Eucharistic Theology:
Meeting of Hindu and Christian
Religious Experiences

The years between 1970 and 1987 marked a significant development in the Eucharistic theology of Joseph Parecattil. Before this period Parecattil had indeed appreciated and advocated the principles of Vatican II regarding restoration, revision and adaptation. From 1970 onwards, he applied them in forming the «Indian Mass», which incorporated elements of Hindu theology and ritual into the Eucharistic liturgy. The Christian mysteries were expressed in Indian terms and thought-patterns, making the Syro-Malabar liturgical adaptation not superficial but substantial. In this way he hoped to realize his understanding of the Syro-Malabar Church as «Hindu in Culture, Christian in Religion and Indian in Liturgy». The theological foundation of the Indian Mass is the analogy between the incarnation of the Word and the inculturation of the local Church. However, in this same period, the opposition to the process of revision and adaptation increased, and only that of restoration was espoused. This opposition finally caused the formulation of the 1985 Missal which is a faithful reproduction of the Chaldean liturgy. Since it practically undid everything that Parecattil had hoped to achieve, he was most troubled by this development. Yet, he trusted that one day his ideas would be regarded as theologically solid and pastorally effective. These themes are treated in the first sub-section of this chapter.

In the field of Eucharistic spirituality, Parecattil attempted a synthesis of Christian and Hindu traditions. One notable development in his thought at this time was his reflection on the need to re-formulate the axiom: *Extra ecclesiam nulla salus*, since it did not correspond to the theology of Vatican II and was detrimental to dialogue with adherents of other religions.

However, Parecattil never questioned the uniqueness of Christ in the economy of salvation, and indeed presented him as the fulfilment of all Hindu religious aspirations. He called his people to foster an Indian-Christian spirituality by which to embody the goal of inculturation, and he encouraged the religious to live with their Hindu counterparts without losing their commitment to Christ and the Church.

Parecattil also concentrated on new areas of social action which are motivated by the desire to live according to Eucharistic grace. Furthermore, he held that human labour is sanctified by this sacrament, since the bread and wine, symbols of nature changed by work, are transformed into the body and blood of Christ. He viewed medical assistance as an important Christian ministry. Providing asylums for leprosy patients was another of his pastoral concerns. He advocated that in India education must assume a democratic nature, and thereby uphold the rights of minorities. Since he considered over-population as a major problem in the country, he proposed natural family planning, and not artificial birth control, as the method of limiting the birth rate.

1. The Syro-Malabar Eucharistic Liturgy:
As Adapted to the Indian Genius

Joseph Parecattil provided great momentum to liturgical adaptation with the formation of «Bharathiya Pūjā» (Indian Mass) in 1973. This Missal was prepared by the Ernakulam Archdiocesan Liturgical Centre under his leadership. On March 31, 1974, it was re-published «pro-manuscripto» with some changes. About the structure of the Indian Mass, Parecattil noted:

> It (Indian Mass) is in line with the principle of «organic development» enunciated by Vatican II in Art. 6 of *Orientalium Ecclesiarum* and Art. 23 of *Sacrosanctum Concilium*. For, it keeps the structure and framework of the Syro-Malabar Mass and reproduces a few prayers thereof. The anaphora is new, but is of an experimental nature in tune with the directives of the Sacred Congregation, dated 9th May, 1969, recommending the compilation of new anaphora[1].

Parecattil admitted that, while the basic structure of the Indian Mass is Syro-Malabar, some might take exception to placing the epiclesis before the words of institution. He justified this change by pointing out that in the early centuries of the Church there were two epicleses, one spoken over the

---

[1] J. PARECATTIL, «Liturgical Reform», 70.

elements, and the other over the faithful. Furthermore, he stated: «in the Raza (Solemn High Mass) there is also an invocation of the Holy Spirit some time before the Consecration»[2]. Parecattil also explained that the anaphora of the Indian Mass is the same as that prepared by the Liturgical Commission of the C.B.C.I and approved by the Bishops Conference in 1972. Moreover, he recalled, in this connection the recommendation of the Congregation for the Oriental Churches that the compilation of new anaphorae be undertaken. He continued: «The pre-anaphora and post-anaphoral portions of the Indian Mass follow the pattern of the Syro-Malabar Mass and reproduce the relevant ideas contained in the same»[3].

However, Parecattil felt constrained to respond to those who criticized him for including Hindu religious literature in the Indian Mass:

> It does not contain any passages from Hindu scripture except the famous sentence «Lead us, Lord, from unreality to reality, from darkness to light, from mortality to immortality». This beautiful passage was quoted by Pope Paul VI in a speech he gave in Bombay in 1964[4].

Parecattil explained the significance of this Hindu prayer in the Christian Eucharistic liturgy. He defended his position: «It is introduced into the Indian Mass just to show that Christ comes to the world as an answer to the yearnings of the human heart, especially the fervent prayers of the people of India»[5]. He pointed out that passages from the Hindu Scriptures are not read in the Mass. Moreover, the usual Christian liturgical dress is used, and the rite is celebrated standing and not sitting on the floor[6]. He claimed that he was inspired to prepare the Missal by the emphasis which Vatican II had given in unequivocal terms to the need to adapt the liturgy to local cultures and contemporary questions and aspirations[7]. He was convinced, therefore, that the introduction of readings from non-Christian scriptures into the Divine Office, even in the Liturgy of the Word, is not in itself objectionable. But he judged that the time may not be ripe for that, because the faithful have been accustomed to look upon non-Christian religions as superstition and idolatry. He viewed this as an attitude which «has to be set right at the earliest»[8].

---

[2] J. PARECATTIL, «Renewal of an Imaginary Prohibition», 114.
[3] J. PARECATTIL, «Renewal of an Imaginary Prohibition», 114.
[4] J. PARECATTIL, «Liturgical Reform», 71.
[5] J. PARECATTIL, «Renewal of an Imaginary Prohibition», 114.
[6] J. PARECATTIL, «Renewal of an Imaginary Prohibition», 114.
[7] J. PARECATTIL, «Liturgical Reform», 71; SC 37-40.
[8] J. PARECATTIL, «Indigenisation and Evangelisation», 243.

Some critics were against the use of the word *OM* in the text due to its «specific Hindu meaning»; Parecattil defended its inclusion:

It is not right to reject *OM* saying that it is a Hindu concept. Nobody can say for certain that everything in Hinduism is right or wrong. What is needed is to learn in depth the origin and meaning of each sound. Even if it seemed a Hindu concept at first sight, one might think of how it could be Christianized. If some reject a language, or rubric just because the Hindus use it, one can only be sorry for him and be ashamed of him[9].

Parecattil went on to explain that *OM* is a combination of the sounds A, U, M. It stands for the creation, preservation and dissolution of all things. Later, *OM* began to signify the unity of three gods: Vishnu (A); Siva (U); and Brahma (M). This reflection led him to make the following comment: «an expert in the Sanskrit language told me that if in Hinduism *OM* signifies the union of three gods, there is nothing wrong in Christianizing it and using it to signify the Trinity of Christian religion»[10]. He defended his position saying that such adaptations had taken place from the beginning of the Church. According to St. John, the second person of the Trinity is the Logos — the Word «through whom all things were made». «Logos» is adopted from Stoic philosophy[11]. Moreover, «Persona» was the mask worn by actors. This term was accepted by the Church to refer to the Father, Son and the Holy Spirit[12]. Parecattil then put a question to his critics: «Does not the sacred syllable *OM*, expressing the creative will of God, convey a similar idea and favourably dispose the mind of the Hindu to accept the doctrine of the Word?»[13].

In the eyes of the critics of the Indian Mass, the use of the word *saccidānanda* is too suggestive of Hinduism. However, Parecattil justified its relevance in the Christian Eucharistic liturgy:

The word *saccidānanda* signifies that God is *sat-cit-ānanda*. We have to appreciate the sages who have coined this term for God a long time before Christ, and we as Indians should be proud of this contribution to philosophy[14].

---

[9] J. PARECATTIL, «Syro-Malabar Church», *Sathyadeepam* 54 (1981 January 28) 3.

[10] J. PARECATTIL, «Syro-Malabar Church», *Sathyadeepam* 54 (1981 January 28) 9.

[11] J. PARECATTIL, «Foreword» to N.K. JOSE, *The Liturgy*, xvi.

[12] J. PARECATTIL, «Syro-Malabar Church», *Sathyadeepam* 54 (1981 January 28) 1; ID., «Foreword» to N.K JOSE, *The Liturgy*, xvii.

[13] J. PARECATTIL, «Research Seminar», 31.

[14] J. PARECATTIL, «Syro-Malabar Church», *Sathyadeepam* 54 (1981 January 28) 3.

According to Parecattil, *saccidānanda* is a «concept underlying the Christian view of the Holy Trinity, comprising three divine Persons, Father, Son and the Holy Spirit. For, the Father is the creative Godhead, the Son, the innermost word or thought of the Father and the Holy Spirit, their mutual love, identical with eternal bliss»[15]. God the Father is being (*Sat*); Word or intellect is the Son (*Cit*); and their mutual love and happiness is the Holy Spirit (*Ānanda*). Being, Intellect, and Bliss, which are infinite in character and express divine inter-relations, are three distinct Persons according to Christian revelation[16]. However, Parecattil held that there is a difference between Trinity and Trimurthy[17].

The Indian Mass, according to Parecattil, is a reflection of the nature of the Syro-Malabar Church, which has cultural, religious and liturgical aspects:

Not a few who have a genuine love for our country and a sincere appreciation for our culture look forward to that happy day when it will be possible to say of the Syro-Malabar Community [...] «Hindu in culture, Christian in religion and Indian in liturgy». That will be the hey-day of Christianity in India and the realization of the catholicity of the Church in our soil. Unless such a cultural integration is effected and a corresponding spirit is created at all levels in the sacred functions [...] the future of Christianity is not going to be very bright. To maintain a proper missionary spirit it is necessary to integrate the Church effectively in the cultural milieu of New India with her characteristic synthesis of East and West, of Old and New. The task should start with the liturgy, to be projected eventually into theology[18].

Parecattil maintained that the Syro-Malabar Church is Hindu in culture insofar as Christians are more or less like their Hindu counterparts in appearance, education and social customs[19]. He firmly stated that the Church has to assimilate and adapt these elements, or rather Christianize and

---

[15] J. PARECATTIL, «Unitive Understanding», 82.

[16] J. PARECATTIL, «Research Seminar», 31; ID., «Foreword» to N.K. JOSE, *The Liturgy*, xviii.

[17] J. PARECATTIL, «Foreword» to N.K. JOSE, *The Liturgy*, xxi.

[18] J. PARECATTIL, «Adaptation and the Future of Christianity», 190.

[19] The phrase: «Hindu in culture, Christian in religion, and Indian in worship» is an improvement of the axiom which has qualified the Syro-Malabar Church as «Hindu in culture, Christian in religion and Oriental in worship» (Cf. P.J. PODIPARA, «Hindu in Culture», 89-94; ID., «The Thomas Christians and Adaptation», 171-177). However, this axiom does not mean that culture, religion and liturgy are separate water-tight compartments of Christian life; rather it tries to specify the nature of the Syro-Malabar Church.

use them, in the Eucharistic liturgy[20]. The right to acculturation is a fundamental and God-given one, deriving necessarily both from human freedom and the mission of the Catholic Church. No one has the right to force an Indian to worship God in the European way. The deposit of faith should be preserved intact (2Tim 1, 14; Gal 1, 8), but freedom of expression in explaining it should also be respected[21].

The Indian Mass brings the process of indianization to a deeper level, while all previous attempts to further it in the Syro-Malabar Church were restricted to externals:

> Evidently those adaptations (in the Syro-Malabar liturgy) were only in the external realm. I would say in the body of the liturgy — and not in its soul or spirit. Therefore, they touched only the fringe of the question. What is more important is the soul of the liturgy, which takes into account the philosophical background, cultural heritage, spiritual patrimony, language, genius, idioms, music, tastes, hopes, aspirations, needs, plans and prospects, in short, the life-situation of the contemporary person to whom the Church is making its diakonia (service) available[22].

Parecattil was of the opinion that the Syro-Malabar liturgy has to be adapted to the Indian genius on a deeper level, removing its semitic overtone[23]. He held that there is no harm in borrowing certain customs, ideas and expressions even from Hinduism because the Catholic Church rejects nothing which is true and holy in non-Christian religions[24]. He emphasised that this Indianization is neither Hinduization[25], nor syncretism of religions[26].

Parecattil based his liturgical adaptations on a firm theological foundation. According to him the theology of the local Church justifies indigenization particularly in the Eucharistic liturgy:

> Many show little or no interest in the question of adaptation in general and liturgical adaptation in particular owing to a lack of understanding, perhaps, of

---

[20] J. PARECATTIL, <«A Friendly Approach»>, 305; ID., «Adaptation and the Future of Christianity», 189; ID., «Foreword» to P. THENAYAN, *The Missionary Consciousness*, xv; ID., «Religious Values», 8; ID., «Thirty Years of C.B.C.I», 27.

[21] J. PARECATTIL, «Foreword» to T. PEREIRA, *Towards an Indian Christian Funeral Rite*, xxi.

[22] J. PARECATTIL, «Adaptation and the Future of Christianity», 190.

[23] J. PARECATTIL, «Adaptation and the Future of Christianity», 190; ID., <«St. Mary's Basilica»>, 104.

[24] J. PARECATTIL, «Foreword» to P. THENAYAN, *The Missionary Consciousness*, xiv.

[25] J. PARECATTIL, «Foreword to N.K. JOSE, *The Liturgy*, xv.

[26] J. PARECATTIL, «Foreword» to P. THENAYAN, *The Missionary Consciousness*, xviii.

the theology of adaptation which, again, requires a proper notion of the local Church. The local Church, still less a particular Church in the sense of a Rite, is not simply an administrative unit or a territorial subdivision of the universal Church. It is the actualization of the mystical body of Christ in a particular place and time. It is the sign and instrument of salvation for the people of those particular life-situations. In other words, it symbolises the incarnation of Christ, assuming flesh and blood, adapting himself to local conditions and dwelling among men. It is the re-enactment of the Paschal Mystery, unifying all believers in the Word and vivifying them in the Spirit[27].

According to Parecattil, the local Church is the concrete realization of the universal Church in a particular time and space[28]. The local Church assumes flesh and blood from a particular culture through a healthy incarnational process[29]. He affirmed that indigenization was started with the incarnate Word of God. By becoming man, he opted to be born a Jew and ratified all that was of perennial value in the cultural and religious traditions of the Jewish religion, and in the life and cultural habits of the people of Palestine[30]. On one occasion, Parecattil stated: «If Christ were to become incarnate in our country today, he would have chosen the local dress, would have whispered the local dialect; he would have been an Indian in its full sense»[31]. Therefore, the incarnation of the Word essentially entailed an inculturation[32].

Parecattil deepened this insight in the following text and pointed to the necessity of indigenization:

> The Church which is the continuation and extension of Christ's incarnation, should become incarnated in the local cultures, elevating them and converting them into instruments of salvation. They are to be assumed in view of the redemption, and purified of what is not consonant with true revelation, for the building up of the body of Christ[33].

---

[27] J. PARECATTIL, «Adaptation and the Future of Christianity», 188.

[28] J. PARECATTIL, «Foreword» to T. PEREIRA, *Towards an Indian Christian Funeral Rite*, xxii.

[29] J. PARECATTIL, «Foreword» to T. PEREIRA, *Towards an Indian Christian Funeral Rite*, xvi.

[30] J. PARECATTIL, «Opening Prayer Service», 1; ID., «Foreword» to P. THENAYAN, *The Missionary Consciousness*, xv-xvi.

[31] J. PARECATTIL, «The Task Ahead», 188; ID., «Foreword» to Z. PARANILAM, *Christian Openness*, xii.

[32] J. PARECATTIL, «Foreword» to P. THENAYAN, *The Missionary Consciousness*, xv-xvi.

[33] J. PARECATTIL, «Adaptation and the Future of Christianity», 6.

Inculturation helps the Church, which really is the sacramental continuation of the incarnation of Christ, to embody itself in a country, or amidst a race of people or a nation as a whole. This process will keep the Church and its liturgy ever ancient and ever new. Hence, inculturation is the practical consequence of the incarnation[34]. Parecattil considered that Christians must draw from the rich religious treasures of the country where they live, and build up a genuinely local Church on the basis of its indigenous cult and culture[35]. The Apostles and their successors followed the same principle. Unfortunately, in subsequent centuries missionaries projected a foreign image of the Church[36]. There were exceptions, as in the case of Fr. Robert De Nobili in India[37]. He firmly believed that Indian culture indeed already enriches Christian liturgy[38]. If the pagan cults of Rome could be assimilated into Christianity, it is not wrong to draw on the rich resources of Hinduism, which is pre-eminent among all non-Christian religions, with its genuine concept of God, its idea of attaining union with God through prayer and contemplation, its asceticism and spirit of renunciation. To bathe in the river Ganga is a symbolic action to which remission of sins is ascribed. St. John the Baptist was baptizing people in the river Jordan to impress on them the need of repentance and reconciliation with God, resulting in the cleansing of the soul from sin[39].

With specific reference to the Eucharist, Parecattil said: «If we want to speak to a Hindu about the Holy Eucharist, reference to the prevalence of sacrifice in Hindu rituals will be a good starting point»[40]. He was of the opinion that it is possible to have an Indian type of Christian culture, and therefore an Indian Eucharistic liturgy which reflects the philosophical

---

[34] J. PARECATTIL, «Foreword» to P. THENAYAN, *The Missionary Consciousness*, xv-xvi.

[35] J. PARECATTIL, «Indianization and Evangelization», 240.

[36] J. PARECATTIL, «Adaptation and the Future of Christianity», 188.

[37] The Italian Jesuit missionary, Roberto de Nobili was a pioneer in the field of adaptation and acculturation. His aim was to build a bridge of understanding between Hinduism and Christianity and evolve a community, that would be at one and the same time authentically Christian and authentically Indian. Joseph Parecattil held in high esteem this method of preaching the Gospel (Cf. J. PARECATTIL, «Opening Prayer Service», 1; ID., «Adaptation and the Future of Christianity», 188; ID., «Foreword» to Z. PARANILAM, *Christian Openness*, xiii; ID., «Foreword» to T. PEREIRA, *Towards an Indian Christian Funeral Rite*, xxi; ID., «Inidgenisation and Evangelisation», 241).

[38] J. PARECATTIL, «Foreword» to N.K. JOSE, *The Liturgy*, xvi.

[39] J. PARECATTIL, «Research Seminar», 31.

[40] J. PARECATTIL, «Research Seminar», 31.

categories and idioms of the country[41]. Indian Christians who have respect for their nation and culture should not be satisfied with a form of worship which employs cultural elements of the West[42]. As is often the case, Parecattil quoted from *Sacrosantum Concilium* to support his points: «anything in their way of life that is not indissolubly bound up with superstition and error it (the Church) studies with sympathy and, if possible, preserves intact» (SC 37). Parecattil boldly stated: «I doubt whether there is any Indian rite that is indissolubly bound up with superstition and error, so much so that it will not stand purification and adaptation»[43]. Without this assimilation and adaptation, the Indian Church will not be able to meet the many challenges which it faces especially in the post-conciliar period[44]. Parecattil insisted on an updated Eucharistic liturgy in accordance with the cultural context of India[45]. He pointed out: «In the last analysis, the liturgical controversy in the Syro-Malabar Church can be reduced to this question: Should we remain with the signs, symbols and prayer formulas embedded in a Chaldean culture, or can we modify them, so that they may suit modern Indian conditions?»[46].

In the history of the Syro-Malabar liturgical experimentation, the «Short Mass» occupies a prominent place. The Central Liturgical Committee of the Syro-Malabar Church gave guidelines to further abridge the 1968 Missal. As a result, the Short Mass was prepared under the leadership of Parecattil. The text was printed «pro-manuscripto» for use at experimental centres especially in the archdiocese of Ernakulam.

Parecattil was sharply criticised by many for the preparation of the text on various grounds. But, he had his own answers for each of the criticisms. Here, the main points are enumerated. Some thought that the Missal is too short, and called it a «Mini Mass». About this Parecattil noted:

> It is not so short as some people imagine. It normally takes at least half an hour and, if properly celebrated with a few words of introduction, a short homily based upon the Scripture, spontaneous prayers of the faithful, silent

---

[41] J. PARECATTIL, *Towards an Indian Christian Funeral Rite*, xix; ID., «Vision of the Church», 26.

[42] J. PARECATTIL, «Foreword to N.K. JOSE, *The Liturgy*, xvi; ID., «A Friendly Approach», 305.

[43] J. PARECATTIL, «Foreword» to T. PEREIRA, *Towards an Indian Christian Funeral Rite*, xv-xvi.

[44] J. PARECATTIL, <«Cultural Adaptation»>, 3; ID., «The Task Ahead», 11; ID., «Updating the Liturgy», 3.

[45] J. PARECATTIL, «Updating the Liturgy», 1.

[46] J. PARECATTIL, «Adaptation and the Future of Christianity», 190.

prayers etc., it takes more than an ordinary unabridged Mass, said in routine way as it is usually done[47].

Parecattil also defended the structure of the Mass as it only leaves out a few «useless repetitions» in accordance with the Art. 34 of the Constitution on the Sacred Liturgy. He judged that the brevity of the text has assured that «the faithful take part knowingly, actively, and fruitfully»[48]. He claimed that the anaphora of the Mass is the «oldest one» discovered by Macomber in 1966[49]. The language of the text was made elegant, and certain modifications were made because, if the ceremonies are unattractive, the people will «desert our churches, in favour of the Latin churches with meaningful, dynamic services»[50].

From 1978 onwards, the reform of Syro-Malabar Liturgy took a quite different turn. It gradually deviated from the path of revision and adaptation, and was directed towards the restoration of the 1962 text. The *Order of the Solemn Raza of the Syro-Malabar Church* has undone almost all the attempts of Parecattil to promote the liturgical reform, and has to a great extent restored the old Chaldean liturgy. Naturally, Parecattil was very sorry to witness these developments. He recorded the various events that occurred at different stages of the formation of the Solemn Raza which was finally promulgated in 1985. The first of these is the preparation of the 1978 Draft. About it Parecattil commended:

> A sub-committee was set up in 1974 to finalise the 1968 text with the changes needed, if any, on the principle of restoration, revision and adaptation [...] the above subcommittee has prepared a new draft in 1978. It betrays an unauthorised attempt to return to the pre-Vatican 1962 text, putting the clock back. Such a mandate was not given by the Bishops' Conference to the sub-committee[51].

Parecattil demanded that the draft had to be re-edited according to the stipulations of the S.M.B.C meeting in 1974[52]. Moreover, the draft contained only the Ordo of the simple Mass without any *propria*. According to

---

[47] J. PARECATTIL, «Liturgical Reform», 72.

[48] J. PARECATTIL, «Renewal of an Imaginary Prohibition», 116.

[49] J. PARECATTIL, «Liturgical Reform», 72.

[50] J. PARECATTIL, «Liturgical Reform», 73.

[51] J. PARECATTIL, «Liturgical Reform», 60-61.

[52] The meeting held on August 4, 1974 accepted the principle of the «restoration, revision and adaptation» in the Syro-Malabar liturgical reform giving due importance to the pastoral and cultural demands of the Church (Cf. J. PARECATTIL, *Liturgy As I See It*, 87).

Parecattil what was urgently needed was the compilation of more anaphoras and *propria* for feasts and various occasions[53].

Another important event was the meeting of the Syro-Malabar Bishops in Rome on August 26, 1980 under the presidency of Cardinal Rubin. All the nineteen bishops of the Syro-Malabar Church and the concerned members of the Oriental Congregation attended the meeting. Parecattil evaluated the latter as follows:

> In his presidential address, Cardinal Rubin categorically affirmed that reform of the liturgy should be based on the 1962 Mass. I felt sorry and disappointed that a decision on a subject which was to be discussed at the meeting was given by the president himself, and that too before the discussion was even started [...] the judgement of Cardinal Rubin on the 30th August was indirectly supporting the minority. Still he said that in liturgical revisions the text of 1968 also should be taken into account [...] We left Rome only after submitting a memorandum to the Congregation pointing out the stipulations in the speech of Cardinal Rubin to which we could not agree. Thirteen bishops out of nineteen had affixed their signatures to the memorandum[54].

Parecattil could not agree that the reform of the liturgy of the Syro-Malabar Church was to be done based on the Missal of 1962. He noted that it was after the promulgation of the 1962 text that the vision of Vatican II on liturgical renewal came out, and that the most ancient copies of the anaphoras were discovered[55]. In his speech at this meeting, Parecattil systematically elaborated the history and theology of the Syro-Malabar liturgy[56]. Later, he wrote a long letter to Cardinal Rubin analyzing the content of his speech. Among other points, he mentioned the identity of the Syro-Malabar liturgy:

> But the basic common denominator of our opinions was only that our Church should maintain its Eastern-Rite character insofar as it is in conformity with its *apostolic identity*, which is not the same as its Chaldean identity. The former extends far back to the times of St. Thomas, who, like all other apostles, would

---

[53] The draft was submitted to the Central Liturgical Committee in 1978 for discussion which took place on February 20, 1978 at CST Study House, Thrikkakara. There was a division of opinions. Some held that the S.M.B.C in 1974 had suggested only a revision of the 1968 Mass with the addition of anaphorae and propria. The others strongly supported the structure of the draft which overlooked the suggestions of the S.M.B.C and showed a trend to return to the 1962 Text (Cf. J. PARECATTIL, «Liturgical Reform», 61; ID., *Liturgy As I See It*, 126).

[54] J. PARECATTIL, *Liturgy As I See It*, 130-131.

[55] J. PARECATTIL, *Liturgy As I See It*, 130.

[56] For details of the Speech, cf. J. PARECATTIL, «Liturgical Reform», 43-92).

have used only the local language and symbols for worship, and the latter not farther than the fourth century, when Chaldean colonisers immigrated into our country. Though we did not object to the preservation of the *good* and *relevant* elements of the Chaldean liturgy, the majority of us did not subscribe to the idea of preserving the Chaldean liturgy in toto, for the simple reason that it is an alien liturgy super-imposed on us Indians by the force of circumstances. To put it briefly, the apostolic identity of our particular Church should take precedence over its Chaldean identity in point of time and importance.[57]

Parecattil asserted that the tradition of the Syro-Malabar Church is apostolic, which means that it is Indian[58]. He believed that the Chaldean traditions were imposed on this Indian Church, and therefore alien as far as the Syro-Malabar Church is concerned[59]. Parecattil added: «We do not understand why some people, or for that matter, the Sacred Congregation itself wants to reimpose it on us. What is our genuine and authentic tradition — Indian or Chaldean? This is the crux of the problem. Art. 6 of "Orientalium Ecclesiarum" speaks only about preserving one's own *legitimate* liturgical rites. In the view of us Indians, the Chaldean rite cannot be termed legitimate»[60].

A new draft of the Mass was prepared and sent to the Oriental Congregation on October 30, 1981. About the draft Parecattil commented:

The difference of view of the minority and majority on a few points were separately intimated. The minority insisted on the following:
1. The celebrant should not offer Mass facing the people.
2. The sign of the cross should not be made along with the prayer «in the name of the Father, the Son and the Holy Spirit, Amen» at the beginning of the Mass.
3. The Credo should be recited after the offertory and after coming down from the altar.
4. The Credo must be recited every day, and that too the Nicene creed.
5. At the offertory, the prayer to accept the sacrifice be made to Christ and not to the Father.
6. In the consecration words «the blood shed for all» must be replaced by «blood shed for many»[61].

---

[57] J. PARECATTIL, «Evaluation of the Meeting», 1-10.

[58] J. PARECATTIL, «Liturgical Reform», 48.

[59] J. PARECATTIL, «Liturgical Reform», 49; ID., «Some Comments» 1-2.

[60] J. PARECATTIL, «Evaluation of the Meeting», 140.

[61] J. PARECATTIL, *Liturgy As I See It*, 132.

In reply, the Oriental Congregation sent a directive on March 1, 1983 in which it was stated that the new text was to be prepared based both on the Latin translation of 1955 and on the Syrian Missal of 1960, and that the Raza had to be prepared before the solemn and simple forms[62]. In his reply to Cardinal Rubin on June 21, 1983, Parecattil pointed out: «That document[63] contradicts the directives given in your speech of August 3, 1980»[64]. He continued: «Your Eminence too accepted the principle when you spoke of «revision, renewal and adaptation» in your speech of August 30, 1980. Now I would like to know if and where exactly «revision, renewal and adaptation» have been effected in the proposed text?»[65].

The Secretary the Oriental Congregation, Archbishop Misroslaw Marusyn, send a letter (Prot. N. 955/65, dated July 24, 1985) to Parecattil with the enclosures: «Final Judgement of the Sacred Congregation for the Oriental Churches concerning the Order of the Syro-Malabar Qurbana» and a copy of the covering letter addressed to Archbishop Antony Padiyara. Parecattil wrote a reply to Archbishop M. Marusyn on May 24, 1986, in which he stated:

I am extremely grateful to you for forwarding these documents to me for my «information and utility». Since they contain insinuations against and reflections on the Syro-Malabar episcopate in general and me in particular, I feel it my duty, as one who has been following with genuine interest the history of the reform of our liturgy and playing my own role in it, to note down my comments, put the records straight and vindicate my position, so that at least future historians may see the other side of the picture, even if my words go unheeded for the moment. Time will however show who was right[66].

In the letter, Parecattil analyzed each point of the «Final Judgement», and clarified his positions. His main contention was that the Raza was not acceptable to the Syro-Malabar Christians in general, since it «has no positive literary qualities nor any progressive liturgical insights to commend itself to the enlightened people of Kerala»[67]. Moreover, he noted: «Of course, since it is imposed on them from above, they have no other alternative but to accept it, though with reluctance and resentment»[68].

---

[62] J. PARECATTIL, *Liturgy As I See It*, 132.
[63] Reference is to the directive on March 1, 1983.
[64] J. PARECATTIL, <«Evaluation on the Directives»>, 1.
[65] J. PARECATTIL, <«Evaluation of the Directives»>, 1.
[66] J. PARECATTIL, «Reply to Archbishop Marusyn», 3.
[67] J. PARECATTIL, «Reply to Archbishop Marusyn», 6.
[68] J. PARECATTIL, «Reply to Archbishop Marusyn», 6.

Archbishop Powathil, the Chairman of the Central Liturgical Committee of S.M.B.C, sent a letter to Cardinal Parecattil on October 29, 1985 forwarding the draft text of the Raza prepared by the episcopal committee and submitted to the Conference for approval. Parecattil sent him a reply on November 4, 1985, in which he stated the following about the Raza:

> While appreciating the good will manifested and the efforts put in by the episcopal committee, I am afraid that the final product is not up to the expectations nor in keeping with the decision made on December 4-5, 1983 at the meeting of the Syro-Malabar Bishops' Conference [...] According to me the text presented evidences of no serious concern for contemporary pastoral exigencies. Nor has it paid attention to the principle of «revision and adaptation», the need of which had been repeatedly emphasized in our earlier meetings[69].

In this letter Parecattil also noted that the draft text is too literal a translation from original Syriac, and does not have the beauty of a Malayalam liturgical text, since the sentences are clumsy and complicated and their meaning is beyond the grasp of the simple people[70]. He concluded the letter in these words: «Anyway I don't share any responsibility if the Conference decides to give approval to the text. I don't enter into further details. Though my comments, made with the best of intentions and in the interests of the Syro-Malabar Church, may prove a cry in the wilderness, I wanted to make a record of it»[71].

The *Order of the Solemn Raza of the Syro-Malabar Church* came into effect on February 8, 1986 with its inaugural celebration at Kottayam by His Holiness Pope John Paul II during his pastoral visit to India. Parecattil made a critical study regarding the theological and pastoral content of the Raza. At the outset of the study he said:

> Its get up is excellent; so too the printing. My hearty congratulations to those concerned. I wish I could say the same about its contents as well. But sorry, I cannot[72].

Referring to the special inauguration of the Mass, Parecattil noted: «His Holiness kept a meaningful silence, abstaining very wisely and prudently

---

[69] J. PARECATTIL, «Letter to Bishop Powathil», 32.

[70] J. PARECATTIL, «Letter to Bishop Powathil», 32.

[71] J. PARECATTIL, «Letter to Bishop Powathil», 33.

[72] J. PARECATTIL, «A Critical Study», 99.

from saying any word about that controversial Raza in his public disco-urse»[73]. According to Parecattil, it was the simple form of the Mass to be prepared, and not the Raza. He held that the Raza sprang up especially in a Semitic climate which was completely different from the Indian cultural background and was further developed in monastic circles. He remarked:

> If anybody is particular to preserve the Raza in its totality as an old curiosity it may be celebrated at least on Sundays in some seminaries, religious houses and other centres emotionally committed to traditionalism. Others who form the majority, must be allowed to break through the Chaldean bottleneck and adopt a progressive liturgy, drawing however inspiration from and accepting the genuine guidelines of the past as directed by Vatican II[74].

Parecattil observed that, in spite of the insistence of the Semitic gestures in the Missal, some Indian forms are allowed occasionally. About them he remarked: «So the pro-Chaldean specialists are slowly realising that what they branded as Latinization is in fact Indianization»[75]. Moreover, since Parecattil considered the length of the Raza as inappropriate for modern times, he suggested removing the repetition of prayers[76]. As his criticism of the theological points is almost identical with the arguments forwarded against the 1962 text, they are not repeated here[77].

Parecattil hoped that the simple and solemn forms of the Mass, which are of greater importance from the pastoral point of view, would be further revised and adapted, and would not consist of an abridged form of the Raza:

> Let us hope and pray that the Syro-Malabar Church and the people of God that compose it will not be let down by the compilation of the Simple Mass and other liturgical texts paying little or no attention to its pastoral dimension, so much insisted upon by the Decrees of Vatican II and other official docum-ents[78].

According to Parecattil the simple Mass should be more in line with adapting to the cultural and pastoral exigencies of the Indian people[79].

---

[73] J. PARECATTIL, «Letter to Bishop Kundukulam», 259; ID., «Reply to Archbishop Marusyn», 6.

[74] J. PARECATTIL, «A Critical Study», 101.

[75] J. PARECATTIL, «A Critical Study», 103.

[76] J. PARECATTIL, <«Pastoral Dimension», 1.

[77] For more details regarding the arguments of Joseph Parecattil, cf. J. PARECATTIL, «A Critical Study», 103-116).

[78] J. PARECATTIL, «Letter to Bishop Kundukulam», 259.

[79] J. PARECATTIL, «Pastoral Dimension», 1.

Regarding the language of the solemn Mass, he thought it was too literal and could not be comprehended by the people[80].

2. The Indian Eucharistic Spirituality:
A Synthesis of Hindu and Christian Elements

During this period Parecattil had also contributed significantly to the development of an Indian-Christian spirituality. He held that the grace which flows from the Eucharist redeems all human beings including non-Christians. They too share the fruits of the cross, and Jesus Christ is the answer to their quest for God. Hence, Parecattil was convinced that the position of the Church regarding the salvation of those outside it needed to be re-formulated.

Since Parecattil believed that Christ has redeemed the entire human race by his blood, it follows that the grace of the cross justifies all. Unfortunately many people do not know that they are saved by the grace of Christ which is continually offered to them in the Eucharist:

> Then he (St. Paul) adds that all are justified through the free gift of His grace by being redeemed in Christ Jesus (Rom 3, 10f, 23) That being so, this grace that has already been given to everyone has not yet become a personal experience for a large majority of mankind. They are ignorant of the fact that they have been already redeemed and they still remain as if they have never regained God's grace. Because of this they are found helpless like a sheep without a shepherd (Mk 9, 36)[81].

Parecattil affirmed that human beings have always been conscious of their sinfulness, and have tried their best to free themselves from it. But most often they could not find a truly satisfying redemption from it, because they sought human forms of self-redemption. The result was tantamount to what Jesus said «What is born of the flesh is flesh» (Jn 3, 6). People are able to attain redemption only through the grace of Christ which made available mainly in the Eucharist[82].

Parecattil thus maintained that, as Jesus Christ has saved the entire human race, his message has a true relevance in India and in fact has entered into its soul with the emergence of an Indian spirituality fostered mainly by the Eucharistic liturgy:

---

[80] J. PARECATTIL, «Pastoral Dimension», 2.

[81] J. PARECATTIL, «Catholic Charismatic Renewal», 1.

[82] J. PARECATTIL, «Catholic Charismatic Renewal», 1.

it is impossible to oust Christ from India, even if one were to wish to expel all those who preach Christianity. For, it has already taken deep roots in the soil and Christ's presence is there, in every walk of human life, at least implicitly and imperceptibly. For us, Catholics, He has become our Emmanuel — God with us — not only by his ideological presence but also by His real presence in the Holy Eucharist[83].

According to Parecattil, the Risen Christ, whom St. Thomas the apostle acclaimed with the words «My Lord and My God», abides with his divinity and humanity in the world through the sacrament of the altar. The spiritual life of sincere Catholics is based on the Holy Eucharist, and draws its warmth and light from the tabernacle as if from a power house[84]. Hence, St. Thomas introduced a living person into India, the risen one who will be with humanity unto the consummation of the world[85]. The Eucharist nourishes the spiritual life and the missionary activity of the Church, and remains their centre[86].

As Christ's saving grace is extended to all people, Parecattil was correct in stating that non-Christians also have a share in it. He developed this idea by focusing his attention on Hinduism as a natural religion. According to Catholic dogma, God's presence could be perceived in some manner or other in such a religion. In particular, Parecattil held that in Hinduism there is evidence of the revelation of the Creator:

> To the aesthetic mind, the whole universe is a manifestation of the power and glory of the supreme, absolute Being. It might sometimes happen that the simple folk worship a tree, an animal or a stone, as symbolising the power of the Almighty; in so doing they pay homage directly or indirectly to the Master of the Universe. Communion with nature and contemplation of the beauty and harmony of the universe will certainly instil in us a sense of the Divine [...] Against this background, we can easily see why the Rishis (sages) of old retired to the forest of India for contemplation and meditation, which are the first steps to a conscious realization of the divine presence in us[87].

Parecattil also asserted that religions like Hinduism bear witness to the Messianic expectations of the human race, and play a providential role in the economy of salvation by preparing the ground for the advent of the

---

[83] J. PARECATTIL, «Prayer and Penance», 15.
[84] J. PARECATTIL, «Prayer and Penance», 16.
[85] J. PARECATTIL, «Prayer and Penance», 16.
[86] J. PARECATTIL, *Letters to Priests*, 106.
[87] J. PARECATTIL, «Unitive Understanding», 81-82.

Redeemer[88]. Parecattil pointed out that one can find the presence of God «in the rain, dew and snow, in the lipid waters that reflect the skies, in the evening breeze that caresses the corn meant for man's food, in the humming of the bee which gathers honey and in the immense ocean that mirrors the infinite»[89].

Parecattil went on to state that Jesus Christ is the answer to the search for God by the Hindu sages and the entire people of India:

> The Hindus had been praying, over the centuries, in the words of the *Bṛhadaranyaka Upanishads*: «Lead me from unreality to reality, from darkness to light, from mortality to immortality» [...] This profound longing of the human soul, echoed and reechoed during the course of the centuries, has met with its adequate response in Christ who said: «I am the light of the world», «I am the way, the truth and the life» and «I have come that they may have life and have it more abundantly»[90].

Parecattil pointed out that the expectation of a divine redeemer was evident among all peoples of the world, a fact that corroborates the Christian message regarding the incarnation of the Divine Word[91]. Jesus Christ is the unmistaken answer to this yearning of the human heart[92]. He is the Word of God, consubstantial with the Father; He is the Light of the world and Life itself[93]. Hence, according to Parecattil, «Christianity is not something opposed to Hindu religious aspirations, but is the fulfilment of its innate cravings, beliefs and experiences[94].

In this context, Parecattil provided a contemporary understanding of the Catholic dogma about the necessity of the Church for salvation. He was of the opinion that an excessively narrow interpretation of this truth hurts the feelings of the Hindus:

> «Extra ecclesiam nulla salus» (outside the Church no salvation) is a time-honoured adage, accepted without questioning in the pre-Vatican period and interpreted in a wide sense so as to include even bonafide non-Catholics and non-Christians in the purview of salvation. Whatever be the interpretations given to mitigate the bluntness and soften the literal meaning of the statement, it was harrowing to the sentiments of those outside the Catholic Church. Hence

---

[88] J. PARECATTIL, «Indigenisation and Evangelization», 242.

[89] J. PARECATTIL, «To Pray is to Discover God», 88.

[90] J. PARECATTIL, «Mater Dei Institute», 3; ID., <«Christ is the Light»>, 360.

[91] J. PARECATTIL, «Research Seminar», 28.

[92] J. PARECATTIL, «Prayer and Penance», 17.

[93] J. PARECATTIL, «Prayer and Penance», 17.

[94] J. PARECATTIL, «Opening Prayer Service», 1-2; ID., «Mater Dei Institute», 5.

in this ecumenical era there is the need of re-formulating or at least of re-interpreting the old maxim, in the light of modern perspectives and contemporary theological thinking[95].

Parecattil was convinced of the providential role which the so-called «pagan» religions are playing in the economy of salvation[96]. He was of the opinion that it is not possible to make definite statements about the salvation of those outside the Church: «Nobody can claim to have said the last word on this delicate issue. But nobody can gainsay either the fact that God, who is the Father of all and not only of «Abraham, Isaac and Jacob», wishes all His children to be saved and places at their disposal at least the minimum means required for it, without, however, intending to tamper with their inborn liberty either to accept or reject the generous offer»[97]. Since Parecattil maintained that God's providence in every religion under the sun has a part to play in leading people to their eternal destiny[98], he was satisfied that there is now much discussion about the gems of truth dispersed in, and the rays of light illumining from, the Hindu religious tradition. He was also encouraged by the fact that there is at present much emphasis on the need to indigenise Christian spirituality especially through Eucharistic worship[99].

In this connection, Parecattil reflected on the conversion from Hinduism to the Catholic faith. He was of opinion that conversion must be neither a forced or a hasty step nor a subtle means to exploit the weaker segments of the population:

> Conversion should not be made to assume the nature of a mental revolution but only of a gradual evolution, that is to say, a salutary process by which one's innate cravings find their adequate fulfilment in Jesus Christ[100].

Parecattil noted that the process of evangelization in India must not be marked by drastic methods[101]. To him the success of evangelization is to be judged not so much by the numerical strength of the Christian community, as by the ideological impact it has on the people of the country and its influence on shaping the ideals and attitudes of the nation. In this respect

---

[95] J. PARECATTIL, «Foreword» to T. EMPRAYIL, *The Emerging Theology* vi.

[96] J. PARECATTIL, «Foreword» to Z. PARANILAM, *Christian Openness*, xi.

[97] J. PARECATTIL, «Foreword» to Z. PARANILAM, *Christian Openness*, xii.

[98] J. PARECATTIL, «A Friendly Approach», 304.

[99] J. PARECATTIL, «A Friendly Approach», 304.

[100] J. PARECATTIL, «Indigenisation and Evangelisation», 241-242.

[101] J. PARECATTIL, «Opening Prayer Service», 1-2; ID., «Mater Dei Institute», 5.

the Christian Church in India is, as a matter of fact, exercising a much deeper influence than its numerical strength would warrant, for it highlights and defends the fundamental eternal values of life[102].

Parecattil understood that the Christian maxim of «no salvation outside the Church» created unnecessary conflict with the advocates of Hinduism. He was of the opinion that, whereas Hinduism was generally tolerant and respectful towards Christianity, the members of the Church here not always responded in kind:

> The encounter between Hinduism and Christianity has perhaps a different story to tell. Hinduism has evinced an admirable receptivity and respect for Christ's teaching and cannot, therefore, be said to have come into conflict with Christ's message as enshrined in the Gospels. On the contrary, it is perhaps Christianity, as it was presented, that came into conflict with Hinduism and other ancient religions of the East. Clearly this conflict was inevitable but was also, to some extent, avoidable, if the mouthpieces of Christianity set their heart on fulfilling, instead of attempting, against the spirit of the gospel, to destroy and then to build up[103].

Parecattil was of opinion that the followers of Hinduism generally are not opposed to Christ, although they may not be willing to accept Christianity in its present form[104]. He remarked: «The Hindus, in general, are full of respect for Christ and His teachings, in spite of the short-comings of individual Christians»[105]. Parecattil explained this statement by noting that Christians have been rather slow to discover and appreciate the rich treasures of non-Christian religions[106]. Christianity will be capable of making a strong appeal to Hindus only if it could be presented as fulfilment of Indian cultural patterns and national aspirations[107]. He added that the time is ripe «to ask pardon to God for the unsympathetic attitude we have adopted towards our fellowmen and the followers of other religions. God is charity. Love of God must necessarily reflect itself in love of man, whatever be his religion, education or social status»[108].

---

[102] J. PARECATTIL, «Indigenisation and Evangelisation», 240; ID., «Adaptation and the Future of Christianity», 187.

[103] J. PARECATTIL, «Mater Dei Institute», 4.

[104] J. PARECATTIL, «Mater Dei Institute», 5.

[105] J. PARECATTIL, «Mutual Sharing of Life», 160.

[106] J. PARECATTIL, «Foreword» to T. PEREIRA, *Towards an Indian Christian Funeral Rite*, xvi.

[107] J. PARECATTIL, «Mater Dei Institute», 6.

[108] J. PARECATTIL, «Unitive Understanding», 83.

Parecattil was convinced that in the modern context of India it is imperative that Christians adopt a new outlook regarding Hinduistic culture and spirituality:

A theologian, really Catholic in outlook, is one who, without allowing himself to be blown off his feet in regard to his Christian commitment and without letting his faith suffer any set-back, examines the non-Christian sources of religion, and the life and thought of the people of other faiths, with a readiness to assimilate, adopt and absorb «those things that are true, noble, right, pure, lovely and honourable» (Phil 4, 5) whatever be the milieu in which they are found[109].

Parecattil thought that, if Christians are sincerely to appreciate the values of Hinduism, they must engage in a dialogue with it regarding the deepest meaning of life[110]. Only if Christians learn to respect all that is true, noble and beautiful in the life and thought of non-Christians, can they practice real ecumenism[111]. In one of his writings, Parecattil asserted the following: «A deep study of Hinduism will go a long way for a salutary and fruitful encounter with them and for a friendly dialogue in a climate of mutual respect»[112]. It is necessary that the preachers of the Gospel manifest greater admiration for the religious traditions and the ethical customs of the people they want to evangelise[113]. In his opinion, this approach, apart from the rich dividends it would pay in fostering Christian witness, would also add a new dimension to ecumenism, since it would unite members of the Church on the basis of the rich spiritual heritage of India[114]. In other words, the adherents of both religions would be enriched through such mutual sharing[115].

Parecattil appreciated the efforts of the bishops at Vatican II to promote dialogue between Christians and non-Christians. He viewed this development as a sign that the Holy Spirit is calling Christianity to leave behind its isolation, and to take an active part in the field of world religions:

---

[109] J. PARECATTIL, «Paganism in Christianity», 22.

[110] J. PARECATTIL, «Adaptation and the Future of Christianity», 190.

[111] J. PARECATTIL, «Opening Prayer Service», 1.

[112] J. PARECATTIL, «Foreword» to T. EMPRAYIL, *The Emerging Theology*, vii.

[113] J. PARECATTIL, «Foreword» to T. EMPRAYIL, *The Emerging Theology*, viii; ID., «Unitive Understanding», 83.

[114] J. PARECATTIL, <«Ecumenical Movements»>, 169.

[115] J. PARECATTIL, «Foreword» to Z. PARANILAM, *Christian Openness*, xii.

The Catholic Church which, for several centuries past, was living in a world of its own has emerged from the Vatican Council II with a growing enthusiasm to enter into dialogue with other religions of the world[116].

Parecattil clearly seconded the need of sincere dialogue with those who do not fully share its affirmations and attitudes[117]. Furthermore, he was conscious that such dialogue would be effective, if it were to be carried out in a spirit of humility and mutual respect rather than of arrogance and aggressiveness[118]. He reiterated his conviction that this communication would benefit the adherents of both religions, and serve the greater glory of God[119]. He encouraged Christians to «be prepared to meet co-religionists on a footing of equality and friendliness»[120]. Of course, Christians rightly believe that Jesus Christ is the fullness of divine revelation and that acknowledgement of his person leads to eternal life[121]. But this fact does not and should not stand in the way of Christian engagement in mutually enriching dialogue with non-Christians[122]. It would be a disservice to Jesus Christ, who «came not to destroy but to fulfil», if Christians were to try to put out the light of truth lit by God in all human minds and hearts, and fan the flame of interreligious rivalry and antipathy[123]. Parecattil knew that the sharing about religious beliefs demands a profound sense of love among the dialogue partners, even when they have to disagree in major points: «A Christian cannot be blind to the spiritual earnestness, sincerity and work of God's grace in those who profess a faith different from his own»[124]. Hence, the overtures towards dialogue are to be made with an open mind[125]. Parecattil was pleased to note that since Vatican II many Christian theologians have published statements and treatises, high-lighting the positive role of Hinduism in the economy of salvation[126].

---

[116] J. PARECATTIL, «Unitive Understanding», 84.

[117] J. PARECATTIL, «Pope John Paul II», 363.

[118] J. PARECATTIL, <«Cultural Adaptation»>, 3; ID., «Foreword» to T. EMPRAYIL, *The Emerging Theology*, viii; ID., «Foreword» to Z. PARANILAM, *Christian Openness*, xii; ID., «Cultural Adaptation», 3.

[119] J. PARECATTIL, «Fourth Centenary», 3.

[120] J. PARECATTIL, «A Friendly Approach», 304.

[121] J. PARECATTIL, «Foreword» to Z. PARANILAM, *Christian Openness*, xii.

[122] J. PARECATTIL, «Foreword» to Z. PARANILAM, *Christian Openness*, xii.

[123] J. PARECATTIL, «The Mutual Sharing of Life», 160.

[124] J. PARECATTIL, «Swami Ranganathananda», 67; ID., «The Mutual Sharing», 160.

[125] J. PARECATTIL, «Foreword» to Z. PARANILAM, *Christian Openness*, xii-xiii.

[126] J. PARECATTIL, «Foreword» to Z. PARANILAM, *Christian Openness*, xii-xiii.

Parecattil lamented that Christians generally know very little about Hinduism, just as Hindus comprehended Christianity only superficially. A more sympathetic understanding of the religious tenants of the others will prevent both from making unwarranted and offensive statements[127]. He thought in fact that God could only be pleased if His children, from Hindu, Muslim and Christian traditions, would offer joint prayers to Him[128]. Indeed, all forms of fostering unity between the adherents of different religions demand allegiance to one's own convictions, as well readiness to overcome divisive prejudice:

> Participation in meetings of this kind (ecumenical) does not imply a renouncement of one's own faith or religious commitments. Loyal to one's own convictions, one gets an opportunity to make common cause with men of other religions[129].

Parecattil pointed out that it is necessary that at such meetings Christians should be ready to express their convictions frankly without making undue compromises and to value at the same time, whatever is noble, good and beautiful in other religions[130]. He expressed these insights succinctly by saying that there is scope for «concrete Hindu-Christian dialogue in this age of ecumenism by sharing one another's life at the deepest level of religious experience, having of course, due regard to the limitations imposed by one's own religious commitments»[131].

Parecattil encouraged ecumenical dialogue as an effective and healthy way to present the Gospel in terms which respect the soul of India:

> Personally, I believe that, far from being losers, we will only be gainers if we establish contacts with Hindu asceticism and Indian modes of thought. On several occasions I have advised priests — religious and diocesan priests — to spend some time, if possible, in some Hindu Ashram with the view not only of imbibing Indian spirituality but also of bridging the gulf, as far as possible, between the two religions, by an encounter between the two at the deepest level and in a spirit of mutual concern and co-operation. I am sure, it will pay rich dividends in our apostolic endeavour, and in our efforts to discover the soul of India[132].

---

[127] J. PARECATTIL, «Unitive Understanding», 84; ID., «Foreword» to Z. PARANILAM, *Christian Openness*, xii; ID., «Foreword» to T. EMPRAYIL, *The Emerging Theology*, vii.

[128] J. PARECATTIL, «A Friendly Approach», 305.

[129] J. PARECATTIL, «Unitive Understanding», 86.

[130] J. PARECATTIL, «A Friendly Approach», 304.

[131] J. PARECATTIL, «The Mutual Sharing», 160.

[132] J. PARECATTIL, «Mater Dei Institute», 12.

With a view to internal spiritual renovation and re-orientation of religious formation, Parecattil affirmed that it is high time that India's cultural and religious heritage become better known by Christians who can be enriched by them[133]. In this way he hoped that from India would emerge a Christian vision faithful to the Gospels, but at the same time rich in the spiritual legacy of the country[134]. He was highly optimistic that the genius of the Indian people[135] add a new dimension to traditional Christian spirituality, which still bears the stamp of western thought[136]. These insights can be summarized in the following forceful statement: «Christ has still to be born in India, in her mythical, ethical, mystical and theological dimensions. He is to be re-articulated in Indian thought-patterns, which is a great challenge for us»[137].

Parecattil specified some aspects of Hinduism that could be accepted by the Church in its pursuit of a distinctly Indian-Christian spirituality. First of all, he pointed out the Hindu quest for God:

Its (religion) long influence on the people has made spirituality a second nature to the Indian who is really obsessed with God. A craving to experience God is his life-breath. He is inebriated with God. The great Indian ideal in religious life is *saksatkara*, realisation of God in one's own self[138].

Parecattil often noted that the life and the thought of Indians are permeated by their religious faith[139]. The scriptures and other books of Hinduism contain the wisdom of the ages, and they have taught the masses of India many sublime truths through edifying examples of virtue and whole-hearted devotion[140]. Since a close union with God is the *Mōksha* (liberation or salvation) which an Indian seeks to attain[141], the other objectives of life, namely *dharma* (righteousness), *artha* (wealth) and *kama* (sexuality) are subservient to it and lead to it[142].

---

[133] J. PARECATTIL, «Adaptation and the Future of Christianity», 187.
[134] J. PARECATTIL, «Religious in the Indian Context», 3.
[135] J. PARECATTIL, «Religious in the Indian Context», 2.
[136] J. PARECATTIL, <«Indian Cultural Heritage»>, 2-3.
[137] J. PARECATTIL, <«Christian Religious Experience»>, 2-3.
[138] J. PARECATTIL, «Religious in the Indian Context», 2.
[139] J. PARECATTIL, «Religious Values», 2.
[140] J. PARECATTIL, «Swami Ranganathannanda», 65.
[141] J. PARECATTIL, «Monasticism, Christian and Indian», 2-3.
[142] J. PARECATTIL, «Spiritual and Moral Renewal», 2.

Since *Sannyāsa* is the way of life by which to achieve this realization of God, Parecattil held that an Indian Christian spirituality should be articulated in terms of it:

> *Sannyāsa* or religious life, is nothing new to India. It is part and parcel of India's spiritual heritage and age-old tradition. This fact is typically expressed by the very synonym of our land, *Ārshabhāratha*, which means the land of *ṛṣis* or sages. In fact, monastic life was the highlight of Indian spirituality and there were Hindu *Āshrams* or Buddhist *vihārās* throughout the length and breadth of the country[143].

According to Parecattil, the ultimate goal of *sannyāsa*, is God-realization[144]. A *sannyāsi* attains God through the three-fold *mārga* of *karma* (worship and other actions), *jñāna* (divine enlightenment from within) and *bhakti* (unwavering devotion to the Lord)[145]. Moreover, *Sannyāsa* also means renunciation not only of purely material things, but primarily of one's own ego. To emphasize this truth, Parecattil referred to the following saying: «Space is garment of a *sannyāsi*, the palm of his hand his begging bowl, the earth his couch» (*Bhāgavatam* 2, 2)[146]. Catholic religious whose existence is made pure and spotless by the vows of poverty and chastity[147], could interpret *sannyāsa* as the attitude that nothing is ultimately worthwhile unless it leads to God-consciousness[148]. In Parecattil's view, the value and nature of a *sannyāsi* could serve as a genuine foundation of an Indian-Christian spirituality[149].

Thus, Parecattil hoped that the Indian Church would be able to carry out its evangelizing mission by explaining Christ's message of total liberation in indigenous categories[150]. What modern Indians need today are such Indian seers, who live the Gospel credibly in their country, and whom they can look for further religious inspiration[151].

---

[143] J. PARECATTIL, «Third National Convention», 1; ID., «Religious in the Indian Context», 1.

[144] J. PARECATTIL, «Third National Convention» 1.

[145] J. PARECATTIL, «Religious in the Indian Context», 2.

[146] J. PARECATTIL, «Religious in the Indian Context», 3.

[147] J. PARECATTIL, «Religious in the Indian Context», 2-3.

[148] J. PARECATTIL, «Third National Convention», 2; ID., «Religious in the Indian Context», 3.

[149] J. PARECATTIL, «Indian Cultural Heritage», 1.

[150] J. PARECATTIL, «Thirty Years of C.B.C.I», 28; ID., «Priest for Tomorrow's India», 6.

[151] J. PARECATTIL, «Religious in the Indian Context», 4.

3. Bread and Wine: As Symbols of Human Labour

Since all the activities of Christians are centred on Eucharist, their work itself is oriented towards this sacrament:

> It is true that the Christian, like other men, must work to earn his daily bread, to sustain his family and to secure the material basis of the good life [...] Men can bring their offerings to God, including all the labours of their hands. This profound mystery is given sacramental expression in the Church's central act of worship, the holy Eucharist[152].

Parecattil often reminded his people that in the Eucharistic sacrifice the fruits of human labour, bread and wine, are brought forward and offered to God as symbols of all their activity. Through this offering of the Church, God gives back to the followers of his Son the very gifts they have brought to him once they have become the sacred body and blood of their Redeemer. Parecattil thus linked the Eucharist to human work: «In the Eucharist, then, is enshrined the whole mystery of man's labour as well as the whole drama of man's redemption»[153]. In his view the Eucharist is the perfect symbol of the wholeness of Christian life, the unity of work and worship — the marvellous and inextricable link that exists between the bread that is won by the sweat of one's brow and the bread of life that comes down from heaven[154]. For any kind of work, whether manual or intellectual, the strength to fulfil it responsibly comes from the Eucharist[155]. Moreover, all forms of work should provide Christians a holy satisfaction[156]. Therefore, Parecattil instructed his people to offer to the Lord, along with the bread and wine, all the efforts of their work in the Eucharist[157].

Parecattil maintained that, since every work has its own dignity, it is not proper to disregard one:

> It is sometimes said that the Bible teaches that work is a curse laid upon the human race as a punishment for disobedience, for we read, «In the sweat of thy face shalt thou eat bread» (Gen 3, 19). The book of Genesis does not in fact teach that work is a curse. In the story of creation man is put into the world to

---

[152] J. PARECATTIL, «Catholic Workers' Association», 4.
[153] J. PARECATTIL, «Catholic Workers' Association», 4.
[154] J. PARECATTIL, «Catholic Workers' Association», 4.
[155] J. PARECATTIL, *Letters to Sisters*, 168.
[156] J. PARECATTIL, *Letters to Sisters*, 200.
[157] J. PARECATTIL, *Letters to Priests*, 51.

be a worker. Before he is fallen from grace, he is placed in the Garden «to till it and to keep it» (Gen 2, 15)[158].

Parecattil was of opinion that Bible in fact never speaks of work as degrading, because it is the will of God for human beings[159]. He pointed out that it is of great significance for Christians that the Redeemer of the world came in the person of a village workman[160]. The incarnation, the divine penetration of human existence, would be carried out through the life and work of Jesus of Nazareth[161]. Furthermore, Christians should never forget the words of Jesus: «Insofar as you did this to the least of my brethren, you did it to me. Insofar as you disowned the least of my brethren, you disowned me» (Mt 25, 40-45). Parecattil thought the main reason why the Church promote the social welfare of the people is to continue the mission of Jesus who desired to transform the divided world into a brotherly unity. The Spirit of Christ disturbs the consciences of the rich for the atrocities they commit, consciously or unconsciously against millions of poor people[162]. The purpose of the Church's involvement in social betterment is a response to the presence of the divine Spirit, who transforms this world into a more peaceful and habitable place for the children of God[163].

Parecattil urged Indian Christians to engage themselves in society by upholding the priority of moral and spiritual principles:

> So a positive remedy (to the problems of India) that I have to suggest, apart form economic and political measures [...] is a return to the source of all happiness, of all justice, truth, honesty and love of God and the due appreciation of spiritual and moral values which we must try to inculcate into the minds of children at the school level[164].

The basic solution for all the ills affecting modern India, according to Parecattil, is a return to the values of that Supreme Power who ordains human affairs and guides the destinies of nations. God alone is the final judge meting out rewards or punishments according to the deeds of

---

[158] J. PARECATTIL, «Catholic Workers' Association», 2.

[159] J. PARECATTIL, «Catholic Workers' Association», 2-3.

[160] J. PARECATTIL, «Catholic Workers' Association», 3.

[161] J. PARECATTIL, «Priest for Tomorrow's India», 8.

[162] J. PARECATTIL, «The Catholic Church», 4.

[163] J. PARECATTIL, «The Catholic Church», 9.

[164] J. PARECATTIL, «Spiritual and Moral Renewal», 5.

individuals and groups[165]. Parecattil reminded Indian Christians that the pursuit of both money and sensual satisfaction must be regulated and controlled by the precept of *dharma* or justice[166]. To be made up of blind worshippers at the altar of the goddess either of wealth or of sex means to be a country heading towards ruin[167]. Parecattil thought that the economic planners of modern India are often in danger of putting the economic cart before the moral horse. Since there are certain things which may be economically feasible but morally undesirable, the right decisions in such cases can be made only by those who have an equal concern for material welfare and spiritual values[168].

In his attempt to foster moral and spiritual principles, Parecattil concentrated his attention on medical care, inspired by the intelligence and compassion of the good Samaritan:

> The parable of the good Samaritan is applicable [...] to those working in the medical field [...] Coupled with breadth of vision — a quality of the head, the Samaritan was outstanding also in compassion — a quality of the heart. He has the capacity to share another's grief and feel another's pain[169].

Parecattil perceived three apparent reasons which prompted the protagonist of the parable to act the way he did. The first was empathy: the projection of one's own feeling into another being. When the Samaritan saw a fellow being lying there on the wayside, he did not merely observe him but rather became part of him[170]. The second was courage: those who passed by the wounded man were afraid of anything unusual or challenging; they were scared away by the fear of getting involved, as many people usually are, when they come across a victim of a road accident. The Samaritan, pushing aside these fears, courageously translated his concern into action[171]. The third reason must have been his regular habit of helping others. This instance certainly was not his first act of kindness. He must have trained himself for years to respond affirmatively to other's needs[172]. Parecattil instructed the Christians to be of the service to others like the good

---

[165] J. PARECATTIL, «Spiritual and Moral Renewal», 1.

[166] J. PARECATTIL, «Over-population», 3; ID., «The Well-being of Christian Families», 4.

[167] J. PARECATTIL, «Spiritual and Moral Renewal», 3.

[168] J. PARECATTIL, «Seminar on Education», 4.

[169] J. PARECATTIL, «Practice Brotherhood», 2.

[170] J. PARECATTIL, «Practice Brotherhood», 2.

[171] J. PARECATTIL, «Practice Brotherhood», 2.

[172] J. PARECATTIL, «Practice Brotherhood», 2.

Samaritan by a kind word, a sympathetic look, an understanding attitude and a readiness to extend a helping hand. These efforts bring cheerfulness into the hearts of the suffering, and hope to their troubled spirits[173].

Parecattil who was particularly concerned with leprosy patients whom he regarded as the neglected section of society and in need of deserved sympathy, help and support:

> It is gratifying for me that our archdiocese turned its attention to leprosy relief as early as 1942 establishing a leper asylum at Green Gardens, Shertallai, which now affords shelter and protection to nearly 200 patients. Of late, that institution has added a new dimension to its activities through a mobile dispensary, making medical aid easily available to leper-patients in the surrounding areas and helping the detection and treatment of the disease at an early stage[174].

Parecattil who was well aware that in India leprosy was the deadly disease which should have top priority in official and voluntary circles[175]. Only through preventive methods can India eventually succeed in stamping out the disease and saving future generations from contagion[176]. Parecattil pointed to the statistics from Europe where the incidence of the malady was far from being at a low ebb until recent years[177]. In this context, Parecattil appreciated the great services done to humanity by medical doctors and nurses. Addressing a conference of Indian nurses, he said: «The nurse stands at the bedside of a patient as an angel of peace and consolation, breathing hope and trust in the midst of the encircling gloom. Next to the doctor, she is the beacon of light to one beset with physical and mental suffering»[178]. According to Parecattil, serving the sick is more of a profession; it is a divine call to the mission of saving lives and helping suffering brothers: «In the degree in which we help others, wipe their tears, lighten their burdens, heighten their joys and brighten their lives, we will be able to hear the rewarding words from the Divine Master, "Well done, good and faithful servant"»[179]. Parecattil appreciated the role which the Church rendered to Indian society especially in the field of caring the sick and the dying after

---

[173] J. PARECATTIL, *Letters to Sisters*, 159.
[174] J. PARECATTIL, «Refresher Course», 1.
[175] J. PARECATTIL, «Nursing Profession», 3.
[176] J. PARECATTIL, «Refresher Course», 1.
[177] J. PARECATTIL, «Refresher Course», 1.
[178] J. PARECATTIL, «Nursing Profession», 1-2; ID., *Letters to Sisters*, 197.
[179] J. PARECATTIL, «Nursing Profession», 3.

the example of Jesus who looked at them with mercy (Mt 11, 4-6; Lk 5, 31)[180].

While treating any physical illness, medical personnel were encouraged by Parecattil not to neglect the need of mental and spiritual cure which belongs to integral healing:

> Man being composed of body and soul, these two elements have their mutual repercussion, Physical illness may cause mental illness, and vice versa. What we call psychosomatic diseases have their roots in some mental disorders. Inner conflicts, psychological tensions and depressing thoughts adversely affect bodily functions[181].

Parecattil was of opinion that a complete cure of the physical disease of patients demanded that their mental and spiritual problems also have to be first attended to; and conversely, in order to restore the mental health of patients, their physical well-being has necessarily to be looked after[182]. Mental disorders often arise from guilty consciences and from the loss of spiritual equilibrium[183]. In this connection Parecattil said «We speak of saving lives; but surgery and medicine simply postpone the inevitable. Man has in his heart a vacuum which only God can fill. Real savings of life comes about when we help men and women fill that vacuum, so that they may find happiness in this life and in eternity»[184]. Hence, Parecattil urged that those who suffer physical ailments be advised to make their peace with God by sincere repentance and fervent prayer[185]. Apart from the divine help that prayer brings, a change in the mental attitude of patients effected through this means, and the restoration of their physical health is aided.[186] He thus requested the people to make a «Prayer of the Faithful» at the daily Mass for the sick and dying of the parish[187].

Education was another field of Christian social action which Parecattil analyzed in terms of the democratic character of India:

> The kind of education that befits an aristocratic society is easy to define. It is the education of the elite by an elite for an elite. This, however, is a thing of

---

[180] J. PARECATTIL, <«Day of the Sick»>, 342-343; ID., «Religious Values», 7; ID., «Objective History», 97; ID., «Religious in the Indian Context», 2.

[181] J. PARECATTIL, «The Role of Confession», 348.

[182] J. PARECATTIL, «The Role of Confession», 350.

[183] J. PARECATTIL, «Day of the Sick», 346.

[184] J. PARECATTIL, «Nursing Profession», 3.

[185] J. PARECATTIL, «The Role of Confession», 350.

[186] J. PARECATTIL, «The Role of Confession», 353.

[187] J. PARECATTIL, <«Day of the Sick»>, 347.

the past. In a democratic society the system of education has naturally to follow the democratic pattern. What we need is a democracy in education of the whole people[188].

Parecattil was convinced that thorough re-thinking of the Christian educational apostolate in India was necessary so as to adjust it to the chief need of the time, that is to say, that it has to reach the ordinary people of the country. A democracy must ensure the formation even of the unfit because education is a primary right of every citizen[189]; however, in doing so, it must not prevent the best students from developing their skills for the greater benefit of all[190]. Moreover, Parecattil pointed out that, since education shapes the attitude and character of the people and sharpens their skills, it thus plays a decisive role in the economic growth and development of societies[191]. Yet, education today is not meant simply to train individuals to take their place in society as it exists; it must promote the overall good of the country[192] with an emphasis on national integration[193]. For this reason he stated that Catholic institutions, in order to be relevant must not be afraid of striking out on new paths which meet the problems of the people[194].

In Parecattil's view, over-population was indeed a major problem in India. However, he was against introducing artificial devices to control the population. Instead, he advocated natural family planning methods, because they are faithful to moral and spiritual values:

> To my mind, what is most important is to revitalise our spiritual outlook, deepen our faith in God, enliven our awareness in the eschatological dimension of life and rekindle our hope in the reward that God will accord to His faithful followers. Earthly life is a passing phenomenon, and eternal life is our cherished goal. Created things should help us to achieve that goal instead of putting obstacles on the way. There is the need of realizing the supremacy of spiritual values over material comforts and passing pleasures. Unless these ideas are driven home to the minds of men, any amount of programmes, including

---

[188] J. PARECATTIL, «Social Institute», 2.

[189] J. PARECATTIL, «Education», 2.

[190] J. PARECATTIL, «Thirty Years of C.B.C.I», 30; ID., «Social Institute», 2-3.

[191] J. PARECATTIL, «Seminar on Education», 2.

[192] J. PARECATTIL, *Letters to Sisters*, 123.

[193] J. PARECATTIL, «National Integration», 4.

[194] J. PARECATTIL, «The Role of Women», 3; ID., *Letter to Sisters*, 131.

Natural Family Planning which demands a good measure of self control from the couples, will not solve the problems with which we are faced[195].

Since Parecattil was perturbed to learn that in Kerala the rate of abortion was increasing, he made the following public appeal: «It is our duty to raise our voices in defence of the millions of innocent human beings whose lives are thus nipped in the bud, and that too in *Arshabhāratha*, wedded to the principles of *Sathyam* and *Ahimsā*».[196] Parecattil pointed out that, while voluntary sterilisation itself is dehumanising, compulsory sterilisation is much more so. Furthermore, to provide the incentive of material gifts in order to make the programme acceptable to poor people is an exploitation of their plight[197]. Abortion as a way of limiting the number of children should at once be ruled out, since it goes against God's command, «Thou shalt not kill». If human life is sacred at every stage, the unborn child is all the more to be respected, because it is the life of an innocent and defenceless[198]. On this point, Parecattil was quite adamant: «Abortion can never be considered a means of family planning. Its malice is much more serious than that of artificial methods of birth prevention»[199].

All the same, agreed that over-population is a serious problem confronting India while condemned methods of birth-control that are artificial and thus debase to human dignity, Parecattil did state that those within the framework of the natural and positive laws given by God are permissable[200]. However, he thought that problems arising out of over-population can be remedied by an all-out effort to attain self-sufficiency in food and in the other necessities of life[201]. Even natural family planning is not going to succeed in India, unless the people set great store by the ultimate values of life. He firmly held that this would be much easier for Christians who, besides being illumined by natural reason and guided by the noble examples of innumerable sages and saints, have access to the supernatural means of Holy Mass and the other sacraments[202].

---

[195] J. PARECATTIL, «Family Problems», 33.

[196] J. PARECATTIL, «Family Problems», 32; ID., <«Sanctification of Christian Families»>, 116.

[197] J. PARECATTIL, «Family Problems», 33; ID., <«Sanctification of Christian Families»>, 117.

[198] J. PARECATTIL, <«Sanctification of Christian Families»>, 117.

[199] J. PARECATTIL, «Over-population», 2; ID., «<Christ is the Light»>, 363.

[200] J. PARECATTIL, «Family Problems», 33; ID., «Family Planning», 1; ID., *Letter to Sisters*, 156.

[201] J. PARECATTIL, «Family Problems», 33.

[202] J. PARECATTIL, «Over-population», 3.

With regard to giving voice to the moral concerns of the Syro-Malabar Church and partaking in its social apostolate, Joseph Cardinal Parecattil did not deem it right to motivate his people chiefly by means of convincing references to philosophical principles, Scriptural texts and magisterial teaching. Instead, he judged a Eucharistic motivation to be more conatural to their religious experience, more appropriate in their economic environment, and more credible to their Hindu countrymen. In an article entitled «The Mission of Christ», Parecattil reveals that his preference for a Eucharistic motivation to social action was not only based on Catholic sacramental theology, but also on Hindu religious sentiment: «Gandhi once said that God comes to the poor today in the form of bread»[203]. The fact that Parecattil quotes this astounding saying certainly does not mean that for him the mysterious goodness and mercy of God should be reduced, in the eyes of the poor, to a piece of bread which keeps them from starving.

But the use of the quote does indicate his conviction concerning the relationship between orthodoxy and orthopraxy in Catholic Eucharistic devotion. In his vision, the Church must serve its members not only as a centre of liturgical worship, but also as one of social relief for the under-privileged, the poor and the suffering[204]. Parecattil noted that one of the most impressive features of the Church in the post-conciliar period is its mounting concern for the down-trodden through social work carried out by lay people, religious and priests.[205] Such attitudes and activities, if properly motivated and orientated, will lead many Indians to the God of Jesus Christ[206]. The phrase «if properly motivated and oriented» can be interpreted to mean «if based on true Eucharistic faith and oriented to the practice of justice and love». For, Parecattil believed that, in the light of the many problems of India, an essential requisite to ensure communal harmony among all sections of the people is to do justice to everyone, especially to the underprivileged through truth and love[207]. Radical openness to others, genuine concern for others and sincere love alone can bring about peace in our midst[208]. Where do these traits of openness, concern and love spring from, according to Parecattil? And how would he say that they are to be kept vital in the minds and hearts of Indian Christians? From all that has

---

[203] J. PARECATTIL, «The Mission of Christ», 303.

[204] J. PARECATTIL, «Cultural Adaptation», 3-4; ID., «Religious Values», 3.

[205] J. PARECATTIL, «Objective History», 96.

[206] J. PARECATTIL, «Religious Values», 7.

[207] J. PARECATTIL, «The Catholic Church and the Problem of World Peace», 2-3; ID., «Spiritual and Moral Renewal», 4-5.

[208] J. PARECATTIL, «The Catholic Church and the Problem of World Peace», 2.

been stated in the expository chapters of this study, his answer would undoubtedly be that they spring from the self-giving of the Eucharistic Christ, and that they are kept vital by the Holy Spirit acting through Eucharistic grace.

The chapter has analyzed the Eucharistic theology of Cardinal Parecattil in the second phase of the post-Vatican II period. His main contribution to Syro-Malabar Eucharistic theology was undoubtedly the Indian Mass, which introduced what he considered acceptable elements of Hindu theology and culture. At the same time, he played a significant role in other liturgical reforms as well. With regard to spirituality, he advocated a Hindu-Christian synthesis based on a profound appreciation of the importance of Hinduism in the economy of salvation. As the followers of a natural religion, Hindus search for God constantly, and are called to find in Christ the fulfilment of their quest. In his view, rigid interpretations of the teaching that there is no salvation outside the Catholic Church needed to be re-formulated. With regard to the social apostolate, he thought that all human labour is sanctified by the Eucharist, in which it is included by means of the symbols of bread and wine. Christians should engage in different kinds of humanitarian activities, such as medical care and education, so as to be signs of God's presence there. In order to control the over-population of India, Parecattil promoted natural family planning and improvement of living conditions rather than artificial methods. In order to find continual moral energy to achieve this social betterment, Parecattil urged Christians not only to know and venerate the Eucharistic Christ, but also to grasp and imitate his generosity in sharing bread with the needy for whom God is distant when no one places nourishment in their hands.

PART THREE

A CRITICAL EVALUATION
OF THE EUCHARISTIC THEOLOGY
OF JOSEPH PARECATTIL

The Eucharistic Theology of Joseph Parecattil
as an Inspiration and a Challenge
to the Syro-Malabar Church

This Chapter critically evaluates the strengths and limits of the Eucharistic theology of Joseph Parecattil. At first it points to the merits of his Eucharistic thought. Thereafter, the limits of his study are sketched out, and some means are proposed to overcome them so as to enhance the merits. While doing so, one finds that his contribution to the Eucharistic theology of the Syro-Malabar Church is indeed both substantial and lasting. His primary concern was to reform the Indian Oriental Church in the light of the Vatican II documents. He influenced the liturgical, spiritual and apostolic life of Christians by means of this renewal. He developed his Eucharistic thought by showing the close connection of these three areas of Christian life.

However, the Eucharistic theology of Joseph Parecattil is marked by some limitations, since he left out some of the important dimensions indicated by Vatican II. The eschatological significance of the sacrament is hardly touched. The Eucharist as the pledge of the future glory of Christians needed to be included in his theology, especially in order to underscore the connection between the heavenly and earthly liturgies. Moreover, when treating Eucharistic grace, he emphasized the personal sanctification of Christian individuals, rather than that of the Church as a whole. Parecattil rightly claimed that the Eucharist is the driving force for the social work of the Church. But he did not explore sufficiently the relationship between the real presence of Christ in the Eucharistic elements and his social presence in the poor.

1. Positive Aspects: A Faithful Interpretation of Catholic Eucharistic Theology in the Syro-Malabar Church

This section of the chapter delineates the achievements of Joseph Parecattil. As this study has already pointed out, his merit lies in the earnest attempt to develop a Eucharistic theology for the Syro-Malabar Church. His contribution to the Eucharistic theology of the Indian Church can be summarized in the following three sub-divisions.

1.1 *The Unique Sacrifice of the Eucharistic Christ, the Personal Sacrifice of Indian Christians, and the Spirit of Sacrifice in Hinduism*

It is the merit of Parecattil that, while formulating the Eucharistic theology of the Syro-Malabar Church, he affirmed the uniqueness of the sacrifice of Christ in this sacrament. At the same time, he underlined the active role of the faithful in joining their personal sacrifice to the sacramental self-offering of Christ. Moreover, he tried to comprehend the Hindu spirit of sacrifice, and integrate it into the Christian sense of offering.

Joseph Parecattil maintained that all the assembled participants have an active role in the Eucharistic liturgy. They celebrate Mass as those who share in the common form of Christian priesthood. A valid reception of Baptism confers on Christians the sacerdotal office through the pneumatic imprinting of the seal of Christ[1]. The baptized, by this anointing of the Holy Spirit, are consecrated to a Royal Priesthood[2]. Parecattil was also convinced that through Baptism Christians become the active members of the mystical body of Christ. This incorporation into the Church confers upon the faithful the right to participate in the Christian cult, especially at the Eucharistic liturgy[3], because the People of God gather together so that they may offer a living sacrifice, acceptable to God (Rom 12, 1)[4].

In the liturgical context of the Eucharist, Parecattil dealt with the uniqueness of the sacrifice of Christ. He believed that the Mass is the effective memorial of the death and resurrection of Christ[5]. Parecattil brought together the three dimensions — past, present and future — of the

---

[1] L. OTT, *Fundamentals of Catholic Dogma*, 309.

[2] LG 4.

[3] L. OTT, *Fundamentals of Catholic Dogma*, 310.

[4] PO 2.

[5] E. LUSSIER, *The Eucharist*, 140.144; L.C. HAY, *Eucharist, A Thanksgiving*, 69.

sacrifice of Christ[6]. In the Eucharist, the memorial is not simply a symbolic representation; it is the making present of the very reality of the self-offering of Christ here and now[7].

Parecattil viewed the Eucharist as the offering of Christ the High Priest after the order of Melchizedek, and thus as the fulfilment of the prophecy articulated in Psalm 110: «You are a priest forever, after the order of Melchizedek» (v. 4; Cf. Gen 14, 18; Ps 110 [109] 4; Heb 7, 11)[8]. He considered Christ's sacrifice as a unique one which was offered in complete submission to the will of the Father, and which went to the extent of dying on the Cross (Ph 2, 8; Lk 23, 46)[9].

Parecattil established a logical connection between the Last Supper, the Cross and the Eucharist. He held that the immolation on the Cross was pre-figured at the Last Supper, and that both are re-presented on the altar. He faithfully followed the positions of Thomas Aquinas and the Council of Trent,[10] stating that the reality of what takes place in the celebration of the Eucharist is inextricably bound to the event of the Last Supper, in which the Church has always claimed that the institution of the Eucharist took place[11]. Again, given the background of the Last Supper, Parecattil considered the Eucharist as a Meal[12]. At the same time he maintained that the Last supper was a pre-figuration of the Cross[13]. Thus, he insisted that the concepts of sacrifice and meal are complementary[14].

After establishing the uniqueness of the Eucharistic sacrifice, Parecattil turned to the personal sacrifice of the Christians in the context of the Syro-Malabar Church. He stated that in the Mass the faithful offer themselves together with the sacramental sacrifice of their Lord; they offer Christ, the

---

[6] ND 1583; E. KILMARTIN, *Christian Liturgy*, 338; L.C. HAY, *Eucharist, A Thanksgiving*, 67; M.B. PENNINGTON, *The Eucharist Yesterday and Today*, 41; M. THURIAN, *The Mystery of the Eucharist*, 14; B. HÄRING, *The New Covenant*, 151.

[7] M.B. PENNINGTON, *The Eucharist Yesterday and Today*, 40; M. THURIAN, *The Mystery of the Eucharist*, 18; D.N. POWER, *The Eucharistic Mystery*, 304.

[8] ND 1546; DS 1739; H.F.G. SWANSTON, *The Community Witness*, 163.

[9] E. SCHILLEBEECKX, *Christ the Sacrament*, 28.

[10] *Summa Theologiae*, III, 73, 5; ND 1514; DS 1637.

[11] J.M. POWERS, *Eucharistic Theology*, 48.

[12] B. HÄRING, *The New Covenant*, 130; M. THURIAN, *The Mystery of the Eucharist*, 13; H.F.G. SWANSTON, *The Community Witness*, 72-73; J.M. POWERS, *Eucharistic Theology*, 56.

[13] Cf. ND 1566; DS 3848.

[14] H.F.G. SWANSTON, *The Community Witness*, 76; E. SCHILLEBEECKX, *The Eucharist*, 127; ID., *Christ the Sacrament*, 21.

divine victim, to the Father, and themselves along with him[15]. They do
what Christ did by offering themselves to the Father in order to obtain the
benefits of their salvation[16]. Parecattil maintained that the celebration
denotes the Christian self-offering to the Father expressed in the symbolical
offering of the Eucharistic gifts of bread and wine[17]. Thus, Christians are
to make their offering of self totally from the heart[18]. What the faithful
live out daily is what they bring to the altar to be transformed by God[19].
They celebrate the unique sacrifice of Christ with a reverent and contrite
heart so as to atone for their own sins and those of the world[20]. Thus,
Parecattil thought that, by celebrating the Eucharist, the Syro-Malabar
Christians join themselves to the sacrifice of Christ to the Father.

Although Parecattil did not deal directly with the notion of sacrifice in
Hinduism — especially the difficulties Hindus have to accept the vicarious
sufferings of Christ — he linked the Christian liturgy to many Indian
spiritual elements. He firmly believed that, in order to facilitate the active
participation of the faithful, it was necessary to reform the Eucharistic
liturgy of the Syro-Malabar Church. He highlighted the teachings of Vatican
II especially re-garding the principles of restoration, revision and adaptation.
His principal contribution was in incorporating cultural elements into the
Eucharistic liturgy; the concrete shape of this renewal was the publication
of the «Indian Mass» (Bhāratiya pūjā) in 1973. Here, Parecattil's intention
was to make the Syro-Malabar Church «Hindu in Culture, Christian in
Religion and Indian in Liturgy». He believed that, if a cultural integration
was not effected in the liturgy, the future of Christianity in India would not
be assured. Thus, his idea was to make the Syro-Malabar Eucharistic liturgy
fully Indian by countering the foreign elements dominant in the Chaldean
liturgy.

Parecattil knew that this was to be achieved by inculturation which entails
a «vital contact and exchange between the Church and different cultures»[21]. He understood that it is a process of dialogue between experience

---

[15] LG 11.

[16] E. KILMARTIN, Christian Liturgy, 338-339.

[17] E. KILMARTIN, Christian Liturgy, 339; M.B. PENNINGTON, The Eucharist Yesterday
and Today, 34.

[18] E. LUSSIER, The Eucharist, 115; L.C. HAY, Eucharist, A Thanksgiving, 82.

[19] P. BERNIER, Eucharist: Celebrating its Rhythms, 21-22.

[20] B. HÄRING, The New Covenant, 132-13.

[21] GS 44; A.R. Crollius marks three stages of inculturation: 1) Translation: the Church
comes across new cultures and preaches the Gospel with minor cultural adaptation; 2)
Assimilation: the missionaries and the local Christians assimilate elements from each
other's culture; 3) Transformation: local culture is transformed through a re-orientation

and faith in which the latter expresses itself through elements of a new culture[22]. Inculturation means the integration, on the part of the Church, of native cultural values, insofar as they are relevant to making the Gospel intelligible to those living in a concrete reality[23]. In his view, this indigenization presupposes a humanly prudent and theologically sound adjustment of Christian teaching and ritual to the living local culture, in order to present the Church as the universal sacrament of salvation[24].

Parecattil considered the theology of the incarnation as the supportive principle for inculturation, and stated that, if Jesus were to have been born in India, he would have been fully Indian[25]. Moreover, according to him, liturgical adaptation has a strong basis in the theology of the local Church[26]. The rootedness of a Church in the native soil is normally manifested in the development of an indigenous Christian praxis, expressed in a particular worship pattern and in a proper discipline and structure[27].

Parecattil considered that, if the Christian faith is well expressed in local cultural idioms, the whole Church is benefited. He was encouraged by the position of Vatican II which states: «[...] anything in their way of life that is not indissolubly bound up with superstition and error she studies with sympathy and if possible, preserves intact»[28]. Parecattil believed that, in the context of the Syro-Malabar Church, the Indian cultural elements are to be corrected and perfected by being incorporated into the Christian tradition[29]. He strongly advocated that the cultural forms that do not go contrary to the fundamentals of the faith of the Church should be integrated into the liturgy[30]. In inculturation, therefore, the Church and cultures are mutually enriched and transformed[31]. Moreover, Parecattil held that

---

of it. The entire process of inculturation thus is one of integration of the Christian faith and life in a given culture and the integration of a new expression of the Christian experience in the life of the universal Church (Cf. A.R. CROLLIUS, *What is So New about Inculturation?*, 14).

[22] Y. CONGAR, «The Role of the Church», 220-221.

[23] D.S. AMALORPAVADASS, *Efforts Made*, 15.

[24] L.J. LUZBETAK, *The Church and Cultures*, 347.

[25] D.S. AMALORPAVADASS, «Theological Bases», 5.

[26] EN 20; A.R. CROLLIUS, *What is so New About Inculturation?*, 16-16; A. SHORTER, *Toward a Theology of Inculturation*, 5; S. ELAVATHINKAL, *Inculturation and Christian Art*, 239.

[27] A.M. MUNDADAN, «Emergence of the Missionary Consciousness», 34.

[28] SC 37

[29] AG 9; D.S. AMALORPAVADASS, *Theological Bases*, 6.

[30] L.J. LUZBETAK, *The Church and Cultures*, 349.

[31] A. SHORTER, *African Christian Theology*, 145.

liturgical adaptation should not remain only on the level of externals. According to him, this process should touch the spirit of the liturgy. In his view, the Syro-Malabar Eucharistic liturgy should absorb the philosophical categories and theological thought-patterns of India. Thus, true inculturation is not a matter of external adaptation, for it concerns the transformation of authentic cultural values through their integration into Christianity[32]. Thus, Parecattil interwove in his Eucharistic treatise the uniqueness of the sacrifice of Christ, the active personal offering of the faithful, and the inclusion of appropriate elements of Hindu culture.

1.2 *The Universal Love of the Eucharistic Christ, the Interior Sanctification of Indian Christians, and the Search for Holiness in Hinduism*

The Eucharist is the self-gift of Christ to humankind, his love for the world expressed by his real presence in the consecrated elements. As a sign of love, he imparts his grace to all who approach him in this sacrament. Parecattil considered the Eucharist as the primary source of grace for Christian life, since it is the memorial of the death and resurrection of the Lord. The Eucharist gives spiritual nourishment by causing a loving union between Christ and the faithful[33]. He followed the teachings of the Vatican II which describe the Eucharist as «the summit toward which the activity of the Church is directed, and as the source from which all her powers flow»[34]. All the other sacraments, and all ecclesiastical ministries and works of the apostolate, are bound up with the Eucharist and are directed towards it[35]. He held that, through the Eucharistic presence of Christ in the world, the new covenant announced by Jeremiah as an interiorization of religion (Jer 31, 31-34) and by Ezekiel as a new heart created by the Spirit of God (Ezk 36, 26-27) is effected in the world. The interior force and efficacy of the new covenant manifest themselves in the exterior acts of love which Christians do for one another[36].

Parecattil explained the Eucharist as the source of sanctification for all Christians. He stated that Jesus provides his life to the people as a spiritual nourishment so that they may be transformed into himself. The primary effect of receiving the Eucharist is that it fosters a life of union with God

---

[32] RM 52.

[33] *Summa Theologiae*, III, 79, 6.

[34] SC 10; LG 11; Eu. M 58.

[35] PO 5; H.F.G. SWANSTON, *The Community Witness*, 162; M.B. PENNINGTON, *The Eucharist Yesterday and Today*, 2.

[36] E. SCHILLEBEECKX, *Christ the Sacrament*, 17.

through Christ: «He who eats my flesh and drinks my blood, lives in me and I live in him. As I who am sent by the living Father, myself draw life from the Father, so also whoever eats me will draw life from me» (Jn 6, 56-57). Parecattil also maintained that the Eucharist grants spiritual satisfaction according to the devotion «of the offerers», and «of those for whom the sacrifice is offered»[37].

Parecattil often affirmed that the effects of Eucharistic grace should be perceived by others in the daily life of the faithful. What they have received in the celebration of the Eucharist should leave its mark on their way of life[38]. The Eucharist redeems and sanctifies the daily existence of the faithful with all its joys and sorrows[39]; in the Eucharist, Christians accept their share in the death and resurrection of Christ[40].

Parecattil noted that Jesus died for the sins of humankind, and that the Eucharist thus communicates divine forgiveness. He maintained that, through Eucharistic grace, the Christians have an antidote against sin[41], since the sacrament is the «covenant in the blood of Christ», a sacrifice making atonement for sins[42]. He believed that the power of the Eucharist to forgive sins stems from its nature as the sacramental memorial of Christ's redemptive act[43].

Parecattil also claimed that the Eucharistic sacrifice implores God to accomplish the sanctification of believers until the return of Christ, and to grant liberation to all who do not know him as yet[44]. The non-Christians are peo-ple in whom God is interested, because he extends salvation to all, and ena-bles them to respond either by acknowledging him as the Creator, or by searching for him in shadows and images (Act 17, 25-28; 1Tim 2, 4)[45]. Following Vatican II, Parecattil held that those who without fault on their part do not know the Gospel of Christ and his Church, but seek God with a sincere heart through the promptings of their conscience attain salvat-ion[46]. Therefore, Parecattil desired that Christians acknowledge with respect the spiritual and moral values of various non-Christian religions, and

---

[37] *Summa Theologiae*, III, 79, 5.

[38] SC 9-10; GS 38; Eu. M 13.

[39] SC 9-10; Eu. M 13; E. LUSSIER, *The Eucharist*, 140.

[40] E. LUSSIER, *The Eucharist*, 173.

[41] E. SCHILLEBEECKX, *Christ the Sacrament*, 182; E. LUSSIER, *The Eucharist*, 189.

[42] B. HÄRING, *The New Covenant*, 130.

[43] L.C. HAY, *Eucharist, A Thanksgiving*, 87.

[44] M. THURIAN, *The Mystery of the Eucharist*, 25.

[45] LG 16.

[46] LG 16; R. PANIKKAR, *The Unknown Christ*, 5.

join with them in promoting and defending common ideals[47]. The non-Christian religions which come under the cosmic covenant, or that made with Noah, are still means of salvation; they are «real although essentially incomplete», and they fulfil a mediatory role in relation to Jesus Christ[48]. Parecattil affirmed that God wills that all human beings to be saved and he gives all people this possibility by offering them graces through different religions[49]. Hence, Hinduism also has a place in the universal saving plan of God[50]. For, the followers of this religion, according to Parecattil, are «anonymous Christians» and not non-Christians[51]. Moreover, he presented Christ as the real goal of Hinduism since his grace is present in this religion[52].

Parecattil was convinced that Christianity must show great respect towards Hinduism as the Indian religion that has manifested great appreciation for Christ's teaching. He felt the need for a mature dialogue with Hinduism, which must be undertaken with an attitude of mutual understanding, avoiding all aggressiveness and sense of superiority[53]. Here, his views are perfectly in line with Vatican II: «[...] Through dialogue and collaboration with the followers of other religions, and in witness to the Christian faith and life, Christians acknowledge, preserve and promote the spiritual and moral good, as well as the socio-cultural values found among them»[54].

---

[47] ABHISHIKTANANDA, «The Depth-Dimension», 215.

[48] J. DUPUIS, *Jesus Christ*, 140; R. PANIKKAR, *The Unknown Christ*, 24; D.S. AMALORPAVADASS, *Theological Bases*, 6.

[49] Rahner says: «If however, man can always have a positive saving relationship to God, and if he always had to have it then he has always had it within that religion which in practice was at his disposal by being a factor in his sphere of existence» (Cf. K. RAHNER, «Christianity and the Non-Christian Religions», 128).

[50] R. PANIKKAR, *The Unknown Christ*, 54.

[51] K. RAHNER, «Christianity and the Non-Christian Religions», 131.

[52] R. PANIKKAR, *The Unknown Christ*, ix.

[53] E. SCHILLEBEECKX, *God the Future of Man*, 122. He adds: «It would be misleading to regard dialogue as possible only because, and insofar as the Church can recognize something of herself in others — in other words, insofar as she can interpret others as "implicit" Christians and thus, in the final analysis, not allow others to be other, but secure them in advance for Christianity by interpreting their outlook on life as Christian. That would make all dialogue impossible — because, for example, a Buddhist from his point of view can just as well regard a Christian of good will as an "implicit" Buddhist. This does not mean that I wish to deny the reality of what is called "anonymous" Christianity. But it is necessary, if dialogue is to be sincere, for others to be involved in that dialogue precisely as others and therefore precisely as non-Christians» (Cf. *God the Future of Man*, 122).

[54] NA 2; GS 92.

Parecattil believed that a fruitful encounter will lead to a mutual sharing between the two religions. He clearly stated that a sincere dialogue does not demand the sacrifice of one's own religion; instead, by being loyal to one's own religious convictions, one has the opportunity to find a common ground and to learn about those of others[55]. He specified the mutual sharing in the field of spirituality, and pointed out that the Church must treasure the precious insights of other religions, especially the moral values dominating the thoughts of the sages of Hinduism.

Parecattil viewed the Indian practice of *Sannyāsa* as beneficial to Christianity, since it summarizes the Hindu quest for transcendental experience. From the beginning of her history India has admired religious leaders who declared the reality of the unseen world, and led a fervent spiritual life[56]. The aim of human life is God- realization. One realises the unmanifested Supreme Self only by the knowledge of the depths of one's inner self through a life of interiorization and detachment[57]. In order to attain self-realization, one has to reach the level of impersonal, universalized and absolute transcendence. At this stage, the self will be identified with Brahman[58]. Therefore, a *Sannyasi* has to renounce all desire for the world[59], and to abandon all attachment to sensual enjoyments[60]. In short, a *Sannyāsi*'s life is a living symbol of renunciation and poverty[61]. This total renunciation facilitates the attainment of God-realization[62]. Gitā teaches a detachment from everything, even when one actively engages in daily works[63]. A *Sannyāsi*, by leading a life of concentration on Brahman,[64] experiences God in silence and solitude[65]. Meditation is important in order to gain both self-knowledge and God-realization[66].

Parecattil considered that the Indian monastic lifestyle of *Āśram* could be adapted by Christianity. Close contacts should be formed between the Hindu

---

[55] M.M THOMAS, «A Reply», 64; A. PUSPARAJAN, «Prospects of Christian Dialogue», 269; VANDANA, «Dialogue», 326; S.J. SAMARTHA, *Courage for Dialogue*, 43.

[56] S. RADHAKRISHNAN, *Eastern Religions*, 34.

[57] I.C. SHARMA, *Ethical Philosophies*, 87-88.

[58] I.C. SHARMA, *Ethical Philosophies*, 100.

[59] *Brhadāraṇyaka Upaniṣad*, III, 5, 1.

[60] Manu. VI: 38, 49.

[61] D. ACHARUPARAMBIL, «Monasticism in Hindu Tradition», 448.

[62] D.S AMALORPAVADASS, «Poverty of the Religious», 69.

[63] *Bhagavad Gitā* III: 6-7; B. GRIFFITHS, *Christ in India*, 11; J. NEUNER, «Non-Attachment», 99.

[64] Manu, VI: 41-43; *Maitrāyaṇa Upaniṣad*, VI: 34.

[65] A.J. MONCHANIN – H. LE SAUX, *A Benedictine Ashram*, 59.

[66] A. ELENGIMATTAM, *Monasticism*, 131.

and Christian *Āśrams* through short or long visits and exchanges of views. Through the practice of prayer the members of the *Āśrams* try to «enter more deeply into the experience of God and a close union with him[67]. The *Āśrams* provide an atmosphere of Hindu-Christian experiments in liturgy, spirituality and social commitment[68]. By being committed to their own faith and at the same time open to those adhering to other creeds, they seek to form one family on the basis of the truths they share. Thus, by adapting Hindu religious experiences, Parecattil wished to enrich Christian spirituality.

1.3 *The Humanitarian Values of the Eucharistic Christ, the Ethical Life-style of Christians, and the Ideals of Truth and Non-violence in Hinduism*

Joseph Parecattil often stressed the role of the Eucharist in the social actions of Christians. They try to conduct a Eucharistic life in their society, because they are guided by the Christian principle of love of neighbour. In this respect the Hindu ethical principles of truth and non-violence can be of great help to Indian Christians.

Parecattil maintained that the Eucharist instills in Christians the humanitarian values of Christ. According to him, the celebration of the Eucharist induces the Christians to engage in social activities, since these express the Christian love to which all are called in Jesus Christ[69]. Parecattil thought that, if Eucharistic worship is to be authentic, it must make Christians grow in awareness of the dignity of each person as the deepest motive of their apostolic work[70]. He was convinced that the weak, the suffering, the underprivileged and the children, are to be particularly cared for by those who take part in the Eucharistic liturgy[71]. Thus Parecattil stated that the Eucharist involves not only correct doctrine (orthodoxy) but also right action (orthopraxy)[72]. In his view, the celebration of the Eucharist urges the faithful to work for the betterment of the social order in line with the values of the kingdom of God[73]. He believed that, if human dignity is denied to others, there is no real faith in the Eucharistic

---

[67] B. GRIFFITHS, *Christ in India*, 47.

[68] D.S. AMALOPAVADASS, «*Ashram* Aikya», 308.

[69] DC 5; P.J. ROSATO, *Introduzione alla teologia*, 82-83; S. RAYAN, «Asia and Justice», 13.

[70] DC 6; OA 23; LC 68; D.N. POWER, *The Eucharistic Mystery*, 313.

[71] P. BERNIER, *Eucharist: Celebrating its Rhythms*, 48.

[72] L.C. HAY, *Eucharist, A Thanksgiving*, 150.

[73] D. LANE, *Foundations for a Social Theology*, 142; E. LUSSIER, *The Eucharist*, 118.

presence of Christ. The Eucharist must lead Christians to comprehend, and to manifest in action, the primacy and centrality of human beings[74].

Parecattil considered the Eucharistic Lord himself as the model and source for Christian humanitarian activities. Jesus of Nazareth was the friend of the poor (Lk 4, 18; Mt 11, 5). He healed the sick, gave food to the hungry and cured the illnesses of those who came to him with faith. In him, God is revealed as he who saves his creatures from misery, oppression and exploitation[75]. Jesus was born in complete poverty (Lk 2, 7); he had to work for his own bread (Mk 6, 3); he had no stone to lay his head on (Mt 8, 20); he died naked (Jn 19, 23-24)[76] Jesus was moved by the misery of his mankind. In the Sermon of the Mount Jesus urged his disciples to be defenders of the poor and the needy, because in this way they would announce the kingdom of God[77]. Parecattil thought that for Jesus, the salvation of each person ultimately depends on one's attitudes and actions towards the poor[78].

Parecattil held that the Church of today has to continue to do the same work of Jesus who «went about doing good». The example of Jesus inspires the Church to adapt a preferential option for the poor[79]. The Church has, therefore, a vocation to be present at the heart of the world by proclaiming the good news to the poor, freedom to the oppressed, and joy to the afflicted[80]. According to Parecattil, the Church serves the poor through works of charity, relief, defence and liberation[81]. He held that from the Church's Eucharistic liturgy arises the mission of serving human beings in the existential situation of the world[82].

Parecattil specified different areas of social work by which Christians could extend Eucharistic grace. He reminded the people to help the poor with food, clothing, housing, medical assistance and education[83]. The

---

[74] S. RAYAN, *Asia and Justice*, 14.

[75] J. FULLENBACH, *Hermeneutics Marxism*, 73.

[76] J. FULLENBACH, *Hermeneutics Marxism*, 76; P. ARRUPE, *Witnessing to Justice*, 38; J. DESROCHERS, *Christ the Liberator*, 246.

[77] J.J. ALFARO, *Theology of Justice*, 25.

[78] T. PUNNAPADAM, *Justice as Spirituality*, 163.

[79] LG 17; AG 1.

[80] DIM 5.

[81] J. SOBRINO, *Jesus in Latin America*, 138; G.V. LOBO, «Rome Accepts Liberation Theology», 218.

[82] E. SCHILLEBEECKX, *God the Future of Man*, 108; P. BERNIER, *Eucharist: Celebrating its Rhythms*, 26.

[83] AA 8.

Church rightly understands its medical, educational and charitable work as the continuation of Christ's service to the needy of the world[84].

Parecattil advocated that Christians adapt the principles of truth and non-violence, the great ideals of Hinduism put into practice by Gandhi in his religious and socio-political career[85]. The particular motivation of Christians is the similarity between the behaviour of Gandhi and that of Jesus. Thus Parecattil advises Indian Christians to follow the example of Gandhi, and to avoid violence out of love for the Eucharistic Christ. He foresaw that, if India does not abide by these principles, the future of the country will be adversely affected. In his writings Parecattil combines the humanitarian values of Jesus, the social witness of Christians among the weak and the poor and the lofty ideals of Hindu reformers and prophets.

2. An Indication of the Unresolved Issues and a Proposal of Some Means to Overcome Them

The purpose of this section is to point out some aspects of the Eucharistic theology of Vatican II which Joseph Parecattil left unmentioned for the most part, and to propose some insights by which his thought might be made more balanced. Hence these pages of the thesis focuses on three such undeveloped aspects: 1) The eschatological dimension of the Eucharist; 2) The sanctification of the Church through the sacrament; and 3) The analogy between the real presence and social presence of Christ.

2.1 *The Failure to Develop Adequately the Eschatological Dimension of the Eucharist as the Anticipation of the Ultimate Goal of the Spirituality and the Social Involvement of Christians*

The goal of the Christian life as a pilgrimage on the earth is ultimately the attainment of the kingdom. Therefore, the Eucharist as the primary source of energy for the Christian journey in history, has a direct relation to eschatology. The eschatological perspective of the Eucharist is evident in the passages dealing with the Last Supper. Although Parecattil showed the connection between the Last Supper, the Cross and the Eucharist, he did not deal with their eschatological significance. At the Last supper, Jesus said: «Truly, I say to you, I shall not drink again of the fruit of the vine until that day when I drink it new in the kingdom of God» (Mk 14, 25; Mt 26, 29; Lk 2, 18; 22, 16-18; 1Cor 11, 23-25; 6, 26). The Last Supper with the

---

[84] J. DESROCHERS, *Christ the Liberator*, 46.
[85] I. JESUDASAN, *A Gandhian Theology*, 23.

disciples was a symbolic action by which Jesus gave them a share in the eschatological blessings he was to receive. At the last meal Jesus was looking forward, not just to his approaching death, but also to the kingdom of God which would come along with it[86].

In the Eucharistic meal of the Church the faithful receive the eschatological «bread of heaven» that was promised in Psalm 78: «He commanded the skies above, and opened the doors of heaven; and he rained down upon them manna to eat, and gave them the grain of heaven. Men ate of the bread of the angels; he sent them food in abundance» (vv. 23-25). The Eucharist is the manna which gives future life to pilgrims on the way to the kingdom. In the sacrament, the manna points forward to the messianic banquet[87]. By communion in the body and blood of Christ, the faithful come to share in his resurrection and in the gift of eternal life. This share in Christ's glory transforms their human life and gives them hope in times of stress. The full import of this is expressed in Christian faith in the second coming of Christ, the meaning of which it is impossible to express in conceptual terms[88].

Jesus' death on the Cross is the final realization of the central theme he preached, the coming of God's eschatological rule. This death is the form in which the kingdom of God exists under the conditions of this age — glory in powerlessness, wealth in poverty, love in desolation, abundance in emptiness, and life in death[89]. The attainment of heaven is an effect of the sacrament of the Eucharist. Those who receive this sacrament worthily are given an anticipation of eternal glory[90]. St. Thomas Acquinas maintained that the Eucharist is the consummation of the Christian life[91]. Vatican II clearly states the eschatological nature of the Eucharist: «Christ left to his followers a pledge of this hope and food for the journey in the sacrament of faith, in which natural elements, the fruits of human cultivation, are changed into his glorified body and blood, as a supper of brotherly fellowship and a foretaste of the heavenly supper»[92]. Parecattil clearly

---

[86] W. KASPER, *Jesus the Christ*, 118; G. WAINWRIGHT, *Eucharist and Eschatology*, 59.

[87] H.F.G. SWANSTON, *The Community Witness*, 169.170.

[88] D.N. POWER, *The Eucharistic Mystery*, 294.

[89] W. KASPER, *Jesus the Christ*, 119.

[90] *Summa Theologiae*, III, 79, 2.

[91] *Summa Theologiae*, III, 73, 3.

[92] GS 38; Cf. J. NEUNER, «The Eucharist and the New Man», 161-166; G.V. LEEUWEN, «The Eucharist», 404-443.

stated that the Eucharist is the food which nourishes the spiritual life of Christians and stimulates their social witness; however, he did not show the connection between these truths and the eternal life which the sacrament anticipates.

Christians live in the interim period between the «already» and the «not yet». The Church is not yet fully the eschatological kingdom[93]. The Eucharist is «a paschal banquet in which Christ is consumed, the mind is filled with grace, and a pledge of future glory is given to us»[94]. The Eucharist anticipates «the eschatological banquet in the kingdom of the Father, proclaiming the Lord's death until his coming»[95]. The Eucharist is the food of the pilgrim Church which gives it hope and zeal[96]. It is the food of the Church today on earth and it will be its everlasting happiness to come[97]. In short, the Eucharist already grants Christians on earth the foretaste of future glory[98].

The Eucharist represents the Church as sharing in the eschatological meal of the kingdom with Christ as High Priest, host, and nourishment. The celebration of the Eucharist should keep alive Christians' longing for the final consummation, the expectation of the day when he who now dwells amongst them in a hidden way will come again[99]. It is the connection between the Eucharist and coming kingdom of God from which the Church derives meaning and life[100]. The truth that Christians are an eschatological people, living according to Christ's promises, is highlighted each time the sacramental action is performed. Receiving in communion the eschatological gift of Christ, the Church does not confound present reality with the gift promised[101].

The Eucharistic liturgy illustrates symbolically the relationship between the earthly and the heavenly liturgies. Christ is present in the earthly liturgy as the Saviour who unites the worshipping community with himself

---

[93] E. SCHILLEBEECKX, *God the Future of Man*, 103.

[94] SC 47.

[95] Eu. M, 3; Cf. P.J. ROSATO, *Introduzione alla teologia*, 88; JOHN PAUL II, «Annunciate l'anno», 369.

[96] PAUL VI, *The Teachings*, X, 76.

[97] PAUL VI, *The Teachings*, IX, 36.

[98] PAUL VI, *The Teachings*, V, 284-285; JOHN PAUL II, «Annunciamo al mondo», 733-734.

[99] B. HÄRING, *The New Covenant*, 162.

[100] E. KILMARTIN, *Christian Liturgy*, 341.

[101] D.N. POWER, *The Eucharistic Mystery*, 298-299.

in the passover he suffered before entering into glory[102]. The Eucharist is the festal meal, the effective sign of the eternal banquet of love in heaven[103]. The Eucharist, which is celebrated as a meal, assures Christians that all that it promises will be fulfilled for them in unspeakable glory, in the eternal banquet[104]. At the Eucharist, Christians recall their faith that the Church shall celebrate the final banquet with Christ in the kingdom of God. This goal renews their confidence and hope[105]. It is true that Parecattil based his theology on the liturgy of the Eucharist. Yet, if he had treated the relation between the heavenly and earthly liturgies, his views would have been much more comprehensive.

2.2 *The Lack of Reflection on the Sanctification of the Entire Church which Emerges from the Eucharistic Celebration and Grants a Broader Perspective to the Holiness of Individual Christians*

Parecattil's main concern in stressing the active participation of the faithful in the Eucharistic liturgy was that they derive grace from it for their day-to-day life. However, he was more preoccupied with the sanctification of individual Christians than with that of the Church as the people of God. Yet, the entire assembly of the faithful as a community offers the sacrifice together with Christ[106]. Therefore, the Church as a holy community, is the pre-requisite for participating in the Lord's Supper. The body of the faithful as an assembly, united always but still in need of greater unity, eats the one bread and drinks the one cup[107]. The Eucharist is the centre of the whole Christian life both for the universal Church and for the local congregation of that Church. The Church first «makes the Eucharist» so that «the Eucharist builds it up»[108]. Thus, Eucharist is the very heartbeat of the assembly of the faithful[109]. The Church is built up on the Eucharist which is its basis and centre[110]. The sacrament reflects God's love for his people,

---

[102] E. KILMARTIN, *Christian Liturgy*, 342.

[103] B. HÄRING, *The New Covenant*, 136.

[104] B. HÄRING, *The New Covenant*, 136.

[105] L.C. HAY, *Eucharist, A Thanksgiving*, 68; Cf. M. PENROSE, «Cosmic Dimensions», 433-441.

[106] Cf. J. DUPUIS, «Toward a Communal Eucharistic Celebration», 401-417.

[107] SC 10; E. LUSSIER, *The Eucharist*, 162.

[108] Eu. M 6; DC 4.

[109] PO 5.

[110] PO 6.

and their dependence on him[111]. Therefore, no celebration of the Eucharistic mystery is possible without a community of faithful, the Church[112]. The first community partook in the breaking of bread, and recognized that Christ was with them[113]. Furthermore, the presence of Christ in the elements is not seen as an end in itself, but as a means of unifying and enlivening the Church[114]. In the Eucharist, therefore, the Lord is present in those who have come together in his memory: «Where two or three of you are gathered together in my name, there I am in the midst of you» (Mt 18, 20)[115].

Therefore, the Church is the community constituted by the everlasting covenant. It is not limited with regard to race or nationality, or any other factor, for it must offer universal praise to God[116]. As the covenant community, the Church lives out the witness to God required of it, and is marked by the hope that the liturgical remembrance of Christ's saving passion inspires. Through eating the bread which is Christ's body and through sharing the cup which is Christ's blood, the Church expresses and appropriates time and again its reality as a covenant people[117]. Thus, the Eucharist sanctifies the Church: «The renewal in the Eucharist of the covenant between the Lord and human being sets the faithful aflame with Christ's insistent love [...] from the Eucharist, grace is poured forth upon them as from a fountain[118]. The Eucharist is, therefore, the source of the perfection of the Church[119]. The Eucharist contains «the whole of the Church's spiritual treasure, namely Christ himself, our Pasch and the living bread who gives life to men by His flesh made living and vivifying by the Holy Spirit»[120]. Communion with God on the part of individual Christians is achieved in the context of the Church, the visible mystical body[121].

The silent conversation between the Saviour and the individual soul is neither the only, nor even the main purpose of the Eucharist. For, the latter

---

[111] L.C. HAY, *Eucharist, A Thanksgiving*, 99.

[112] E. LUSSIER, *The Eucharist*, 164.

[113] H.F.G. SWANSTON, *The Community Witness*, 168.

[114] L.C. HAY, *Eucharist, A Thanksgiving*, 108.

[115] P. BERNIER, *Eucharist: Celebrating its Rhythms*, 37.

[116] H.F.G. SWANSTON, *The Community Witness*, 167.

[117] D.N. POWER, *The Eucharistic Mystery*, 298.

[118] SC 10.

[119] AG 39.

[120] Eu. M 6.

[121] E. SCHILLEBEECKX, *Christ the Sacrament*, 182.

is primarily meant to incorporate Christians into the Church of Christ[122]. Therefore, the Eucharist is the chief means of the sanctification of the community of the faithful[123]. Modern theologians, while affirming the real presence of Christ in the Eucharist, and the legitimacy of venerating the Lord in the species, tend to emphasize that the end of the Eucharist is the sanctification of the community[124]. The Eucharist must remain on the level of an interpersonal relationship — of the union of Christ with all in the community, and of all in the community with their brothers and sisters[125].

Since the Holy Spirit sanctifies the Church, the celebration of the Eucharist is a pneumatological event[126]. The Spirit, who enabled the crucified Christ rise from the dead, enables the Church to fulfil the promise contained in the words of the institution at the Last Supper. Hence, the Holy Spirit's role in the Eucharist is to make actual and vital the historical words of Christ[127]. The epiclesis invokes the Father to send the Holy Spirit upon the Eucharistic gifts and upon the participants so that they may become «one body, one spirit in Christ»[128]. Since the Spirit dwells in the Church, Christ's gift of himself to his followers is mediated through the divine Pneuma[129]. As the internal principle, or soul, of the visible Church, the Spirit unites all the members to Christ their head[130].

Thus, the views of Parecattil on the role of the faithful in the Eucharistic liturgy would have been more reinforced, if he had described the communitarian aspect of this sacrament more fully. The active participation of the faithful, the theme stressed by Parecattil, would have a deeper significance, if the Church itself were viewed as sanctified by the Holy Spirit at the celebration of the sacrament. Although individual Christians receive grace by participating in the Mass, this gift is communicated in the context of the community of the faithful, which is the Church.

---

[122] B. HÄRING, *The New Covenant*, 145.

[123] A. SCHMEMANN, *The Eucharist*, 255.

[124] E. SCHILLEBEECKX, «Transubstantiation», 187.

[125] E. SCHILLEBEECKX, «Transubstantiation», 187.

[126] M. THURIAN, *The Mystery of the Eucharist*, 22.

[127] M. THURIAN, *The Mystery of the Eucharist*, 22; L.C. HAY, *Eucharist, A Thanksgiving*, 93.

[128] Cf. L.C. HAY, *Eucharist, A Thanksgiving*, 94.

[129] LG 4; J.M. POWERS, *Eucharistic Theology*, 169.

[130] W. KASPER, *The God of Jesus Christ*, 229.

2.3 *The Absence of Analogy between the Real Presence of Christ in the Transformed Eucharistic Species and His Social Presence in the Emarginated Poor as the Motivation of Christian Diaconia*

Joseph Parecattil established a close connection between the Eucharist and the mission of the Church by stating that the Eucharist nourishes the interior life and stimulates the social activities of the faithful. However, his Eucharistic theology lacks an analogy between the real presence of Christ in the Eucharistic elements and his social presence in the poor. If this analogy were properly developed, the link between the participation in the Eucharistic liturgy and the practice of social love would be better understood.

The real presence of Christ, which is hidden in the bread and wine, is visibly manifested in his social presence in the poor who are the sign and image of his ingoing passion in the world[131]. It is to be strongly held that there is a relationship between the real presence of Christ in the Eucharistic elements and his social presence in the poor; the poor are the sacrament of Christ[132]. A genuine participation in the Eucharistic liturgy and a serious commitment to the social mission of the Church are closely related[133]. The Eucharistic experience of the faithful makes them aware of the presence of Christ in the needy[134]. Therefore, the social mission of the Church is actually contained in the Eucharistic elements[135]. People's hungers and needs are indeed expressed in the bread and wine brought to the sacred table[136]. The Eucharist, therefore, has a social significance by promoting mutual service, the sharing of goods, and the crossing of social barriers[137]. It is to be noted that contemporary Eucharistic theology points out the relationship between the celebration of the sacrament and the practice of charity[138]. In short, the Eucharist signifies this charity, and at the same time brings it about[139]. Eucharistic worship, therefore, is the expression of charity which is the authentic and deepest characteristic of the Christian

---

[131] PAUL VI, *Insegnamenti*, VI, 377; P. J. ROSATO, *Cena del Signore*, 83.

[132] Cf. J. SOBRINO, *The True Church*, 125-159.

[133] DIM 58; Cf. J. THEISEN, «Images of the Church», 118-129.

[134] DC 6.

[135] P. BENOIT, «The Holy Eucharist», 106-115.

[136] D.N. POWER, *The Eucharistic Mystery*, 61.

[137] P.J. ROSATO, *Introduzione alla teologia*, 83; D.N. POWER, *The Eucharistic Mystery*, 30.

[138] D.N. POWER, *The Eucharistic Mystery*, 18.

[139] DC 5.

vocation: «This worship springs from the love and serves the love to which we are all called in Jesus Christ»[140]. The Early Church linked the «agape» to the Eucharistic supper, showing itself as one body around Christ united by the bond of charity; it claimed charitable works as its own mission and right[141]. Thus, it can be said that «charitable action today can and should reach all people and all needs»[142]. Inspired by the Eucharistic grace the Church is involved in many kinds of service, especially of organised charity[143]. This love springs from the Eucharist has urged Christians to devise and realize social development programmes[144].

Moreover, Parecattil could have shown that the Eucharist is the sacrament in which the participants experience the social justice preached by Jesus[145]. The awareness of the presence of Christ in the poor stimulates Christians to work for the establishment of justice in society. The Church teaches that justice needs to be practised in various areas of social life. *Mater et Magistra* says: «We consider it opportune to call attention to fundamental principle of social justice, namely, that social progress should accompany and be adjusted to economic development in such a way that all classes of citizens can participate in the increased productivity»[146]. The document continues to say that justice is to be observed not only with respect to the distribution of wealth acquired by production, but also with respect to the exercise of responsibility in perfecting the personalities of tolerance[147]. Furthermore, the affluent nations «should not remain indifferent to those nations whose citizens suffer from internal problems that result in poverty, hunger and inability to enjoy even the more elementary human rights»[148]. On the one hand, there are many who are deprived of the absolute necessities of life, and on the other, there are some who live in riches and squander their wealth[149]. Economic and social disparity

---

[140] DC 5.
[141] AA 8.
[142] AA 8.
[143] A.P. BARNABAS, «Christian Concern», 60.
[144] M.M. THOMAS, «Theological Aspects», 20.
[145] P.J. ROSATO, *Introduzione alla teologia*, 84; P. BERNIER, *Bread Broken and Shared*, 69-78.
[146] ND 2116.
[147] ND 2117/1; DS 3947.
[148] ND 2122; Cf. O. CUMMINGS, «The Eucharist and Social Justice», 207-212.
[149] GS 63.

between individuals and peoples is a source of scandal and militates against human dignity, as well as international peace[150].

God created the earth with the goods necessary for the well-being of all. Justice and charity must regulate the distribution of created goods so that they are actually available to all[151]. It is not to be forgotten that, if the world is made to furnish each individual with the means of livelihood, each person therefore has the right to find in the world what is necessary for himself[152]. Hence, each individual shares responsibility in establishing justice in society[153]. Everyone must become particularly sensitive to all human suffering, to all injustice and wrong, and seek the way to redress them effectively: «Let us learn to discover with respect the truth about the inner self of people, for it is precisely this inner self that becomes the dwelling-place of God present in the Eucharist»[154]. Thus, the Eucharist provides the basis for social action aimed at establishing justice in the world.

One's response to the love of God is expressed in the love and service of others. Christian love of neighbour, however, cannot be separated from justice: «For love implies an absolute demand for justice, namely, a recognition of the dignity and rights of one's neighbour»[155]. Divine love impels the Church to solidarity with everyone who suffers[156]. It should be remembered that the demands of justice must first of all be satisfied, and that which is already due in justice is not to be offered as a gift of charity[157]. Therefore, justice and charity are closely related, and some-times even identified[158].

The Eucharist fosters the mission of social justice by promoting the fundamental rights of human beings[159]. The Church, which is bound to give witness to justice, recognizes that anyone who ventures to speak to people about justice must first be just in their eyes[160]. Participation in the struggles of people for liberation from oppressive forces that stifle their

---

[150] GS 29.
[151] GS 69.
[152] PP 22.
[153] OA 48.
[154] DC 6.
[155] DM 34.
[156] LC 61.
[157] AA 8.
[158] EN 31; RH 16; Cf. G. OUTKA, *Agape, An Ethical Analysis*, 75-88.
[159] R. MAHONY, «The Eucharist and Social Change», 52-61.
[160] DIM 40.

human existence is an important aspect of the Church's mission today. Those who are oppressed by poverty are the object of a love of preference on the part of the Church which, since her origin and in spite of the failings of many of her members, has not ceased to work for their relief, defence and liberation[161]. Therefore, the Church is involved in a variety of social activities, especially those which mitigate the sufferings of the underprivileged. Thus, the theology of Parecattil would have been more comprehensive, if he would have established a direct link between the presence of Christ in the Eucharistic and his presence in those who suffer because of social injustice.

In conclusion, it can be said that Parecattil established a clear link between the Eucharistic liturgy, spiritual life and social action. The faithful must actively participate in the Eucharistic liturgy. For this reason, the liturgy should be reformed, especially by being adapted to the living situations and cultural background of the people of the Syro-Malabar Church. Such a full and sincere participation bestows more grace for their spiritual life. The sacrament urges Christians to be one even with the followers of non-Christian religions. Moreover, a genuine participation in the Eucharist activates the social apostolate of the faithful. A better treatment of the eschatological dimension of the Eucharist, of the sanctification of the entire Church which it brings about and of the analogical relationship between the presence of Christ in the Eucharistic elements and in the poor, would indeed provide correctives to the theology of Joseph Parecattil, and place its many positive traits in even higher relief.

---

[161] LC 68.

GENERAL CONCLUSION

The following pages intend to depict in a concise form the major trends that run through the chapters. This thesis, which treats the Eucharistic theology of Joseph Cardinal Parecattil, has pointed out the various factors by which his thought-pattern was influenced; analyzed in detail his Eucharistic texts; and critically evaluated his positions regarding the subject matter of this study. The results of the research disclose that the principle contributions of Parecattil are his systematic interpretation of the Eucharistic theology of the Syro-Malabar Church, and his provision of a strong foundation on which the ever more perfect inculturation of this theology in the Indian context may rest. He has successfully done this, by developing an original synthesis in which he has inter-connected the three aspects of Eucharistic liturgy, spirituality and social action, and has shown the relevance of each of them for dialogue with Hinduism.

As is pointed out in the first chapter, the theology of the Syro-Malabar Church, in which Joseph Parecattil was born and brought up, depended on the *lex orandi* of its Eucharistic liturgy which was almost identical with that of the Chaldean Church. This liturgy can be characterized as determined by three Eucharistic prayers: 1) *the Anaphora of Addai and Mari*; 2) *the Anaphora of Theodore of Mopsuestia*; and 3) *the Anaphora of Nestorius*. Nevertheless, in his formal theological training Parecattil grasped the various dogmatic teachings of the Western Church which were expressed at the time in Post-Tridentine and Neo-Thomistic categories. Moreover, both at home and in seminary he became familiar with the popular devotions to the Eucharist, such as visits to the Blessed Sacrament, attendance at benediction and dedication to the Sacred Heart of Jesus, the symbol of the outpoured love of the Father in his obedient and self-giving Son.

Apart from these factors of his formation, Joseph Parecattil was inevitably exposed to the religious pluralism of India. Early in his life he came to appreciate Hinduism as a religion possessing rich spiritual treasures, even though most Christians did not have such admiration for it since they considered it thoroughly pagan. The social situation of India had its impact on Parecattil the young pastor who worked hard to improve the living conditions of the poor masses, by promoting various welfare programmes. As one committed to the freedom of India, he followed the political development of the nation in the first half of the twentieth century with great interest, and absorbed the social and political principles of Mohandas Karamchand Gandhi, whom he viewed as having applied the teachings of the just and non-violent Jesus to the independence movement.

Then Vatican II instilled in Parecattil a strong desire for the revitalization of the Church. Inspired by it, he tried to reform the different aspects of the life of his own Syro-Malabar tradition. With regard to the renewal of the Eucharistic liturgy, he was totally dedicated to the three connected principles of restoration, revision and adaptation of the Missals which are proposed by *Sacrosanctum Concilium* (SC 23).

The positive attitude of Vatican II toward the inherent value of non-Christian religions confirmed the thinking of Parecattil. In *Nostra Aetate* reference is made to the wisdom and sanctity often found in other religions, and it is stated that: «the Catholic Church rejects nothing of what is true and holy in those religions» (NA 2). The Latin Church in India soon adapted elements from the Hindu culture, so as to indigenize the Eucharistic liturgy. The renewal took on concrete shape with the preparation of two Indian Missals: 1) «An Order of the Mass for the Indian Church» composed at Dharmaram College, Bangalore, and 2) «An Order of the Mass for India» published by the N.B.C.L.C, Bangalore. Inspired by these texts Parecattil initiated the composition of a similar text for the Syro-Malabar Eucharistic liturgy called *Bhāratiya Pūjā* (Indian Mass).

Parecattil incessantly stated that active participation in the Eucharistic liturgy leads Christians to adopt a spirituality centred on this sacrament, which in turn is directed to social action based on fraternal charity. He was convinced that by means of an active participation in the Eucharistic liturgy, the faithful make a self-offering of themselves with Christ. By their baptismal character, which renders them members of the mystical body of Christ and partakers in his royal priesthood, the faithful offer the Eucharistic sacrifice along with the ordained priests, albeit in a different manner. Parecattil went on to explain why the unique self-sacrifice of Christ is understood to exist in three ways: symbolically at the Last Supper, physically on the Cross, and sacramentally on the altars of the Church. During the Last Supper Jesus instituted the Eucharist by changing the bread into his broken body, and the wine into his poured-out blood. This self-giving gesture was the pre-figuration of the sacrifice on the Cross. The Mass is the ritual re-presentation both of the Last Supper and of Calvary.

Parecattil maintained that the primary effect of participation in the Mass is the reception of Eucharistic grace which manifests itself in fraternal love, ecclesial unity and diaconal service of suffering human beings. He therefore urged Christians to view Eucharistic grace as the source for such social love. This explains why he was an advocate of a spiritually oriented concept of social work.

Parecattil attended the four sessions of Vatican II, and made a number of interventions. Thereafter, he initiated the renewal of the Eucharistic liturgy of the Syro-Malabar Church. Yet, when the restored Mass text of 1962 was elaborated by others, he lamented its over-emphasis on the restoration of the Chaldean liturgy, and its failure to stress the connected principles of revision and adaptation. As a result, under his leadership efforts were made to revise the Missal which led to the publication of the 1968 Missal.

Parecattil pointed out that the Eucharist strengthens Christians to imitate the virtues of Jesus Christ who is present in the Eucharist: his humility, his merciful character and his submission to the will of the Father. With an aim to make Christian families Eucharist-centred, he propagated the devotion to the Sacred Heart. He also maintained that Eucharistic grace stimulates efforts to work for the reunion of Christians, and thus is directly related to ecumenism. He fostered the teachings of *Unitatis Redintegratio*, and referred to the friendly relationships between the Catholic and the Jacobite Churches in Kerala as positive effects of the Council. Moreover, according to Parecattil, ecumenism in the context of modern India also includes better understanding and collaboration among followers of different religions.

Christians who receive the Eucharist have the responsibility to promote the welfare of all the members of the mystical body of Christ. In order to encourage them to fight against poverty and homelessness, Parecattil frequently referred to the Conciliar decree *Apostolicam Actuositatem*, and reminded his people of their duty to provide the needy with food, housing, medicine, education and work (AA 8). Thus, Parecattil urged Christians to produce more food and to build houses for those living in simple huts. He was also conscious of the need to enhance the role of women in social life. For these reasons, he believed that the welfare of the nation depended on safeguarding consistently the principles of democracy. He reminded the faithful that Gandhi had waged war against a foreign domination simply with the weapons of *Satyam* and *Ahimsā*, and pointed to their responsibility to abide by these principles so as to avoid the outbreak of hostility in the country.

Parecattil courageously contributed to the reform of the Syro-Malabar Eucharistic liturgy. In the *Bhāratiya Pūjā* he claimed to have followed the principle of «organic development» put forward by two documents of Vatican II: *Orientalium Ecclesiarum* (OE 6) and *Sacrosanctum Concilium* (SC 23). He adopted Hindu philosophical categories and idioms to express the Christian mysteries. By means of this reform, Parecattil tried to render the Syro-Malabar liturgy more reflective of the theology of the incarnation of the Word, so that the local Church could become «Hindu in culture, Christian in faith and Indian in liturgy». When he introduced the Indian Mass, he also strove to revise the existing Missal of 1968. As a result, the «Short Mass» was printed «pro-manuscripto», and was used in an experimental manner at certain centres. But from 1978 onwards the reform of the Syro-Malabar liturgy took a different turn, deviating from revision and adaptation, and stressing restoration alone. «The Order of the Solemn Raza of the Syro-Malabar Church» of 1986, by restoring the Chaldean liturgy, undid to a great extent what Parecattil had achieved, and caused him much sorrow.

Parecattil maintained that the Eucharist contains Christ who has redeemed and justified all humanity by the blood he shed on the Cross. He thus presented the Eucharistic Christ as the fulfilment of the search for liberation on the part of Hindus. He contended that a Syro-Malabar spirituality entails a proper synthesis of Hindu and Christian elements. He also espoused that the Christians of India should know more about Hindu religious and ascetical practices, and incorporate them in their own spirituality.

Parecattil claimed that the unity between worship and work could be noted in the Eucharistic bread and wine which are the products of human labour. Strengthened by the sacrament, Christians work for their own sustenance as well as for that of their needy neighbours. He also urged Christians to engage in social work by caring for the physically and mentally sick, by promoting sound education, and by curbing overpopulation through natural family planning and increased production of consumer goods.

Parecattil's treatment on Eucharistic theology carries great worth. It is to his credit that he has established a close link between the Eucharistic liturgy, the spiritual life and the social witness of Christians. Moreover, as a traditionally formed person open to ecclesial renewal, he contributed to the broad-mindedness of the Council and laboured heroically to translate its vital spirit into action in the context of the Syro-Malabar Church. The unique trait of the Eucharistic theology of Parecattil is its conjoining of

patent faithfulness to Catholic teaching and prophetic insistence on idigeni-
zation.

The main focus of his theology is that he attributed to the faithful an
indispensable role in the Eucharistic celebration, since they are sharers in
the priesthood of Christ through the anointing of the Holy Spirit at Baptism.
He treated forthrightly the Catholic dogmas on the Eucharist, maintaining
that the Mass is the memorial, or sacramental re-enactment, of the saving
death and resurrection of Christ. He concentrated particularly on the
sacrificial nature of the Eucharist, viewing it as the self-offering of Christ
the High Priest with whom the faithful offer themselves together to the
Father. Parecattil stressed the identity of the three forms of one sacrifice of
Christ: at the Last Supper, on the Cross and in the Eucharist. This rite,
instituted at the Last Supper, was a pre-figuration of the Cross, and the
Mass is the sacramental re-presentation of both. Moreover, he held that the
crucified and risen Lord is really present in the ontologically changed or
transubstantiated bread and wine. Parecattil also stated that the union with
the Eucharistic Lord through Holy Communion perfects the participation of
the faithful in the Mass.

Precisely in order to facilitate this active, full and sincere participation,
Parecattil advocated the thorough restoration, revision and adaptation of the
rituals. His intention was to accentuate the Indian character of the Syro-
Malabar liturgy, so as to resist those who claimed instead that it is
Chaldean. He was instrumental in the preparation of the Missal of 1968, the
«Indian Mass» of 1974 and the «Short Mass» of 1974. In these texts he
introduced Indian elements into the Eucharistic liturgy, so as to inculturate
it along the clear guidelines provided by the various Papal teachings of this
century and by the documents of Vatican II.

Parecattil forcefully stated how authentic Christian spirituality is
continually strengthened and activated at the Eucharist, the primary source
of divine grace in the Church. The sacrament brings about an ever stronger
bond between Jesus Christ, who is the author of sanctity, and Christians
who are a holy people. Thus, the sacrament causes the sanctification of the
faithful according to their interior freedom and sincere intention to receive
grace and live by it. Hence, Parecattil fostered Eucharistic devotions as
means of responding all the more to sanctifying grace. This sacrament also
fosters an ecumenical spirit among Christians and opens them to dialogue
with the adherents of other religions. Since Parecattil affirmed that the
Eucharistic sacrifice sanctifies all humankind, even those who do not
directly confess Christ have a share in its grace through the holiness they
attain in these religious communities. He considered Hinduism as a natural

religion containing an aspect of the primitive revelation of God, and participating in the economy of salvation. Thus, Parecattil never considered Hinduism as opposed to Christianity, but viewed it as complementary to it, maintaining that Christ himself fulfils the Hindu yearning for God. Moreover, he held that through constant and honest dialogue, Christianity and Hinduism can each be enriched, without losing their identity.

Parecattil incessantly pointed out that the reception of the Eucharist encourages Christians to be engaged in social welfare activities for the poor. The Eucharistic Lord himself, who in his earthly life was the friend of the emarginated, is the model of all Christian charity. The Church in the modern world has to extend the love of the Lord to the poor through good works. Thus, the love of neighbour, which is fostered by the sacrament, obliges Christians to care for their less fortunate brethren. Parecattil appreciated the different fields of social work undertaken by the Church, especially those providing the basic necessities of life such as food, clothing, shelter, medicine and education.

However, in his writings, Parecattil did not treat certain aspects of Catholic Eucharistic theology in a sufficient way. The eschatological dimension of the Eucharist as the «foretaste of the heavenly supper» deserves a proper treatment. The Eucharist anticipates the end-time banquet by rendering it already present as the bread of heaven within history. Moreover, in this way, Parecattil could have underlined the close relation between the earthly and heavenly liturgies, and shown that the Mass in the privileged locus of Christian hope. Another aspect which Parecattil did not stress adequately is the sanctification of the entire Church which is effected by the Eucharist. The Church is not simply a group of individuals, but a community which, without the celebration of the Mass, could not exist as it should. The Eucharist is thus the vitalizing centre of the entire life and mission of the Church. Parecattil did indeed refer to the mystical body of Christ which is nourished by the Eucharist, but he tended to perceive it as composed of individuals.

Finally, it can be said that, in showing the connection between the Eucharist and social work, Parecattil did not deal with the important analogy between the real presence of Christ in the Eucharistic elements and the social presence of Christ in the poor. He certainly insisted that the experience of the Eucharistic Lord at the celebration makes the faithful more keenly aware of their moral responsibilities of caring for the needy. But Parecattil did not state that the social mission of the Church is already contained in the Eucharistic elements, because the broken bread in the hands of Jesus at the Last Supper symbolized the broken poor whom he fed, and with whom he wished to identify himself. Thus, the social mission of Christians lies on the altar with Christ, and is carried out after the celebration by viewing the poor as «sacraments» of Christ himself.

At the end of the introduction to this study a question was posed concerning how a traditionally trained son of an ancient Oriental Church in Asia could end his days celebrating the Eucharist in the vernacular Malayalam and, surrounded by oil lamps and incense sticks, pronouncing the words of institution spoken by Jesus in the Cenacle along with the Hindu prayer asking God to lead humankind from darkness to light and from falsehood and enmity to truth and non-violence. This study has tried to provide the answer by means of formal historical, analytic and evaluative methods; it has tried to show the lasting achievement of Parecattil, while it has not failed to indicate further ways in which his thought can be consolidated by the next generations of Indian theologians. Even if this study has striven to focus on the understanding of the Eucharist which Joseph Parecattil advocated, it has had *per force* to enter into questions of adaptation and inculturation, recent Indian history and contemporary social problems.

This is because Parecattil, a son of an Oriental Church in Asia, could not declare that the Eucharist celebrated in his land could be full and sincere, if it did not lead Indian Christians to extend the self-giving love of Jesus to their Hindu neighbours, Moslem social workers, male or female, and to low cast people without food and housing. Joseph Parecattil in effect made his own the content of the fifth paragraph of the conciliar document *Presbytero-rum Ordinis,* for he was sure, and wanted the people of his Church to be sure, that the Eucharistic celebration and the spiritual way of life it fosters, would be incomplete and insincere today if it did not lead to the practice of works of charity, to mutual help and to all forms of missionary activity and Christian witness.

ABBREVIATIONS

< >	This sign used in this work indicates that the title of the article given inside it is coined by the author, since the original article appears without a proper title.
AA	*Apostolicam Actuositatem* (Decree of Vatican II on the Apostolate of Lay People)
AG	*Ad Gentes* (Decree of Vatican II on the Church's Missionary Activity)
AThR	*Anglican Theological Review*
Brh. Up.	*Brhadāranyaka Upanishād*
C.B.C.I.	*Catholic Bishops' Conference of India*
CD	*Christus Dominus* (Decree of Vatican II on the Pastoral Office of the Bishops in the Church)
CleM	*The Clergy Monthly*
CleR	*The Clergy Review*
CW	*The Collected Works of Mahatma Gandhi.* This work was published by «The Publication Division», Ministry of Information and Broadcasting, Government of India. The book appears in 90 volumes consisting of all the writings of Gandhi between 1884-1947. The volumes are published from Ahmedabad in the years beginning from 1969 to 1984.
DC	*Dominicae Cenae* (Apostolic Letter of John Paul II on the Mystery and Worship of the Eucharist)

DS	DENZINGER – SCHÖNMETZER, ed. *Enchiridion Symbolorum, Definitionum et Declarationum de Rebus Fidei et Morum*
EAAI	*Ernakulam Archdiocesan Archive Index.* A number of writings and discourses of Joseph Parecattil remain unpublished. They are kept in the archive of the Archdiocese of Ernakulam, arranged in an index. These works are quoted in this thesis, within the brackets after *EAAI*, with the serial number and the title as assigned to them in the index.
ECQ	*The Eastern Churches Quarterly*
ed.	Editor
eds.	Editors
EU	*Euentes Docete*
EL	*Ephemerides Liturgicae*
EM	*Ernakulam Missam.* This is the bulletin of the Archdiocese of Ernakulam.
ER	*The Ecumenical Review*
Eu. M	*Eucharisticum Mysterium* (Instruction of Sacred Congregation of Rites on the Worship of the Eucharistic Mystery)
GS	*Gaudium et Spes* (Decree of Vatican II on the Pastoral Constitution on the Church in the Modern World)
IO	*Inter Oecumenici* (Instruction of Sacred Congregation of Rites on the Proper Implementation of the Constitution on the Sacred Liturgy)
JD	*Jeevadhara*
JDh	*Journal of Dharma*
JThS	*The Journal of Theological Studies*
LC	*Libertatis Conscientia* (Instruction of the Congregation for Doctrine of Faith)
LE	*Laborem Exercens* (Encyclical Letter of John Paul II)
LG	*Lumen Gentium* (Decree of Vatican II on the Dogmatic Constitution on the Church)
MM	*Malabar Mail*
MS	*Misericordiam Suam* (Introduction of the Sacred Congregation for Divine Worship to the New Order of Penance)

NA	*Nostra Aetate* (Declaration of Vatican II on the Relation of the Church to Non-Christian Religions)
N.B.C.L.C.	*National, Biblical, Catechetical and Liturgical Centre*
NCE	*New Catholic Encyclopedia*
ND	J. NEUNER – J. DUPUIS, *The Christian Faith*
OrChr	*Oriens Christianus*
OCP	*Orientalia Christiana Periodica*
OE	*Orientalium Ecclesiarum* (Decree of Vatican II on the Catholic Eastern Churches)
OS	*Ostkirchliche Studien*
PO	*Presbyterorum Ordinis* (Decree of Vatican on the Ministry and Life of Priests)
PP	*Populorum Progressio* (Encyclical Letter of Paul VI)
RM	*Redemptoris Missio* (Encyclical Letter of John Paul II)
RfR	*Review for Religious*
RS	*Religion and Society*
Sat. Brahm.	*Śatapata Brāmana*
SD	*Sathyadeepam*
SC	*Sacrosanctum Concilium* (Decree of Vatican II on the Constitution on the Sacred Liturgy)
Scrip.	*Scripture*
StLi	*Studia Liturgica*
S.M.B.C.	*Syro-Malabar Bishops' Conference*
StPatr	*Studia Patristica*
tr.	Translation
TS	*Theological Studies*
UR	*Unitatis Redintegratio* (Decree of Vatican II on Ecumenism)
VJTR	*Vidya Jyothi*
WoWo	*Word and Worship*
ZKT	*Zeitschrift für Katholische Theologie*

BIBLIOGRAPHY

1. Primary Sources (Writings and Discourses of Joseph Parecattil)

PARECATTIL, J., *Augustine vs Pelagius on Grace*, Ernakulam 1948.

———, <«The Church and Politics»>[1]. Reply to the Toast Proposed on the Occasion of His Elevation as Archbishop, Cochin, January 9, 1956, *EM* 27 (1957) 44-46.

———, «Look to the Party and Its Ideals». Talk at Sacred Heart College, Thevara, October 27, 1956, *EM* 27 (1957) 219-220.

———, «Clear Thinking and Vigourous Action». Presidential Address at the Annual Session of the Catholic Association of St. Thomas College, Palai, February 5, 1957, *EM* 27 (1957) 222-224.

———, «The Progress of Our Country» (*Nammude Nādinte Purōgati*). Talk on the Occasion of Laying the Foundation Stone of the Social Services Centre, Kalamassery, February 25, 1957, *EM* 27 (1957) 224-226.

———, «Circular on the Youth Festival» (*Yuvajanavarṣattepattiyulla Sarcular*)[2]. Circular Letter, Cochin, January 20, 1958 *EM* 28 (1958) 9-12.

———, <«Lisie Hospital Day Celebration»>. Welcome Speech, Ernakulam, September 25, 1961, *EM* 31 (1961) 269.

———, «Serve in a New Spirit» (*Navachaithnyathode Pravarthiunmmukarakuka*), Inaugural Talk at the 43 Anniversary Celebration of the Kerala Catholic Congress, Undated, *EM* 31 (1961) 60-67.

---

[1] This sign used in this work indicates that the title of the article given inside it is coined by the author, since the original article appears without a proper title.

[2] When books, articles, or discourses have a title in Malayalam, an English equivalent is quoted in this dissertation, with the Malayalam title in the brackets in transliterated form.

PARECATTIL, J., <«Mary and Evangelization»>. Pastoral Letter, September 26, 1963, *EM* 33 (1963) 147-152.

————, <«Homes for the Homeless»>. Pastoral Letter, Cochin, November 30, 1963, *EM* 33 (1963) 189-196.

————, «The Syro-Malabar Church». Speech on the Occasion of the Interview granted by His Holiness Pope Paul VI to the Syro-Malabar Bishops, December 5, 1963, *EAAI* (699 S [LXXIX] Syro-Malabar Church) 1.

————, «Forward» to G. KANDATHIL, *Syro-Malabar Missal*, Kulanada 1963.

————, <«International Eucharistic Congress in Bombay»>. Pastoral Letter, January 31, 1964, *EM* 34 (1964) 15-24.

————, <«The Spirit of Parish Feasts»>. Pastoral Letter, March 1, 1964, *EM* 34 (1964) 39-46.

————, <«Housing Project»>. Sermon at St. Bruno's Church, Cologne, May 10, 1964, *EAAI* (674 S [LIV] Housing) 1-4.

————, <«Disrespect Shown towards the Eucharist»>. Pastoral Letter, Cochin, une 1, 1964, *EM* 34 (1964) 81-88.

————, <«Devotion to the Holy Eucharist»>. Talk at Sacred Heart College, Thevara, August 10, 1964, *EAAI* (180 E [VLV] Eucharist) 1-6.

————, <«Silver Jubilee of My Priestly Ordination»>. Pastoral Letter, August 30, 1964, *EM* 34 (1964) 227-232.

————, «Dialogue with Hindus». Intervention at the Third Session of Vatican II, September 29, 1964, *EM* 35 (1965) 128-130.

————, <«Mar Ignatius Yakub I, Patriarch of Antioch»>. Presidential Address at a Gathering Organized to Welcome the Patriarch and to Congratulate the Newly installed Catholicos, Kottayam, Undated, *EM* 34 (1964) 90-94.

————, <«The Social Projects of the Archdiocese of Ernakulam»>. Pastoral Letter, August 8, 1965, *EM* 35 (1965) 119-125.

————, <«The Vatican Council II»>. Pastoral Letter, November 15, 1965, *EM* 35 (1965) 179-183.

————, <«Hard Work for Better Life»>. Pastoral Letter, Ernaklam, March 1, 1966, *EM* 36 (1966) 51-57.

————, <«The Sacred Heart of Jesus»>. Pastoral Letter, June 1, 1966, *EM* 36 (1966) 107-112.

PARECATTIL, J., <«The Role of the Bishops»>. Felicitations to Newly Consecrated Bishops of the Malankara Orthodox Church, Kolenchery, August 24, 1966, *EAAI* (33 B [XI] Bishop) 1-7.

―――, <«Dharma»>. Felicitation at the Opening Ceremony of the New Building of the «Dharmodayam Company» September 4, 1966, *EAAI* (135 D [XVI] Dharmodayam Company) 1-6.

―――, <«Mothers' Mercy Trust»>. Presidential Address at Its Meeting, Ernakulam, September 9, 1966, *EM* 36 (1966) 238-240.

―――, «Catholic Charities». Pastoral Letter, Cochin, September 16, 1966, *EM* 36 (1966) 205-208.

―――, <«Reception to Prime Minister Indira Gandhi»>. Welcome Speech on the Occasion of Her Visit to Lisie Hospital, Ernakulam, September 23, 1966, *EM* 36 (1966) 236-237.

―――, <«English Education»>. Inaugural Talk at the English Medium School, Palai, October 9, 1966, *EAAI* (154 E [XIX] Education) 1-8.

―――, <«Council Jubilee Celebrations»>. Address at Its Concluding Ceremony, Cochin, December 4, 1966, *EM* 36 (1966) 253-258.

―――, <«Felicitations to Justice Isaac»>. Felicitations to Mr. Isaac on His Appointment as a High Court Judge, Cochin, December 18, 1966, *EAAI* (232 I [XVI] Isaac, Mr.) 1-6.

―――, <«The Need of Repentance»>. Pastoral Letter, January 20, 1967, *EM* 37 (1967) 1-5.

―――, «Y.M.C.A and Ecumenism». Talk at the Y.M.C.A. Gathering, Alwaye, February 2, 1967, *EAAI* (153 E [XVIII] Ecumenism and Y.M.C.A) 1-3.

―――, <«The Role of the Catholic Church in Fighting Hunger and Illness»>. Pastoral Letter, February 25, 1967, *EM* 37 (1967) 1-4.

―――, <«Dedication of Christian Families to the Sacred Heart»>. Pastoral Letter, Cochin, June 2, 1967, *EM* 37 (1967) 76-82.

―――, <«Nineteenth Centenary of the Matrydom of Sts. Peter and Paul»>. Pastoral Letter, June 15, 1967, *EM* 37 (1967) 105-111.

―――, <«Rome-the Eternal City»>. Pastoral Letter, October 8, 1967, *EM* 37 (1967) 175-182.

―――, <«Themes of the Synod of Bishops--1967»>. Talk on Vatican Radio, October 28, 1967, *EM* 37 (1967) 203-210.

―――, <«Growing in the Spiritual Life»>. Pastoral Letter, Cochin, November 21, 1967, *EM* 37 (1967) 195-199.

PARECATTIL, J., «Christmas Message». Talk on All-India Radio, Trivandrum, December 24, 1967, *EM* 38 (1968) 3-7.

———, <«Evangelization Activities»>. Pastoral Letter, Cochin, February 1, 1968, *EM* 38 (1968) 27-33.

———, «Be at the Service of Bharata Mata». Presidential Address at the College Day Celebrations of Bharata Mata College, Thrikkakara, February 10, 1968, *MM* 32 (1968 February 19) 3.

———, «Irrigation and Food Production». Talk on All-India Radio, March 25, 1968, *SD* 41 (1968 May 1) 1.

———, <«The Role of the Catholic Church in Ecumenism and Dialogue»>. Pastoral Letter, May 1, 1968, *EM* 38 (1968) 109-116.

———, <«Growth in Christian Faith»>. Pastoral Letter, Cchin, June 1, 1968, *EM* 38 (1968) 129-135.

———, «Circular Letter regarding the Approval of the 1968 Mass». Written to all the Syro-Malabar Bishops, Cochin, July 25, 1968, EM 47 (1977) 73.

———, <«Thirty-ninth International Eucharistic Congress»>. Pastoral Letter, August 1, 1968, *EM* 38 (1968) 161-164.

———, <«The Role of the Church in the Field of Education»>. Pastoral Letter, November 21, 1968, *EM* 38 (1968) 277-284.

———, <«Rubber Plantation»>. Release of the Souvenir of the Rubber Planter's Conference, Ernakulam, December 14, 1968, *EM* 39 (1969) 4-5.

———, «The Role of Women in National Integration». Meeting of the National Council of Catholic Women of India at St. Theresa's College, Cochin, January 1, 1969, *EM* 39 (1969) 23-28.

———, «Toast to Dr. Sushila Nayar». January 15, 1969, Cochin, *EAAI* (693 S [LXXIII] Sushila Nayar) 1-3.

———, <«Love-the Corner-stone of Ecumenism (*Snēham Ecumenisattinte Ānikallu*)»>. Talk at the Ecumenical Meeting at Thrikunnath Seminary, Alwaye, January 25, 1969, *EM* 39 (1969) 43-47.

———, «*Satyam* and *Ahimsā*». Talk at the Flag-hoisting Ceremony at Bharata ata College, Thrikkakara, January 26, 1969, *EM* 39 (1969) 48-51.

———, <«The Crucifix is Our Hope»>. Pastoral Letter, February 3, 1969, *EM* 39 (1969) 36-42.

———, «Fire Services». Address at the Public Gathering Conducted by the Fire Forces, Cochin, April 14, 1969, *EAAI* (200 F [XI] Fire services) 1-4.

PARECATTIL, J., <«The Office of the Cardinal»>. Address at the Press Club Meeting, Ernakulam, April, 19, 1969, *EAAI* (39 C [V] Cardinal, Office) 1-4.

————, <«The Kerala Church»>. Talk on Vatican Radio, May 1, 1969, *EAAI* (249 K [IX] Kerala Church) 1-5.

————, <«Helping the Missions»>. Inaugural Address at the Mission Exhibition, Bregenz, May 4, 1969, *EAAI* (307 M [XXXI] Mission Exhibition) 1-3.

————, <«A Few Words of Thanksgiving»>. Reply at the Public Reception Hosted on May 5, 1969 to Congratulate Joseph Parecattil at His Elevation to the Cardinalate, Cochin, *EM* 39 (1969) 242-247.

————, «A Common Feeling». Reply at the Reception Accorded to Joseph Parecattil, Trivandrum, July 6, 1969, *EAAI* (714 U [I] Unity) 1-3.

————, «Baroda Bank». Inaugural Talk at the Opening Ceremony of Its New Branch, Ernakulam, July 11, 1969, *EAAI* (24 B [II] Banking [Private]) 1-4.

————, «Modern Bread». Talk at the Modern Bread Factory, Edappally, July 18, 1969, *EAAI* (308 M [XXXII] Modern Bread) 1-3.

————, «Christmas--1969». Talk at the Ecumenical Christmas Carol Concert, Ernakulam, December 12, 1969, *EM* 39 (1969) 406-412.

————, «Concluding Remarks At The 'Church In India Seminar'». Alwaye, Undated, *EM* 39 (1969) 21.

————, «Social Institute, Kalamassery». Talk at the Closing Function of the Academic Year, February 2, 1970, *EAAI* (685 S [LXV] Social Institute) 1-3.

————, «Malabar Liturgy». Letter Addressed to Maximilian Cardinal de Furstenberg, Prefect, Congregation for the Oriental Churches, May 6, 1970, *EAAI* (Serial Number not mentioned) 1.

————, «Refresher Course in Leprosy». Inaugural Address, Cochin, September 9, 1970, *EAAI* (260 L [IV] Leprosy) 1-2.

————, «Development of Villages». Occasion not mentioned, September 20, 1970, *EAAI* (723 V [VIII] Village Development) 1.

————, «Seminar on Education for Development». Talk at the Seminar, Thrikkakkara, December 29, 1970, *EAAI* (163 E [XXVIII] Education) 1-5.

PARECATTIL, J., «The Role of Women in Shaping the Future of the Nation». Presidential Address at the Silver Jubilee Celebration of St. Mary's College, Trichur, January 31, 1971, *EAAI* (736 W [V] Women) 1-9.

———, «Unitive Understanding--The Aim of the World Parliament of Religions». Presidential Address at the Conference of the World Parliament of Religions, Christian, Cochin, March 24, 1971, *EM* 41 (1971) 79-86.

———, «Mater Dei Institute». Talk at the Graduation Ceremony, Goa, March 27, 1971, *EAAI* (122 D [III] Dialogue, Hindu-Christian) 1-13.

———, «The English-Hindi Missal». Letter to Maximilian Cardinal de Furstenberg, May 27, 1971, *EAAI* (42/71) 1.

———, <«Sanctification of Christian Families»>. Pastoral Letter, July 1, 1971, *EM* 41 (1971) 113-120.

———, <«The Revised Missal of 1968»>. Letter to the Prelates of the Syro-Malabar Church, July 2, 1971, *EAAI* (B\84\71) 1.

———, «Remarks about the 1968 Edition of the Syro-Malabar Mass». Letter to His Eminence Maximillian Cardinal de Furstenberg, August 24, 1971, *EAAI* (L4\82\71) 1.

———, <«Cultural Adaptation»>. Letter addressed to Mr. Pius Joseph, Cochin, June 15, 1971, *EAAI* (118. a. C [LXXXIV] Indigenization) 1-5.

———, <«Holy Qurbana according to the Syro-Malabar Rite»>. Letter to Msgr. Januarius, July 8, 1971, *EAAI* (B/79/71) 1-8.

———, «To Pray is to Discover God». Opening Prayer at the Meeting of the Secretariat for Christian Unity, Rome, February 12, 1972, *EM* 42 (1972) 88-89.

———, <«Ecumenical Movements in Different Churches»>. Presidential Address at the Ecumenical Meeting, Madras, April 6, 1972, *EM* 42 (1972) 162-169.

———, «The Mutual Sharing of Life». Speech at a Public Meeting, Madras, April 15, 1972, *EM* 42 (1972) 156-161.

———, <«Our Liturgy»>. Letter Addressed to Maximilian Cardinal de Furstenberg, Prefect, Congregation for the Oriental Churches, August 22, 1972, *EAAI* (L4/116/72) 1-9.

———, *A Call to Support the Rights of Minorities*, Cochin 1972.

———, «Prayer and Penance». Inaugural Address at the Fourth National Convention, Ernakulam, January 25, 1973, *EM* 43 (1973) 16-20.

PARECATTIL, J., «Arakulam Church». Message at the Golden Jubilee Celebration of the Church, Arakulam, February 4, 1973, *EAAI* (95 C [LXI] Place of Worship)1-4.

———, <«Indian Cultural Heritage»>. Cochin, May 14, 1973, *EM* (109 C [LX XV] Inculturation) 1-3.

———, «Opening Prayer Service». At the Meeting of the Secretariat of Christian Unity, Rome, October 10, 1973, *EAAI* (110 C [LXXVI] Inculturation) 1-2.

———, <«Christ is the Light and Hope of the World»>. Pastoral Letter, Cochin, December 8, 1973, *EM* 43 (1973) 359-367.

———, «Adaptation and the Future of Christianity in India», in *The St. Thomas Christians Encyclopedia of India*, ed. G. Menachery, Trichur 1973.

———, «Religious Values and Emerging Culture». Talk at the Symposium in Honour of Fr. Zacharias, Alwaye, February 16, 1974, *EAAI* (368 R [XIV] Religious Values and Emerging Culture) 1-9.

———, «Indianization and Evangelization». Intervention at the Synod of Bishops, Rome, September 30, 1974, *EM* 44 (1974) 239-243. A copy of the original is found in *EAAI* (117. a. C [LXXXIII] Indigenisation) 1-5.

———, «Paganinsm in Christianity». Convocation Address at the Pontifical Seminary, Alwaye, December 3, 1974, *EM* 45 (1975) 21-27.

———, «Research Seminar on Non-Christian Scriptures». Inaugural Address, Bangalore, December 11, 1974, *EM* 44 (1974) 28-32.

———, <«St. Mary's Basilica»>. Sermon at the Consecration of the Reconstructed Basilica, 1974, *EM* 44 (1974) 98-105.

———, <«Day of the Sick»>. Pastoral Letter, Cochin, September 8, 1975, *EM* 45 (1975) 341-347.

———, «The Role of Confession and Prayer Therapy in the Healing Ministry». Presidential Address at the 12th Annual Convention of the Trained Nurses' Association of India, Ernakulam, Undated, *EM* 45 (1975) 348-354.

———, «Vision of the Church and the Role of the C.B.C.I.». Presidential Address at the C.B.C.I. General Body Meeting, Hyderabad, January 5, 1976, *EM* 46 (1976) 12-35.

———, «Renewal of an Imaginary Prohibition». Letter to the Congregation for the Oriental Churches, February 7, 1977 *EM* 53 (1983) 106-107.

PARECATTIL, J., «Pope John Paul II». Message on the Election of the Pope, Vatican, October 22, 1978, *EM* 48 (1978) 363-364.

————, <«Christian Religious Experience»>. Convocation Address at Dharmaram Pontifical Institute, Bangalore, December 12, 1978, *EAAI* (1. a. 778 E [I] Ecclesiastical Studies) 1-5.

————, «The Catholic Church and the Problem of World Peace in the Nuclear Age». Talk at the Republic Day Celebrations, Cochin, January 25, 1979, *EAAI* (1. a. 807 P [III] Peace, [World] and Church) 1-10.

————, «The Priest for Tomorrow's India». Presidential Address at the Centenary Celebrations of St. Joseph's Seminary, Mangalore, December 6, 1979, *EAAI* (1. a. 810 P [VI] Priest for Tomorrow's India) 1-8.

————, «Family Planning». Inaugural Address at the National Family Planning Meeting, Manjummel, December 9, 1979, *EAAI* (1. a. 782 F [I] Family Planning) 1-4.

————, «Foreword» to N.K. JOSE, *The Liturgy (Ārādhana)* Vaikom 1979.

————, <«Syro-Malabar Liturgical Identity»>. Letter to His Excellency Mario Brini, Secretary, Congregation for the Oriental Churches, July 22, 1980, *EAAI* (L4/RN 70/80) 1-2.

————, «Liturgical Reform in the Syro-Malabar Church». Talk at the Meeting of the Syro-Malabar Bishops under the Presidency of the Congregation for the Oriental Churches, Rome, August 26, 1980, Appendix 3, *Liturgy As I See It*, Ernakulam 1987.

————, «Evaluation of the Meeting in Rome». Letter to Cardinal Rubin, Cochin, December 2, 1980, *EM* 53 (1983) 135-144.

————, <«Syro-Malabar Church and Its Liturgy» (Syro-Malabar Sabhayum Athinte Aradhanakramavum), Interview allotted to the Editor of *SD*, *SD* 53 (1980 December 17, 1980). The inter-view was published part by part in the weekly between 1980 and 1983.

————, «Foreword» to T. EMPRAYIL, *The Emerging Theology of Religions*, Rewa 1980.

————, «Foreword» to T. PEREIRA, *Towards an Indian Christian Funeral Rite*, Bangalore 1980.

————, «Nursing Profession». Inaugural Address at the 17th Annual Conference of the Trained Nurses' Association of India, Cochin, May 29, 1981, *EAAI* (325. a. N [X] Nursing Profession) 1-4.

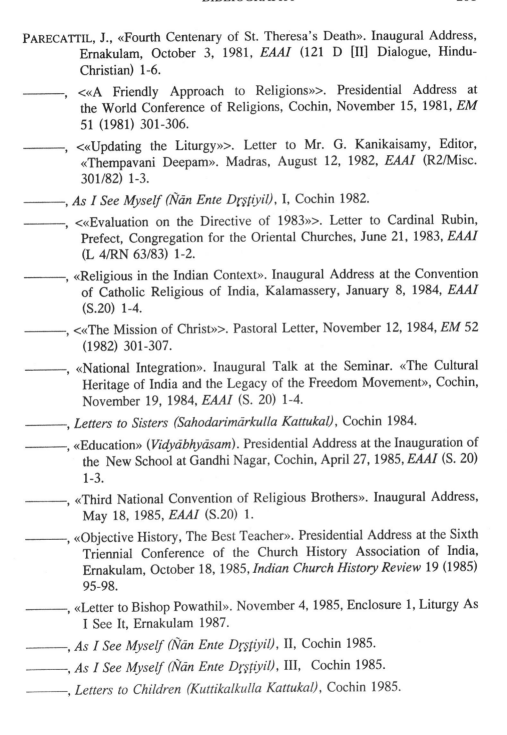

PARECATTIL, J., «Fourth Centenary of St. Theresa's Death». Inaugural Address, Ernakulam, October 3, 1981, *EAAI* (121 D [II] Dialogue, Hindu-Christian) 1-6.

———, <«A Friendly Approach to Religions»>. Presidential Address at the World Conference of Religions, Cochin, November 15, 1981, *EM* 51 (1981) 301-306.

———, <«Updating the Liturgy»>. Letter to Mr. G. Kanikaisamy, Editor, «Thempavani Deepam». Madras, August 12, 1982, *EAAI* (R2/Misc. 301/82) 1-3.

———, *As I See Myself (Ñān Ente Dr̥ṣṭiyil)*, I, Cochin 1982.

———, <«Evaluation on the Directive of 1983»>. Letter to Cardinal Rubin, Prefect, Congregation for the Oriental Churches, June 21, 1983, *EAAI* (L 4/RN 63/83) 1-2.

———, «Religious in the Indian Context». Inaugural Address at the Convention of Catholic Religious of India, Kalamassery, January 8, 1984, *EAAI* (S.20) 1-4.

———, <«The Mission of Christ»>. Pastoral Letter, November 12, 1984, *EM* 52 (1982) 301-307.

———, «National Integration». Inaugural Talk at the Seminar. «The Cultural Heritage of India and the Legacy of the Freedom Movement», Cochin, November 19, 1984, *EAAI* (S. 20) 1-4.

———, *Letters to Sisters (Sahodarimārkulla Kattukal)*, Cochin 1984.

———, «Education» (*Vidyābhyāsam*). Presidential Address at the Inauguration of the New School at Gandhi Nagar, Cochin, April 27, 1985, *EAAI* (S. 20) 1-3.

———, «Third National Convention of Religious Brothers». Inaugural Address, May 18, 1985, *EAAI* (S.20) 1.

———, «Objective History, The Best Teacher». Presidential Address at the Sixth Triennial Conference of the Church History Association of India, Ernakulam, October 18, 1985, *Indian Church History Review* 19 (1985) 95-98.

———, «Letter to Bishop Powathil». November 4, 1985, Enclosure 1, Liturgy As I See It, Ernakulam 1987.

———, *As I See Myself (Ñān Ente Dr̥ṣṭiyil)*, II, Cochin 1985.

———, *As I See Myself (Ñān Ente Dr̥ṣṭiyil)*, III, Cochin 1985.

———, *Letters to Children (Kuttikalkulla Kattukal)*, Cochin 1985.

PARECATTIL, J., *Letters to Priests (Vaidikarkulla Kattukal)*, Cochin 1986.

————, *Letters to the People (Janannlkulla Kattukal)*, Cochin 1987.

————, «Some Comments on the Syro-Malabar Liturgy». Letter to Bishop Gratian Mundadan, October 1, 1986, *EAAI* (185/86) 1-2.

————, «Pastoral Dimension of the Liturgy» (*Liturgyude Ajapalanavasam*), An Evaluation of an Article which appeared in *SD*, December 3, 1987 about the Short Mass, *EAAI* (S.20) 1-10.

————, «A Critical Study of the Restored Raza». Appendix 6, *Liturgy As I See It*, Ernakulam 1987.

————, «Letter to Bishop Joseph Kundukulam». Appendix 2, *Liturgy As I See It*, Ernakulam 1987.

————, *Liturgy As I See It (Liturgy Ente Dṛṣṭiyil)* Ernakulam 1987, tr. K.C. Chacko, Ernakulam 1987.

————, «Reply to Archbishop Most. Rev. Miroslaw Marusyn». Appendix 1, *Liturgy As I See It*, Ernakulam 1987.

————, «Foreword» to Z. PARANILAM, *Christian Openness to the World Religions*, Alwaye 1988.

————, «An Appendix to 'The Holy Eucharist'». Sermon during Mass, Undated, *EAAI* (630 Serm. Eucharist) 1-4.

————, «A Course of Instruction on the Sacrifice of the Mass». Sermon during Mass, Undated, *EAAI* (637 Serm. Mass) 1-22.

————, «Catholic Charismatic Renewal». Message at the Ernakulam Zonal Convention, Undated, *EAAI* (61 C [XXVII] Charismatic Renewal) 1-3.

————, «Catholic Workers' Association». Talk at the Solemn Function of Unveiling the Marble Bust of His Grace Dr. Lourd Mathias, Madras, Undated, *EAAI* (739 W [VIII] Work) 1-4.

————, «Corpus Christi». Sermon during Mass, Undated, *EAAI* (542 Serm. Corpus Christi) 3-4.

————, «Domenica Infra Octavae Nativitatis». Sermon during Mass, Undated, *EAAI* (440 [I] Serm. Sunday Before the Octave of Nativity) 1-4.

————, «Ecumenism». Talk at the Ecumenical Gathering, Cochin, Undated, *EAAI* (152 E [XVII] Ecumenism) 1-2.

————, «Eucharistic Sacrifice». Sermon during Mass, Undated, *EAAI* (626 Serm. Eucharist) 1-4.

PARECATTIL, J., «Family Problems». Inaugural Address at the Kerala Regional Conference, Undated, *EAAI* (196 F [VII] Family Problems) 32-36.

——, <«First Holy Communion»>. Sermon during Mass, Undated, *EAAI* (627 Serm. Eucharist) 1.

——, «How to View the Mass». Sermon during Mass, Undated, *EAAI* (636 Serm.Mass) 1-8.

——, «Practice Brotherhood». Talk at the Third Conference of the Delegates of the Trained Nurses' Association of India, Ernakulam, Undated, *EAAI* (1. a. 816 S [I] Samaritan, Parable of the) 1-2.

——, «Spiritual and Moral Renewal, Pre-Requisite for an Indian Renewal». Undated, *EAAI* (224 I [VIII] Indian Renewal) 1-2.

——, «The Eucharist is the Bond of Charity» (De Eucharistia Prout est Vinculum Caritatis), Sermon during Mass, Undated, *EAAI* (633 Serm. Eucharist) 1-12.

——, «The Eucharist is the Life of the Church». Undated, *EAAI* (632 Serm. Eucharist) 1-20.

——, «The Feast of Corpus Christi» (In Feste Corpus Christi), Sermon During Mass, Undated, *EAAI* (543 Serm. Corpus Christi) 1.

——, «The Hidden Life of the Sacred Heart in the Blessed Sacrament». Sermon during Mass, Undated, *EAAI* (634 Serm. Eucharist) 1.

——, «The Holy Eucharist» (De Sacra Eucharistia), Sermon during Mass, Undated, *EAAI* (630 Serm. Eucharist) 1-12.

——, <«The Last Supper»>. Sermon during Mass, Undated, *EAAI* (629 Serm. Eucharist) 1-6.

——, «The Precious Blood of Jesus» (De Pretioso Sanguine Domini Nostri Jesu Christi) Sermon during Mass, Undated, *EAAI* (602 Serm. Precious Blood) 1-4.

——, «The Preparation for Christ's Coming». Sermon during Mass, Undated, *EAAI* (440 Serm. 4th Advent) 1-2.

——, «The Task Ahead». Address at the Inauguration of the Official Headquarters of the Pastoral Orientation Centre at Palarivattom, Undated, *EAAI* (4 A [IV] Adaptation) 1-15.

2. Secondary Sources

ABHISHIKTANANDA, «The Depth-Dimension of Religious Dialogue», *VJTR* 45 (1981) 214-215.

———, *The Eyes of Light*, Denville 1983.

———, *Guru and Disciple*, Delhi 1990.

ACHARUPARAMBIL, D., «Monasticism in Hindu Tradition», *ED* 30 (1977) 441-464.

ALFARO, J.J., *Theology of Justice in the World*, Vatican City 1973.

AMALADOSS, M., *Becoming Indian: The Process of Inculturation*, Bangalore 1992.

AMALORPAVADASS, D.S., *Towards the Renewal of the Indian Church*, Bangalore 1970.

———, *Efforts Made in the Roman Catholic Church towards Indigenization*, Bangalore 1971.

———, *Towards Indigenization in the Liturgy*, Bangalore 1971.

———, *Indian Christian Spirituality*, Bangalore 1984.

———, *Theological Bases of an Authentic Inculturation*, Bangalore (Undated).

ANDERSEN, W.K. – DAMLE, S.D., *The Brotherhood in Saffron*, New Delhi 1987.

ARRUPE, P., *Witnessing to Justice*, Vatican City 1972.

ATCHLEY, E.G.C.F., *On the Epiclesis of the Eucharistic Liturgy and in the Consecration of the Font*, London 1935.

ATTWATER, D., *The Christian Churches of the East*, I, London 1961.

BACKIANADAN, J.F., *Love in the Life and Works of Mahatma Gandhi*, New Delhi 1991.

BADGER, G.P., *The Nestorians and their Rituals*, London 1852.

BARNABAS, A.P., «ChristianConcern in Peoples' Struggle», *RS* 27 (1980) 54-63.

BENOIT, P., «The Holy Eucharist», *Scrip.* 8 (1965) 106-115.

BERNIER, P., *Eucharist: Celebrating its Rhythms in Our Life*, Notre Dame 1993.

BETHUNE-BAKER, J.F., *An Introduction to the Early History of Christian Doctrine*, London 1903.

———, *Nestorius and His Teaching*, Cambridge 1908.

BOUYER, L., «The Different Forms of Eucharistic Prayer and their Genealogy», *StPatr*, VIII, Berlin 1966.

———, *Eucharist*, London 1966.

BRIGHTMAN, F.E., *Liturgies Eastern and Western*, I, Oxford 1896.

BROCKELMANN, C., *Lexicon Syriacum*, Hirschberg 1928.

CAMELOT, P.T., «Nestorianism», *NCE*, X, Washington 1967.

CATHOLIC BISHOP'S CONFERENCE OF INDIA, *All-India Seminar: Church in India Today*, New Delhi 1969.

————, *Report of the General Meeting of the Catholic Bishop's Conference of India*, New Delhi 1974.

CHADWICK, H., «Eucharist and Christology in the Nestorian Controversy», JThS (New Series) 2 (1951) 145-164.

CHAKIATH, T., «The Social Vision and Commitment of Joseph Cardinal Parecattil», in *Cardinal Parecattil, The Man, His Vision and His Contribution*, ed. A.M. Mundadan, Alwaye 1988, 98-111.

CLARK, F., *Eucharistic Sacrifice and the Reformation*, London 1960.

CODRINGTON, H.W., «The Chaldean Liturgy», *ECQ* 2 (1937) 202-209.

CONGAR, Y., «The Role of the Church in Modern World», in *Commentary on the Documents of Vatican II*, V, ed. H. Vorgrimler, New York 1989, 202-223.

CONNOLLY, R.H., ed. & tr., *The Liturgical Homilies of Narsai*, Cambridge 1909.

COSTELLOE, M.J., «Nestorian Church», *NCE*, X, Washington 1964.

CRICHTON, J.D., *The Church's Worship*, London 1964.

————, «A Theology of Worship», in *The Study of Liturgy*, ed. C. Jones, London 1978, 3-29.

CROLLIUS, A.R., *What is So New about Inculturation?*, Rome 1991.

CUMMINGS, O., «The Eucharist and Social Justice», *CleR*, 71 (1986) 207-212.

CUTRONE, E.J., «The Anaphora of the Apostles. Implications of the Mar Esa'ya Text», *TS* 34 (1973) 623-642.

DEWART, J.M., *Theology of Grace of Theodore of Mopsuestia*, Washington 1971.

DESROCHERS, J., *Christ the Liberator*, Bangalore 1984.

DHALLA, G.M., «Brahmacarya and Christian Virginity», *JD* 3 (1973) 484-485.

DIX, G., *The Shape of the Liturgy*, London 1945.

DUBOIS ABBE, J.A., *Hindu Manners, Customs and Ceremonies*, New Delhi 1983.

DUNN, J.D.G., «Jesus-Flesh and Spirit: an Expression of Romans 1: 3-4», *JThS* (New Series) 24 (1973) 40-68.

DUPUIS, J., «Toward a Communal Eucharistic Celebration», *CleM* 32 (1968) 401-417.

————, *Jesus Christ and His Spirit: Theological Approaches*, Bangalore 1977.

————, *Jesus Christ at the Encounter of World Religions*, tr. R.R. Barr, New York 1991.

EAPEN, K.V., *A Study of Kerala History*, Kottayam 1986.

ELAVANAL, T., *The Memorial Celebration: A Theological Study of the Anaphora of the Apostles Mar Addai and Mari*, Kottayam 1989.

ELAVATHINKAL, S., *Inculturation and Christian Art*, Rome 1990.

ELENGIMATTAM, A., *Monasticism: Christian and Hindu-Buddhist*, Bombay 1969.

EMBREE, A.T., *The Hindu Tradition: Readings in Oriental Thought*, New York 1972.

EMMINGHAU, J.H., *The Eucharist*, Minnesota 1988.

ENGBERDING, H., «Zum anaphorischen Fürbittgebet der ostsyrischen Liturgie der Apostel Addai und Mari», *OrChr* 41 (1957) 116-120.

FARQUHAR, J.N., *The Crown of Hinduism*, London 1913.

FORTESCUE, A., *The Mass: A Study of the Roman Liturgy*, London 1912.

FUENTE, A.G., *Visione liturgica della celebrazione e teologia dell'Ecucaristia*, Roma 1980.

FULLENBACH, J., *Hermeneutics, Marxism and Liberation Theology*, Manila 1989.

GALLAGER, D.A., «Jacques Martin: Thomism», *NCE*, XIV, Washington 1967.

GALVIN, R.J, «Addai and Mari Revisited: The State of the Question», *EL* 87 (1973) 383-414.

GANDHI, M.K., *An Autobiography: The Story of My Experiments with Truth*, Boston 1957.

GERWIN VAN LEEUWEN, J.A.G., *Fully Indian, Authentically Christian*, Bangalore 1990.

————, «Liturgy, the Struggle for Relevance Continues», in *The Church in India: Institution or Movement?*, ed. P. Puthanangady, Bangalore 1991, 25-35.

GRANT, S., *Towards an Alternative Theology: Confessions of a Non-Dualist Christian*, Bangalore 1991.

GRIFFITHS, B., *Christ in India: Essays Towards a Hindu-Christian Dialogue*, Bangalore 1986.

——, *Return to the Centre*, Glasgow 1976.

——, *The Marriage of East and West*, London 1982.

GRILLMEIER, A., «The People of God», in *Commentary on the Documents of Vatican II*, I, eds. H. Vorgrimler et al., New York 1989, 153-185.

GUZIE, T.W., *Jesus and the Eucharist*, Ramsey 1974.

HÄRING, B., *The New Covenant*, London 1967.

HAY, L.C., *Eucharist, A Thanksgiving Celebration*, Delaware 1989.

HEIMSATH, C.H., *Indian Nationalism and Hindu Social Reform*, Princeton 1964.

HILL, W.J., «Thomism», *NCE*, XIV, Washington 1967.

HOECK, J.M., «Decree on Eastern Catholic Churches», in *Commentary on the Documents of Vatican II*, I, eds. H. Vorgrimler et al., New York 1989, 307-331.

JESU RAJAN, *Christian Interpretation of Indian Sannyasa*, Rome 1988.

JESUDASAN, I., *A Gandhian Theology of Liberation*, Maryknoll, New York 1984.

JOHN PAUL II, *The Pope Speaks to India: All the Addresses and Homilies of the Holy Father during His Ten-day Visit to India*, Bandra-Bangalore 1986.

JONES, B.H., «The History of Nestorian Liturgy», *AThR* 46 (1964) 155-176.

JONES, B.H., «The Formation of the Nestorian Liturgy», *AThR* 48 (1966) 277-306.

——, «The Liturgy of Nestorius: The Structural Pattern», *AThR* 48 (1966) 397-411.

JUNGMANN, J.A., «Constitution on the Sacred Liturgy», in *Commentary on the Documents of Vatican II*, I, eds. H. Vorgrimler et al., New York 1989, 1-30.

KANICHIKATTIL, F., *To Restore or To Reform?*, Bangalore 1992.

KASPER, W., *Jesus the Christ*, Kent 1993.

KELLY, J.N.D., *Early Christian Doctrines*, London 1977.

KHER, V.B., ed., *Social Service, Work and Reform by M. K. Gandhi*, Ahmedabad 1976.

KILMARTIN, E., *Christian Liturgy*, Kansas City 1988.

KING, A., «Syro-Malabar Rite», *The Rites of Eastern Christendom*, II, Rome 1948, 417-520.

LAMPE, G.W., *A Patristic Greek Lexicon*, Oxford 1961.

LANE, D., *Foundations for a Social Theology*, New York 1984.

LEEUWEN, G.V., «The Eucharist — a Foretaste of Heaven», *WoWo* 12 (1960) 404-443.

LUSSIER, E., *The Eucharist: the Bread of Life*, New York 1977.

LUZBETAK, L.J., *The Church and Cultures.* An Applied Anthropology for Religious Worker, Illinois 1970.

MACOMBER, W.F., «The Oldest Known Text of the Anaphora of the Apostles, Addai and Mari», *OCP*, 32 (1966) 335-371.

———, «A Theory on the Origins of the Syrian, Maronite and Chaldean Rites», *OCP* 39 (1973) 235-242.

———, «A History of the Chaldean Mass», *Worship* 51 (1977) 107-120.

———, «The Sources for a Study of the Chaldean Mass», *Worship* 51 (1977) 523-536.

MACQUARRIE, J., «Meeting of Theologians in the Modern World: Opportunities and Dangers», *JDh* 1 (1975) 60-67.

MAHIEU, F., «Monasticism in India», *CleM* 7 (1964) 45-47.

MAHONY, R., «The Eucharist and Social Change», *Worship* 57 1983) 52-61.

MANNOORAMPARAMPIL, T., *The Historical Background of the Syro-Malabar Qurbana (Syro-Malabar Qurbanayude caritrapaścāttalam)*, Kottayam 1986.

MAURER, A., «Etienne Gilson: Thomism», *NCE*, XIV, Washington 1967.

McDONALD, A., *The Sacrifice of The Mass*, London 1924.

McKENNA, J.H., *Eucharist and Holy Spirit*, Essex 1975.

MENON, A.S., *Indian History*, Madras 1984.

———, *A Survey of Kerala History*, Madras 1991.

MINGANA, A., *Commentary of Theodore of Mopsuestia on the Lord's Prayer and on the Sacraments of Baptism and the Eucharist*, Cambridge 1933.

MONCHANIN, A.J. – LE SAUX, H., *A Benedictine Ashram*, Douglas 1964.

MONIER-WILLIAMS, M., *A Sanskrit-English Dictionary*, Delhi 1976.

MOOKEN, G., (tr.), *The Liturgy of the Holy Apostles Addai and Mari together with the Liturgies of Mar Theodorus and Mar Nestorius and the Order of Baptism*, Trichur 1967.

MUNDADAN, A.M., «Hindu-Christian Dialogue, Past Twenty-Five Years», *JD* 11 (1981) 375-394.

——, *Indian Christians' Search for Identity and Struggle for Autonomy*, Bangalore 1984.

——, «Emergence of the Missionary Consciousness of the St. Thomas Christians in India: Problems and Prospects at the Cross-Roads Today», in *Mission in India Today: The Task of St. Thomas Christians*, ed. K. Pathil, Bangalore 1988, 21-54.

——, *Emergence of Catholic Theological Consciousness in India*, St. Thomas Academy for Research, Documentation 7, Alwaye 1985.

NEALE, J.M., *A History of the Holy Eastern Church*, I, London 1850.

NEUNER, J., «Non-Attachment: Indian and Christian», *CleM* 2 (1954) 92-107.

——, «The Eucharist and the New Man», *CleM*, 28 (1964) 161-166.

——, «Problems of Teaching Theology», in *Theologizing in India*, eds. M. Amaladoss et al., Bangalore 1981.

NEUNER, J. – J. DUPUIS., *The Christian Faith*, Bangalore 1982.

NEUNHEUSER, B., «Mystery Presence», *Worship* 34 (1960) 120-127.

OTT, L., *Fundamentals of Catholic Dogma*, ed. J.C. Bastible, Rockford, Illinois 1974.

OUTKA, G., *Agape, An Ethical Analysis*, London 1972.

PANIKKAR, K.N., «Land Control, Ideology and Reform: A Study of the Changes in Family Organization and Marriage System in Kerala», in *Determinants of Social Status in India*, ed. S.C. Malik, Shimla 1986, 62-89.

PANIKKAR, R., *The Intrareligious Dialogue*, New York 1978.

——, *The Unknown Christ of Hinduism*, London 1981.

PANIKKAR, R., «Hinduism and Christ», in *Spirit and in Truth*, Fs. I. Hirudayam, Madras 1985.

PARANILAM, Z., *Christian Openness to World Religions*, Alwaye 1988.

PATTERSON, L., *Theodore of Mopsuestia and Modern Thought*, London 1926.

PENNINGTON, M.B., *The Eucharist Yesterday and Today*, Slough 1985.

PENROSE, M., «Cosmic Dimensions of the Eucharist», *RR*, 37 (1978) 433-441.

PODIPARA, P.J., «The present Syro-Malabar Liturgy Menezian or Rozian?», *OCP* 23 (1957) 313-331.

————, «Hindu in Culture, Christian in Religion, Oriental in Worship», *OS* 8 (1959) 89-94.

————, *The Thomas Christians*, Bombay 1970.

————, «The Thomas Christians and Adaptation», *ECQ* 3 (1970) 171-177.

————, *The Thomas Christians and their Syriac Treasures*, Allepey 1974.

POWER, D.N., *The Sacrifice We Offer*, Edinburgh 1987.

————, *The Eucharistic Mystery, Revitalizing the Tradition*, New York 1992.

POWERS, J.M, *Eucharistic Theology*, London 1968.

PRASANNABHAI, «Indigenous Forms of Religious Life», *WoWo* 9 (1976) 196-206.

PROBST, F., «Die antiochenische Messe nach den Schriften des Hl. Johannes Chrysostomus», *ZKTh* 7 (1833) 251-303.

PUNNAPADAM, T., *Justice as Spirituality*, Bangalore 1991.

PUSPARAJAN, A., «Prospects of Christian Dialogue with Other Religions», *JDh* 8 (1983) 248-270.

PUTHANANGADY, P., «Liturgy and Theology — The Dialectical Relationship between Liturgy and Theology with a View to a Theology for India», in *Theologizing in India*, ed. M. Amaladoss et al., Bangalore 1981, 141-154.

PUTZ, J., «The Meaning of Christianity», *CleM* 9 (1946) 294-303.

QUASTEN, J., *Patrology*, III, Westminster, Maryland 1986.

RADHAKRISHNAN, S., *Eastern Religions and Western Thought*, Oxford 1969.

RAES, A., *An Explanation of the Syro-Malabar Mass*, Kottayam 1954.

RAHNER, K., «Christianity and the Non-Christian Religions», in *Theological Investigations*, V, London 1966, 115-134.

RATCLIFF, E.C., «The Original Form of the Anaphora of Addai and Mari, a Suggestion», *JThS* 30 (1929) 21-32.

RAYAN, S., «Christian Participation in the Struggle for Social Justice», *VJTR*, 38 (1974) 282-296.

————, «Asia and Justice», in *Liberation in Asia*, eds. S. Arkiasamy – G. Gispersauch, New Delhi 1987, 1-15.

RAZA, H., *The Cultural Role of India*, New Delhi 1968.

REINE, F.J., *The Eucharistic Doctrine and Liturgy of the Mystagogical Catecheses of Theodore of Mopsuestia*, Washington 1942.

ROCHA, P.R., «The Principal Manifestation of the Church», in *Vatican II: Assessments and Perspectives*, II, ed. R. Latourelle, New York 1989, 3-26.

ROSATO, P.J., *Introduzione alla teologia dei sacramenti*, Casale Monferrato 1992.

———, *Cena del Signore e amore sociale*, Ponteranica 1994.

SAMARTHA, S.J., *Courage for Dialogue: Ecumenical Issues in Inter-Religious Relationships*, Geneva 1981.

SCHILLEBEECKX, E., *The Eucharist*, London 1977.

———, «Transubstantiation, Transfinalizaiton, Transignification», in *Living Bread, Saving Cup*, ed. R.K. Seasoltz, Collegeville 1982, 175-189.

———, *God the Future of Man*, London 1986.

———, *Christ the Sacrament of the Encounter with God*, London 1989.

SCHMEMANN, A., *The Eucharist*, New York 1988.

SHARMA, I.C., *Ethical Philosophies of India*, London 1965.

SHORTER, A., *African Christian Theology: Adaptation or Inculturation?*, London 1975.

SINGH, K., «The Hindu Renaissance», in *Freedom, Progress and Society*, eds. R. Balasubramanian – S. Bhatacharyya, New Delhi 1986, 1-16.

SMITH, V.A., *The Oxford History of India*, New Delhi 1981.

SOBRINO, J., *The True Church and the Poor*, London 1984.

———, *Jesus in Latin America*, Maryknoll, New York 1987.

SPINKS, B.D., «The Consecratory Epiclesis in the Anaphora of St. James», *StLi* 11 (1976) 19-38.

———, «Eucharistic Offering in the East Syrian Anaphorae», *OCP* 50 (1984) 347-371.

STUART, J., *Swami Abhishiktananda*, Delhi 1989.

SULLIVAN, F.A., *The Christology of Theodore of Mopsuestia*, Rome 1956.

SWANSTON, H.F.G., *The Community Witness*, London 1967.

THEISEN, J., «Images of the Church and the Eucharist», *Worship*, 58 (1984) 118-129.

THENAYAN, P., *The Missionary Consciousness of the St. Thomas Christians*, Cochin 1982.

THOMAS, M.M., «Significance of Marxist and Barthian Insights for a Theology of Religion», *RS* 21 (1974) 58-66.

———, «A Reply», *RS* 23 (1976) 59-65.

———, «Theological Aspects of the Relationships between Social Action Groups and Churches», *RS*, 31 (1984) 17-23.

THOMAS, M.M., «The Absoluteness of Jesus Christ and Christ-Centred Syncretism», *ER* 37 (1985) 387-397.

———, *Risking Christ for Christ's Sake: Towards an Ecumenical Theology of Pluralism*, Geneva 1987.

THOTTAKKARA, A., ed., *Gandhian Spirituality*, Rome 1992.

THURIAN, M., *The Mystery of the Eucharist*, tr. E. Chisholm, Oxford 1983.

UNNITHAN, T.K.N., *Gandhi and Social Change*, Jaipur 1979.

VADAKKEL, J., *The East Syrian Anaphora of Mar Theodore of Mopsuestia*, Kottayam 1989.

VANDANA, *Gurus, Ashrams and Christians*, Delhi 1989.

WIGRAM, W., *Introduction to the History of the Assyrian Church*, London 1910.

YOUSIF, P., «Divine Liturgy according to the Rite of the Assyro-Chaldean Church», in *The Eucharistic Liturgy in the Christian Orient*, ed. J. Madey, Kottayam 1983, 125-237

———, «An Introduction to East Syrian Spirituality», in *East Syrian Spirituality*, ed. A. Thottakkara, Bangalore 1990, 1-97.

GLOSSARY

Ācārya	master, teacher, preceptor, head of an *āshram*
Advaita	non-duality
Advaita Vedānta	a Hindu philosophical system of non-dualism
Agni	fire
Ahimsā	non-violence, non-injury
Ānanda	joy, bliss, one of the characteristics of the Godhead
Ārati	waving of light before deity or before one we wish to honour
Ārṣabhārata	the land of rṣis or sages
Asat	non-being
Āśram (Āshram)	hermitage, abode of a guru, a type of monastery. It also refers to one of the four stages of life in Hinduism
Āshramite	one who lives in an *āśram*
Ātman	the Spirit, the Self, the Suprme Universal Self
Ātmasākṣātkāra	self-realization
Avatāra	descent of God, incarnate form of God
Avidya	ignorance
Gīta Bhagavad	«The Song of the Lord» A section of Mahabharatha, one of the epics of the Hindus
Bhakta	devotee
Bhakti	loving devotion
Bhakti mārga	the path of loving devotion
Bhāratīya pūja	Indian Mass
Bhūta yajña	offring to various species of creatures
Brahmacāri	a celibate student
Brahmacarya	the students stage of life; conduct adopted to attain Brahman.

Brhaman	the Suprme Principle of all; the Absolute
Brahmasāksātkāra	God-realization
Carya	course of conduct
Devās	gods
Deva Yajña	offering to gods
Dharma	religious and social norms and duties, righteousness, duty, religion
Dharma-Sāstra	law book
Dhyāna	meditation
Ēzhava	a section of the low caste
Gṛhastha	house holder
Guna	quality
Guru	spiritual guide, a God-realized person who leads others to God
Īsvara	god, the personal deity
Japa	muttered prayers
Jīva	life, soul
Jīvanmukta	one who has found liberation in his life time
Jñāna	wisdom, knowledge
Jñāna mārga	the path of knowledge
Kāma	desire for worldly things
Karma	action, work, the results of acts done in the previous life
Kāvi	the affron coloured cloth worn by Hindu ascetics
Karma mārga	way of disinterested action (one of the three ways of salvation
Khādi	hand spinning cloth
Krsna	an *avatāra* of Visnu
Mahābhārata	one of the two epics of Hinduism
Maharsi	the great sage
Mahātma	«great soul», title of a sage or saint
Mantra	formula of prayer
Mārga	path

Māya	illusion or the undefinable condition of the world of manifestation, the creative power of God
Mōksa	salvation or final libeation
Mukti	liberation, salvation
Nāmajapa	the prayer of the name (of God); repetition of the divine name
Nari yajña	offering to fellow being
Nēti, Nēti	not this, not this, apophatism
Nirguna Brahman	Brahman without attributes, the Godhead beyond all attributes
OM	It is a commbination of the sounds A, U, M. It stands for the creation, preservation and dissolution of all things; signifies to the unity of three gods: Vishnu (A); Siva (U); and Brahma (M).
Paramātman	the Supreme Reality
Prakrti	primordial matter, nature
Pramānās	means for right knowledge, authority
Pūja	ritual worship
Purāna	a body of Hindu scriptures, legend
Pulaya	One of the lowest caste in Hindu religion.
Pūrna	full, complete
Purusa	self, conscious being
Rasa	flavour, quintessence
Rsi	sage, seer
Rsi yajña	offering to grate
Sabda	sound, verbal testimony
Saccidānanda	God conceived as existence (sat), consciousness (cit), bliss (ānanda); the nature of the Suprme Being
Sādhu	a wandering monk, ascetic
Saguna Brahman	Brahman without attributes
Śaiva Siddhānta	one school of Śaivism
Śaivite	a follower of Śiva
Sakṣātkāra	realization of God in one's own self
Sakti	force, power, energy
Sāmkhya	one of the six orthodox systems of Indian philosophy

Samsāra	the phenomenal world, the embodied existence in the cycles of rebirth, death and rebirth
Sannyāsa	renunciation, life total renunciation
Sannyāsi	one who has renounced everything
Śāstra	scripture, systematic knowledge
Sat	truth, being, absolute
Satyam	truth
Siddhānta	doctrinal conclusion
Śisya	disciple
Tapas	austerity
Tat tvam asi	Thou art That
Upanisād	«to sit at a guru's feet»; a class of literature included, along with the Vedās, in the Śruti, and expounding the philosophical significance of the Vedas
Vānaprastha	hermit, forest-dweller
Vēdānta	the end of Vedās, Upanisād, system of philosophy
Vēdās	the ancient sacred texts of Hinduism, the sacred hymns
Visnu	the God Visnu
Yajña	sacrifice
Yōga	union, the discipline of unifying body and mind
Yōgi	one who follows the way of union with God

INDEX OF AUTHORS

TABLE OF CONTENTS

PART TWO

EXPOSITION OF THE EUCHARISTIC WRITINGS OF
JOSEPH PARECATTIL

Riproduzione anastatica: 2 febbraio 1996
Tipografia Poliglotta della Pontificia Università Gregoriana
Piazza della Pilotta, 4 – 00187 Roma